The Exceptional Life
rare; unusually good; superior; outstanding; extraordinary

R-Evolution

A Practical Guide to reach Peak Performance
and create exceptional experiences in our Workplaces,
Homes, and Communities

JESSICA TIETJEN, J.D.

EVOLVING TO
Exceptional

*Welcome to the R-Evolution to help people live Exceptional Lives, I am
confident you will not regret your decision to read this book!*

Photos by David Maupin

For more information, email contact@jessicatietjen.com
Paperback ISBN: 978-1-952566-28-8
Hardback ISBN: 978-1-952566-29-5
Ebook ISBN: 978-1-952566-30-1

Printed in the USA.
Freedom House Publishing Co
Middleton, ID 83644
www.freedomhousepublishingco.com

FREEDOM HOUSE
PUBLISHING CO

Endorsements

"Who doesn't want an exceptional life? Jessica Tietjen's guide to living a meaningful life is full of essential tools and compelling questions that can lead us from simply surviving to thriving. A powerful, practical guide."

-- Shawn Achor, *NYTimes* bestselling author of *The Happiness Advantage* and *Big Potential*

"The Exceptional Life R-Evolution is a new and practical look at what we're doing in the world today and how to rethink tomorrow in order to live our best possible life!"

-- Cy Wakeman, New York Times Bestselling Author of "No Ego"

"Abraham Lincoln stated, "the best way to predict the future is to create it" He would have thoroughly enjoyed reading The **Exceptional Life R-Evolution!** Jessica Tietjen has offered a timely post-pandemic treatise that captures the journey many are navigating regarding the intersection between career and life aspirations. It is a terrific read!"

-- Tom Casey, *Managing Principal, Discussion Partner Collaborative LLC; 5 Times Best Selling Author on Leadership and Executive Transitions; Most Recent Book- Leadership Development-The Next Curve To Flatten!*

"Jessica has written a book for anyone, anywhere, at any age. The only common denominator is that she writes for a reader who truly wants to live as full a life as possible and to maximize their contribution to society. Along the way there are precious lessons to be learned. The author shares the lessons she has learned from others in her life and from her own positive and less-than-positive experiences. Readers will connect with Jessica on one or more of these stories. She is an excellent storyteller and speaks from the heart. I loved the honest glimpse into her life and the people we were introduced to along the way. I will recommend this book to all my friends and colleagues who are ready to reflect and just need the questions to kick-start that exercise."

-- Dr. Beverly Kaye Author of *Help Them Grow or Watch Them Go, Love 'Em or Lose 'Em* and *Up is Not the Only Way*

Table of Contents

SECTION FOUR

Additional Resources

I truly want every person to live an exceptional life and although the book provides a lot of knowledge – we must still *reflect on the concepts*, gain *exposure*, and ultimately *acquire the experience* to reach peak performance.

REFLECT ON THE CONCEPTS:

I created an *Exceptional Life R-Evolution Workbook* for your use as you read or after reading the book to reflect on the concepts and put them into action. After downloading the workbook, you will also get a *FREE course on Creating Exceptional Work & Life Experiences!*

Download the **FREE** Workbook at:
https://www.evolvingtoexceptional.com/free-workbook

GAIN EXPOSURE & ACQUIRE THE EXPERIENCE:

I couldn't imagine writing this book and not providing a venue for more discussion, sharing, and coaching. Not everyone has access to good coaches and even if you do, we can't live every experience, but by sharing we can learn about other experiences and turn it into wisdom!

I created an *Exceptional Life R-Evolution Facebook Group*, please sign up and jump into the conversation sharing your experiences and learning from the experiences of others!

JOIN THE EXCEPTIONAL LIFE R-EVOLUTION PARTNERSHIP PROGRAM:

Are you a coach, healer, leader, teacher, advisor, entrepreneur who is passionate about helping people live Exceptional Lives? Do you provide services or coaching to workplaces, homes (families), and communities that helps to improve lives? To join our partnership program visit our website.

Check out my blog posts and articles for additional insights, advice, and suggestions expanding upon the contents of the book and make sure to keep in touch!

Email: contact@jessicatietjen.com

Follow me on Instagram: @jessicatietjenjd

Follow me on LinkedIn: @jessica-tietjenjd

Follow me on Medium: @jessica-tietjen

Visit my websites:
www.evolvingtoexceptional.com or www.jessicatietjen.com

About the Author

WHO IS JESSICA TIETJEN?

A little background on who I am and why I wrote this book. I will start with what I am not – I am not a researcher, university professor, or famous leader/author/social influencer. I am an everyday person practicing the concepts of this book, learning every day, finding ways to evolve my performance, and applying those strategies so I can live an exceptional life and help others to do so as well. I am a spouse, mother to three amazing children, leader, lawyer, talent management professional, passionate strengths advocate, technology enthusiast, change creator, now a writer, and much more. I serve and perform in many roles and enjoy all of them in different ways!

After graduating from Saint Louis University School of Law, I briefly focused on contracts and legal-related corporate matters. I recognized quickly this was not my passion and pivoted into the role of Talent Development Coordinator. Over the past ten years I have worked to shape Experitec's Talent Management Program from talent acquisition to offboarding. Through this journey, I developed strategies for employees to reach peak performance in their roles. I also became a Certified Gallup®[1] Strengths Coach supporting my ability to coach, support, and evolve the performance of our people. As a result of this work, Experitec has been recognized as a Gallup® Exceptional Workplace three years in a row and a St. Louis Top Workplace four years in a row!

A few things about who I am as a person – I believe in inclusion, I believe in freedom, I believe in a higher power (for me that is God), I believe we can learn from everyone we meet; I believe

---

[1] CliftonStrengths® and the CliftonStrengths 34 Themes of Talent are trademarks of Gallup, Inc. Gallup's content is Copyrighted by Gallup. Used with permission. All rights reserved.

all people are valuable. I believe we can change the world. I believe we can enjoy and be happy in life. I believe everyone deserves that opportunity. I believe evolving our performance can create exceptional work and life experiences. I believe reaching peak performance is possible for everyone. I believe we can all live an exceptional life. And I believe this book will help you to do so.

I hope you will enjoy this book and walk away with actions to improve your life experience.

Introduction

At the beginning of 2020, the world became challenging in ways most never anticipated and many never believed possible. Initially, COVID-19, or coronavirus, seemed far away, a problem in another country and unlikely to impact our lives. While some began preparing, others were denying it would have any impact. Any recorded reality-TV show filmed at the start of the pandemic provides a fascinating reminder of the general public mindset. "This is being blown out of proportion," "It'll be over in a few weeks," "It's the same as the flu." I remember having similar conversations as we daily debated and discussed what might come next.

In March of 2020, the first case of COVID-19 was confirmed in the United States along with the declaration of a Global Pandemic. Many of our workplaces (who had the luxury of doing so) went virtual with employees working remotely from home. Next, daycares and schools closed, sporting events were suspended, events were cancelled, and ultimately the entire country was nearly shut down.

"Unbelievable," "impossible," and "inconceivable" were words uttered as people, in complete shock, were forced to adapt to a completely new world. Families figured out how to work and care for children simultaneously. Workplaces found solutions for employees to work using video, remote access, and new tools. Teachers completely reinvented education into a virtual world. First responders and medical personnel... well, their experience merits a book entirely focused on the tremendous challenges they faced and overcame.

All the changes, necessitated by the pandemic, posed new challenges for the roles in our lives and significantly impacted the way we think about and perform those roles. The impact of challenging circumstances on our roles, lives, and performance is not new. Rather, we know from decades of research and experience that we evolve our performance in response to the challenges we face throughout our lives. Despite the many challenges we experienced throughout the year, the same research applies for reaching peak performance in our lives. We must evolve our performance for the future and these concepts are now more important than ever.

More than a year has passed since the beginning of the pandemic in the United States, and although much has changed with vaccines, we will be tempted to and will, in many cases, return to our lives as they existed before the pandemic. However, the experience of the pandemic provided valuable lessons and insights about how we choose to live our lives. If we recognize these insights and incorporate the lessons into our lives, they will help us be able to live better lives in the future.

The pandemic is only the first of many significant changes we will continue to experience at an ever-increasing pace, an exponential pace of change. These changes are going to challenge each of us in our performance in the workplace, at home, and in our communities. The lessons we learned are essential to help us to go from merely surviving in this new world to thriving in a world with exceptional work and life experiences. In one way, you might consider the last year as God's (or the universe's) plan to prepare us for what comes next.

What do I mean by "what comes next"? As technology gets smarter, as humans get smarter in how they interact with this technology, and as we combine our capabilities into the "superhuman computer" or "super minds," we will be able to accomplish more than we ever dreamed possible. Many authors are writing all about this possibility, and the implications for the speed of changes in technology as we digitally transform. If you are not yet aware of this increasing technology and how changes only imaginable in the movies are going to become reality in our lives very soon, you need to educate yourself, and quickly. This "next" is going to be similar to what we went through with the pandemic, and we will not have a choice to "opt out." We must evolve or fall behind.

Evolving our performance, however, should not be based solely on the fear of falling behind. Rather, evolving our performance has the potential to enhance our lives and truly live exceptional lives. Whether it be in our workplaces, homes, or communities, most desire to perform at their best. Most of us would like to be the absolute "best" version of ourselves and live the best life possible. This book is for anyone who desires to evolve their performance to perform at their best, reach peak performance, and create exceptional work and life experiences.

Upon sharing this book with my 90-year-old grandmother, she shared with tears in her eyes and a smile on her face "I truly feel I lived an exceptional life." Exceptional certainly did not mean easy – she faced significant challenges in her life, losing her father at 9 years old, her 18-year-old son in a car accident, and her husband after he fell down the stairs at home. Despite all the challenges, she grew a family with children, grandchildren, and now 8 great grandchildren! She enjoys fishing, socializing, reading, learning, playing bridge, and especially sharing her wisdom and stories.

Why did I write this book? While I've worked with the concepts in this book for many years, last year really solidified for me their importance to the world. Frankly, this book was meant to be written. I felt it in my bones, and I couldn't have stopped myself from writing it even if I wanted to. I felt inspired that this book is needed in the world today and I was chosen to write it. For me, this inspiration was spiritual, although the contents of the book are not about religion. These principles can and should be applied in any context or situation.

Throughout the book, I share stories about myself and my life experiences. I hope the practicality and real-life experiences will be meaningful and applicable in your own life. Although I do reference external research that informs these concepts, everything I provide is based on my experience. I will also address changes I see occurring, coming soon, or necessary for the future. In addressing these topics, some may be controversial depending on your beliefs. I try to address each topic in a respectful way that can be applied in any life situation. However, I recognize my perspective may make some who desire to hold on to the ways of the past uncomfortable.

The principles are well researched and grounded in best practices. The stories, analogies, and examples I provide to make the principles practical were inspired and provided to me by God based upon my life, my experiences, and those around me. I hope they have the same positive impact on your life as they did on mine while writing this book.

My life's purpose is to help people live their best life – an exceptional life, just like my grandmother has accomplished. This book is meant to help more people evolve their performance to live an exceptional life. After reading this book, you will know how to create these exceptional work and life experiences so you can one day echo my grandma's words.

To do so, we must first understand why evolving our performance is needed to reach our peak performance and climb our personal performance mountain. Next, we need to apply the lessons learned from our experiences, especially during challenging times like those we faced in 2020. Then, we will follow the guide for reaching our peak performance using the four keys: expectations, feedback, development, and accountability. Finally, we will apply these keys to the roles we serve in our workplaces, homes, and communities.

Everyone can live an exceptional life, and the resources in this book will provide you the guidance to do so successfully. The time has come for us to benefit from all the knowledge and technology that are available to us and change how we live our lives. If we can share our knowledge and experiences along our path to peak performance, we will ignite the Exceptional Life R-Evolution and change the world for the better.

I truly hope the insights you glean from this book are useful and applicable to any role you serve. I encourage you to take the time in each section to reflect and consider your own performance and what actions you will take to evolve and reach peak performance!

If you enjoy the book, you can find and follow me for more articles and resources on Instagram at @jessicatietjenjd; at www.JessicaTietjen.com or www.evolvingtoexceptional.com

Section One

PEAK PERFORMANCE CREATES EXCEPTIONAL EXPERIENCES

The sands of time are quicksand...
so much can sink into them without a trace.

Margaret Atwood

Ever watched an hourglass? How the sand drops through a tiny hole between the two glasses? In some instances, and especially at the beginning, watching the sand fall feels as though it is moving so slowly. It feels as though it could be forever before all the sand drops. But then, as time passes, and especially as it gets to the end, it feels as though the time is passing very quickly. Really what makes it *feel* fast or slow is our personal state of mind (need or  desire) at that particular moment in time. Whether the timer's purpose is to mark the ending of something we love versus something we loathe directly impacts how we feel.

Our personal perspectives and perceptions of time develop as a result of our personal experiences. These perceptions of time are noticeable in the difference between the perspective of children (at the beginning of life) and the perspective of the elderly (nearing the end of life). I'm quite certain I'm not the only child who felt an obsessive need to grow up, be like the adults, and have time move faster. As a child, I felt as if time were barely moving, and I might never get to adulthood. Now as an adult, time keeps moving faster and faster. What felt like a year before, now feels like a week. As we grow older, time seems to move more quickly. I was recently told by a fellow twin parent, "If it feels like the seasons are going by fast now, soon seasons will turn into decades."

Part of me would give anything to return to this childlike mindset where I felt I had an abundance of time. But I recognize our mindsets are shaped by our experiences, and these experiences are what create our perceptions of time and ultimately lead us to feel like time is speeding up. Like with the hourglass, how we feel about time is reflective of our experiences and mindsets.

Although many think of time as linear – it does not change, but is always the same and a constant in our world. I (and many physicists) respectfully disagree. Time is dependent on our mindset and our life experiences. Time can be captured and applied in ways that create a meaningful impact in your life. Time can be acquired, applied, and perceived in ways you may never have considered.

For example, compare watching a television show to waiting for medical information. Time watching the television typically flies by and suddenly an hour has passed. Whereas, waiting for the results of a medical test or a surgery, time stands still, every moment feels heavy and long – time passes slowly. Although absolute time doesn't ever change, our mindsets, choices, activities, environment, and approach in life directly impact our use of time and how we feel about it. Whether we feel it was productive, effective, meaningful, valuable, long, short, and anything in between.

All my work with performance for the last ten years is centered around solving the problem of "How should I spend my time?" Where should I allocate my limited time and resources for the *greatest possible outcome?* How do I use my time wisely to *generate meaningful results?* Which approach to time will help me *be happy, successful, and fulfilled?* But what is the greatest possible outcome, what are meaningful results, what does it mean to be happy or successful?

Living an exceptional life by creating exceptional work and life experiences *is* the greatest possible outcome, the meaningful result, and the means for happiness and success. These exceptional work and life experiences are certainly not the same for everyone and truly unique for each individual. However, I know everyone can live a life filled with experiences they feel are exceptional – *better, unique, unusually good, or outstanding.* Evolving our performance to reach peak performance will help us create more exceptional work and life experiences, but we must first prepare for the path to peak performance.

> *Time is dependent on our mindset and our life experiences. Time can be captured and applied in ways that create a meaningful impact in your life. Time can be acquired, applied, and perceived in ways you may never have considered.*

CHAPTER ONE
Creating Exceptional
Experiences

*How does peak performance create
exceptional work and life experiences?*

WHY DOES HAVING EXCEPTIONAL EXPERIENCES
MATTER?

The obsession with time, or more specifically our lack of time, and the inevitable question "How do we get more time?" is misguided. No matter what your personal beliefs, (spiritual, scientific, or any other), we are here on this earth for some purpose or reason. Whether the purpose or reason is to simply exist for a span of time (rise from nature and return to nature at our death), make an impact on the world, or fulfill a mission or calling.

11

Ultimately, whether we learn and choose to fulfill our purpose or reason, is entirely up to us.

Nature does not hurry,
yet everything is accomplished.

Lao Tzu As T

We were placed on nature's never-ending path, which exists regardless of our human choices. Certainly, we are meant to do something meaningful with our time on earth. I invite you to consider that we are meant to experience our lives and this world in the best possible way to live our best life – an exceptional life. What if we are not meant to worry about time or completing enough tasks, achievements, or activities during our time, but rather to appreciate and experience each and every moment of time during our lives?

Most people want to live the best life they can. I call that life an exceptional life. For most of us, work is also a fundamental and frequent part of our life – we must do it, we want to do it, and we feel we need to do it. Therefore, we must have both exceptional work and life experiences to live an exceptional life.

On the cover of the book, under the title, I include the definition of exceptional – *rare; unusually good; superior; outstanding; extraordinary*. Currently, living your best life is truly exceptional or rare for most people but having exceptional work and life experiences *is* achievable by everyone in the world today. With the advance of technology, the lessons we learned during 2020, and the knowledge and capabilities that exist – we certainly have the tools and resources necessary to make it possible. I realize it may be significantly more difficult for some than others but if we can evolve to reach peak performance, we will have exceptional work and life experiences, and we can live exceptional lives. Together we can ignite the Exceptional Life R-Evolution where everyone is able to live their best life!

HOW AND WHEN DO WE LEARN THIS LIFE LESSON?

When do we begin to realize life can be about more than getting through the day? When do we learn we can make more of the time we have each day? When do we learn our experiences can be exceptional and time does not have to be a limiting factor on our happiness, success, or ability to live our best life?

"Still, death is a great teacher. It's just too harsh. I wish I could tell you that through the tragedy I mined some undiscovered, life-altering absolute that I could pass on to you. I didn't. The clichés apply— people are what count, life is precious, materialism is overrated, the little things matter, live in the moment—and I can repeat them to you ad nauseam. You might listen, but you won't internalize. Tragedy hammers it home. Tragedy etches it onto your soul. You might not be happier. But you will be better."

Harlan Coben, in Tell No One

I was nineteen when I first experienced the death of a close family member – my grandfather, the Rev. Dr. John H. Tietjen. Growing up, both of my grandfathers helped shape me as a person. My Grandpa Tietjen was the wise, religious, politically minded human and mission centric leader of our family. I was the oldest of all my cousins (on both sides) and I vividly remember our family dinners where my grandfather would challenge us with debates and discussions on politics, policy, church practices, and so much more.

My grandfather suffered from lung cancer, pancreatic cancer, brain cancer, and ultimately, we believe died of a brain aneurysm. Each time he got cancer he would beat it – and he beat it in miraculous ways. The last time we knew he was getting sicker. In fact, my dad was at the airport on his way to my grandpa's home in Fort Worth, TX. We had family in town and the 'adults' (my mom, aunt, and uncle) sat us down and told the 'kids' (my cousins, sisters, and I) the news about our grandpa. I took the news hard – really hard. I felt the world swirling... like my feet had been kicked out from under me.

I desperately wanted to make my grandfather proud, and I even went to college at George Washington University in Washington D.C. on a path to change the world. I stayed at GW for a year and half, but I could never overcome my homesickness and the culture change. I decided mid-year, just a couple months before my grandfather passed away, to relocate back to Saint Louis University. A few weeks before he died, my grandfather had his fifty-year jubilee celebration celebrating his service in the ministry. I chose not to travel for this event, and I will always regret that decision. I thought I had more time. I thought he would recover like he had before. I thought everything would be ok.

As I heard the words and they sunk in, I responded with vehement denial – you must be wrong, that isn't possible, please tell me this isn't true. I ran out of the house. I wasn't sure where I was going but I just had to get away. You see, I had always been able to debate or discuss my way around any issue. No matter what the situation I could always find an angle, a strategy, a way to fix it. (No surprise I ultimately ended up a lawyer!) But, you see, death is final. You can't debate your way out of it. You can't change it. You can't fix it. You can't even argue about it. Everyone is born, and everyone dies. What we do between those two unavoidable events is up to each of us.

> *Everyone is born, and everyone dies. What we do between those two unavoidable events is up to each of us.*

My grandfather did tremendous work in the Lutheran Church during his time on earth. He was an amazing leader, pastor, and teacher who helped shape my beliefs. He always told me that there is more about us that is the same than is different – we must understand different religions and beliefs, find commonality, and build together. He was also a writer, and his final book before he died was called *"The Gospel According to Jesus,"* where he told the gospel from Jesus' perspective. He saw the value of learning about challenges from different perspectives – including the challenges Jesus faced in his life.

When we consider why having exceptional work and life experiences is important and why we want to have them, I think becoming aware of the finality of death is what ultimately brings us this clarity. When we consider our own death or the death of those we love, everything becomes clearer. We each experience this moment at some point in our lives – we lose someone, and we realize the finality of death. When we experience this moment, we have a choice to ask the questions and consider what death truly means in our lives and the time we spend on earth.

Consider the following questions for a moment: If you were to die tomorrow, would you have regrets? Are there things you wish you had done? Are there things you wish you were doing? If you found out you would die in two weeks, are there things you would want to make sure to do? What would most matter most to you during that time?

How we feel about the time we have shifts and changes as we consider death. When we have what feels like plenty of time – we put off the things that matter most. We delay pursuing our dreams. We focus more on the chores than the moments with our children. We work longer hours rather than spend time in prayer or with family and friends. We put off vacations. We fail to achieve personal goals. We tend to be in a battle with life rather than working in harmony with life.

> *We all feel this constant struggle with time – we want more of it, feel limited by it, dream about having more of it, but rarely do we truly make the most of it or even take steps to improve how we use it.*

Despite feeling like we have plenty of time left on this earth, just about everyone feels the limits and constraints of time on a daily basis. We feel rushed and hurried in our lives. We never feel we have enough time and deciding how to spend our time is one of the biggest challenges we experience. How do I know this is true? If I had a dollar for every time, I heard someone say, "I don't have enough time" or "I don't have time to do more than I'm doing" or "If only there were more time," I'd easily be a millionaire – or maybe even a billionaire!

As time ticks by, so does our opportunity to change and improve the value of our time. We are so busy being busy we don't even see how much time there really is. We let it pass us by – misapplied or even wasted entirely. God does not want us to waste this time on earth. In fact, the time we have here is precious, and we must treat it as such, using it for good.

The many excuses we make for how we spend our time are just that – excuses giving us permission not to change or improve. We can accomplish much more than we realize if we both allow and push ourselves to make the necessary changes. In fact, evolving our approach to how we spend time is the biggest determining factor in whether we reach peak performance and have exceptional work and life experiences. As long as we feel defeated and limited by time, and remain convinced we can't do anything about it, we will stay in this unproductive state.

Why do we take so long to make these changes in our lives?
Why do we choose to perform sub-optimally?
Why do we choose not to operate at peak performance?
Why don't we evolve?

The processes and practices to evolve our use of time are hard. They are hard because if they were easy, we wouldn't actually learn the lessons needed to bring about the change in the first place. Not long ago, while talking about this book with my employee Meldina (you will hear more about her later), she shared a recent experience.

"I was talking to my wedding planner about my beliefs on mindset, life, and change. The wedding planner responded asking me how old I was and when I shared, I was only 26, she said she was surprised someone so young had such tremendous insight. I told her it was all because of the coaching I had received which had transformed my thinking, my results, and my life."

I love Meldina's story because it highlights that we can and likely will learn the lessons contained in this book during our lives. However, the lessons typically take lifetimes to learn. I'm certain you've heard the saying "No one on their deathbed says I wish I had spent more time working!" The lesson from this saying is clearly to make time for family and what we enjoy, and yet, we tend to dismiss or ignore these insights. These lessons learned throughout lifetimes (ours and those who came before us) are what we might refer to as wisdom.

> **Wisdom** is the quality of having experience, knowledge, and good judgment; the quality of being wise[1]

We can benefit from the lessons learned by those who came before us, the knowledge that comes from years of experience, and research from experts around the world. We can collectively refer to all of it as wisdom. We have the opportunity to acquire wisdom by creating experiences where we can harness it earlier in our lives. This wisdom, and the development that precedes it, can be learned, and acquired earlier in our lives. And if we acquire wisdom earlier, while we have more time to act, we can apply it throughout our lives. With this wisdom, we can evolve to truly live exceptional lives.

We know we aren't required to wait for wisdom – so why would we?

WHAT DO WE MEAN BY EVOLVING TO PEAK PERFORMANCE?

I will explain shortly why reaching peak performance is critical to having these exceptional experiences. But before we can reach peak performance, we must understand what we mean by peak performance and why we should care about evolving our performance.

When I think about and refer to performance, I think about the many facets of my life where I am *performing* a particular role – as mother, wife, leader, employee, daughter, friend, sister, advisor, coach, mentor, writer, and more. Each role requires me to perform a particular function with specific responsibilities. Whether we recognize it or not, we are all performing every day, all day, in one role or another. Our actions, our words, and our choices all create our daily performance. We can choose to perform only to meet the bare minimum to survive in a role or we can choose to perform at our very best to thrive in a role, or anything in between these two choices.

We impact our performance with our actions, our competencies, our abilities, our skills, our strengths, our values, our beliefs, and our mindset. Our performance ultimately creates all the results in our life. In the workplace, our performance determines how we progress, get compensated, and deliver business results. At home, our performance determines how we live, how we feel, and the growth of our personal relationships. In our communities, our performance determines how we interact, how we support others, and how we grow as a society dependent on one another for our future.

We all perform – we don't have to do it consciously; we do it because it's what we do as human beings. Like a tree grows, like the clouds drop rain, like the earth circling the sun and the moon circling the earth – performance is our personal gravity, that keeps us moving. Simply, things need to be done (work, housework, childcare) and so (in most cases) we do them.

But we can, in fact, consciously and purposefully perform in a particular way. We can perform poorly – choosing not to put in effort or putting in only minimal effort. Our performance can be average – we can do enough to have things appear acceptable but know internally we are just going through the motions. Or we can be intentional, we can be purposeful, putting in the necessary effort to reach a state of peak performance. Performance we are proud of, performance that creates results for us and our families, performance that generates valuable and meaningful outcomes in our lives and our businesses.

What is peak performance? Let me be clear first with what it is not! I am *not* saying peak performance is *perfect* performance. We cannot perform at perfection in all our roles, for all our lives, and in all situations. Rather, peak performance represents the state in which we operate when performing our daily responsibilities that helps us to perform at our very best.

> **Peak performance** is a state in which the person performs to the maximum of their ability, characterized by subjective feelings of confidence, effortlessness, and total concentration on the task.[2]
>
> **Peak performance** is a state also known as peak experience, the zone of optimal functioning and flow.[3]

Actually, you can't even reach peak performance without falling down, failing, stumbling, hitting hurdles and roadblocks, sometimes choosing not to perform, and even occasionally getting stuck for a period of time. The path to peak performance is filled with challenges but it is the challenges that help us continue to evolve our performance. We must always evolve our performance, learning and continuing to grow in order to succeed. The path where we evolve to reach peak performance is what allows us to have more experiences that are exceptional.

> **Evolve** means to develop gradually, especially from a simple to more complex form; to come forth gradually into being; develop; undergo evolution[4]
>
> **Evolve** means to gradually change one's opinions or beliefs; to develop by a process of evolution to a different adaptive state or condition[5]

For me personally, peak performance is when I am operating at my best, when I am striving to perform at my best, and when, as a result, I am having exceptional experiences at work and in life. I don't claim to be the best performer in the world, always at the top of my performance and never making mistakes. Even writing this I feel the absurdity of that statement. I am not perfect, and my performance is not perfect, but I work every day at evolving to reach my peak performance in the roles I serve because I want to have as many exceptional work and life experiences as possible. And you know what? The more I do this – the more exceptional experiences I have! And as a result, the greater I feel about and enjoy my life!

> *Peak performance is when we have evolved and optimized ourselves to operate at the highest level of our personal capabilities and in a way that produces positive results and creates exceptional experiences in our lives.*

Who doesn't want to have more exceptional work and life experiences? If you don't, then I am not sure the rest of this book will do you much good. Keep in mind following the guide to peak performance is not for those who aren't willing to do the work to reach it. I'm not suggesting all the work is hard – but it does require purposeful, thoughtful, and intentional effort to truly evolve and reach peak performance. You can't just wish it into being. But you can incorporate practical applications into your life, a little bit at a time, and wake up one day realizing you are at peak performance and living an exceptional life!

WHY DO WE (OR SHOULD WE) CARE ABOUT REACHING PEAK PERFORMANCE?

If having exceptional work and life experiences and living your best life is not sufficient motivation for evolving your performance – there are more reasons to do so! We may be motivated by the meaning or purpose of the roles we perform. We may be motivated by the risks that exist if we fail to improve our performance. We may be motivated by our personal needs, values, and strengths.

Motivated by the Meaning or Purpose

Our performance matters because we typically perform roles for the benefit of others. In fact, most of us derive our personal meaning and purpose from the roles we perform. When we care about our roles, we naturally desire to be the very best we can be in that role. The better we perform the roles that matter, the better we feel about our lives and the results we achieve.

All the roles I serve are important to me or I would not choose to perform them. Because the roles I perform are important to me, I personally desire to perform them in the best way possible. I want to be the best mom, best manager, best leader I can possibly be. I've often heard others say, "I work so that I can support my family." That can be meaning enough to perform your role well. To support our family in the best way possible, we must perform the role that supports and makes it possible. Meaning is not loving everything you do. Meaning is finding purpose and a reason why performing the role at your best, or peak performance, matters to you specifically.

Motivated by Risk

We may also derive motivation to perform our roles from the risks that exist if we fail to perform. The only thing that is constant in this world is change. The world is going to just keep on changing. People are going to change, businesses are going to change, and our lives are going to change. When we fail to change or evolve our performance, we suffer the consequences of falling behind. And, unless we constantly evolve our performance to keep up with the pace of change in this world, we will definitely fall behind. The farther we fall behind, the harder it becomes to catch up. This is why those who leave prison after many years struggle so much to assimilate. The world has changed, and they were unable to change with it. I personally prefer not to use negative reasons to provide motivation, but I think the risk of falling behind may sometimes, for some people, be the best motivator until they are able to see the benefits of evolving.

Personal Motivation

Maybe you know you need to evolve your performance, but still struggle to find motivation. Another way to derive motivation is to look inward at your personal attributes. Assess yourself – your strengths, your values, your interests, and your personal needs. Oftentimes when we struggle with motivation, it might be that we lack understanding or familiarity with ourselves. We may need to look internally first and see who we are and how we can help ourselves to be motivated to improve. Everyone in this world has natural talents and, once you've identified yours, they can provide a great tool for finding your motivation to perform. I will provide more information and tools on strengths in the next chapter.

Whatever your source of motivation, you must start by finding a desire to evolve. This desire does not have to be all consuming, it can start small – it will certainly grow over time and with success.

Reflection: *Have you thought about the purpose or meaning of the roles you serve and why those roles matter to you specifically? I encourage you to take a moment and think of all the roles you serve and why performing them (and improving how you perform them) matters to you. Consider if the role is important to you, if so – why, and if not – why do you need to perform it?*

You may be currently serving roles that don't provide you meaning or purpose, or, even worse, you don't care about performing. If this is the case, start by asking if you truly don't care or if you just don't like the role? Consider your options. Can you choose a new role (as is the case in the workplace)? Or do you need to spend more time finding meaning in the role because you must perform it?

DOES REACHING PEAK PERFORMANCE TRULY CREATE EXCEPTIONAL WORK AND LIFE EXPERIENCES?

Alright, let's summarize. I've highlighted why exceptional work and life experiences matter and how you can learn this lesson earlier in life. You know what I mean by peak performance and understand or have a sense of why your performance should matter to you (in at least some of your roles). At this point you might be asking yourself:

How does peak performance help me to live an exceptional life? How does it create exceptional work and life experiences? How do I know if this will work? Will it really make a difference?

I'll be honest, in the beginning I had only hope (not assurance) that my research and the strategies I was promoting and implementing would create the results I believed to be possible. I wasn't sure and didn't really know whether it would actually work. I had to trust the research and resources I relied upon, combined with my own intuition, to see if this path was indeed the right path. Now, after many years of using and applying these strategies in business, in my life, and in the coaching of many employees – I have seen firsthand (over and over and over again) the results that can be achieved.

Peak performance allows us to operate in a way that helps us leverage all our capabilities, the tools and technology we have access to, and the relationships and resources we have available to achieve better outcomes in our lives. When we operate at peak performance, we feel more alive, more in tune, more connected, more committed, and more valuable. We are intentional with what we do to create the results and experiences we want for our lives – at work, at home, and in our communities. We see our experiences and recognize they are exceptional, and they are generating more positive outcomes in our lives.

In my life, I have repeatedly broken through barriers to evolve my performance, taken on new challenges, and successfully learned and performed in new areas. I started in the area of legal contracts, then pursued my passion of talent management. Next, I took on information technology, then order management, project coordination, and customer service. While performing and leading these roles, I have also taken on the roles of wife and mother, battled significant health issues, and managed a number of challenging personal mindsets and situations. And, most recently, I've now become a writer! Through this expansion I have experienced more joy, more exceptional experiences, and a better life than I imagined possible.

Likewise, I have had employees tell me repeatedly, "It's not possible, I can't accomplish more, I can't meet that deadline, I can't take on more work." Ultimately, these same employees successfully achieve twice as much as what they denied they could do in the first place. I'll admit, not all the strategies I started with proved fruitful or delivered value. But every strategy included in the chapters that follow has brought about the changes and results I only *hoped* ten years ago was possible.

As I continue to implement these strategies in my life, I find that I keep getting more time (not less) in my life. I'll admit there are times I stumble, I get stuck, and I need to grow and evolve again. But through each challenge and subsequent growth I learn to appreciate life more, feel good about my contributions, and ultimately create exceptional work and life experiences for myself. I am truly working each day on evolving my performance so I can keep living my best life!

I hope by reading this book you can incorporate these strategies in your own life and see the impact it will make. I hope you will learn where to spend your time and how to get more time back for things you love. I know if you take the principles I provide in this book and apply them to your life – you will see results. And I know that when you do, you will get more time back and you will feel this extra time is creating exceptional work and life experiences.

A review of 18 studies suggests that the prospect of death leads to greater appreciation of life, more rapid formulation of values, more thought about the meaning of life, and stronger social connections… when you consider how short life can be, you create more meaning in the world. [6]

Tom Rath, in Life's Great Question

I want to close this section by coming back to a story about my grandfather. One Thanksgiving, my family met at a Holiday Inn in Arkansas to spend the holiday together. This gathering occurred between two of my grandfather's diagnoses – he had recovered from one cancer and had not yet been diagnosed with the next.

One night, we went out to dinner as a family. When the dessert tray came, my grandfather (who was very much living life to the fullest after beating cancer) stated that the children could have any dessert they wanted. My youngest cousin "wanted" three different desserts – and she got them! As the oldest, I was stunned. This does not happen; we are *never* allowed multiple desserts. I started to argue, but not a parent at the table would cross my grandfather. He survived cancer. If he wants to let the kids have multiple desserts –

then they certainly weren't going to say no! I love this memory because it reminds me of the happiness that evening with my family and the need for these joyful experiences and moments.

We must think of living life on purpose – of living life in a way that honors the finality of death – of living a meaningful and fulfilling life our whole lives rather than just as we approach the end. Evolving our performance to create exceptional work and life experiences is not about a destination. It is a strategy and path to experiencing life in a better, more meaningful way – a way that brings us success, satisfaction, peace, joy, and happiness. If every person were to define what exceptional work and life experiences are or look like for them – they would be as different as the snowflakes that fall from the sky! However, the key to living a life that creates exceptional experiences is evolving to peak performance and the strategies are all similar.

Occasionally, consider enjoying life, your children, and have that extra dessert!

CHAPTER TWO
Evolving to
Peak Performance

How do I reach peak performance?

> ### Key Insight:
>
> I must prepare to reach peak performance by building a strong set of personal capabilities for having productive and effective performance coaching conversations.

A quick Google search for improving performance will solicit hundreds of thousands of articles, models, opinions, and insights on the best way to improve performance. I've spent years reading, researching, and learning about improving performance as an employee, manager, leader, and talent management professional. I truly believe evolving our performance is so important that I'm even writing this book (which I truly hope you will find valuable).

Despite this, I have found that all the models, articles, opinions, and insights are basically the same concepts. They are all based on the same themes and theories, each providing a nuanced way to think about and approach performance. Although strategies for how to apply the concepts, coach and manage performance, and improve performance continue to evolve with the latest research and advances in technology, the fundamental principles for evolving our performance remain unchanged.

Early in my career I was searching for an approach for Experitec to successfully manage and improve performance. I read all of the latest articles and most books on the topic, trying to find the best practice or approach. At the time, a lot was starting to change with performance management – you may remember Adobe had just thrown out the performance review![7] One book, in particular, had a tremendous impact on me early in my career – *First Break all the Rules* by Marcus Buckingham.[8] Initially, I chose the book because, frankly, I like breaking the rules and I thought breaking all the rules of performance sounded like a great idea! Ultimately, the book started me on my journey to evolving performance.

When I read the book, I thought it was brand new – the latest in how to think differently about performance. Only after reading the book, I checked the publication date and found, to my surprise, it was written 20 years prior. I couldn't believe this research and insight existed for many years with so few companies capitalizing on it. Since first reading this book, I have spent years researching, creating, and maximizing my personal approach to performance. During this time, I've added to and refined the foundational concepts, and most importantly, I have personally practiced each and every technique extensively.

HOW DO WE REACH PEAK PERFORMANCE?

In his book, Buckingham uses the analogy for our performance as a mountain.[9] We each have our own performance mountain to climb, and they each look different and have unique challenges. I love this analogy and it works well with the concept of peak performance. Reaching peak performance is never a destination, it's the state of our performance as we climb our performance mountain creating exceptional work and life experiences. The performance mountain is different from career ladders whose only purpose is to take you from rung to rung up to the top. Rather, each performance mountain is to be experienced as you progress on your journey – and you will climb many in your lifetime, both in and outside the workplace.

 We've established why we want to reach peak performance (we truly care about our roles), but how do we get there? How do we prepare, develop the strengths, acquire the tools, and then embark on our journey? Before we can go up the mountain – we must spend time preparing to climb. Think of the preparation as climbing a rock wall – learning skills, developing competencies, and gaining experiences to help us on our journey. This development prepares us to perform our roles at our best, peak performance.

Once on the mountain, we work through a series of challenges and experiences unique to each mountain, or each role we perform. The performance mountain is just the location or the experience we have in a role, we are still creators of that experience. So, how do we create experiences to evolve our performance and reach our peak? Think about this in terms of an athlete or Olympian. They certainly don't reach peak performance by sitting on the couch watching Netflix – it takes effort, intention, and good old fashioned hard work!

You can find hundreds of books, articles, and approaches to improving performance. Everyone approaches it a little differently, uses a different word, or comes at it from a different perspective. Over the years, I have learned a lot about performance through direct experience and, more importantly, trial and error. I think many different approaches to performance can be successful – and anything that moves you towards evolving your performance is worthwhile.

However, I wanted something simple, something practical, something I could remember, and something I could use to easily think about performance. With a framework, we can quickly get to the heart of the topic and what is required to evolve performance. I struggle with models that list 10, 12, 14 things to make you successful! I want something I can remember and will help me when the challenges arise.

WHAT ARE THE KEYS FOR REACHING PEAK PERFORMANCE?

The framework I created uses four keys to peak performance. (Note: Our organization uses a different, albeit similar, word to "peak" that is part of our corporate vision. I have changed it for this book to make it a more universally understandable and applicable word.) To reach peak performance, you must: (1) Set clear expectations, (2) Provide ongoing feedback, (3) Use strengths-based development, and (4) Cultivate a personal accountability mindset.

Expectations, Feedback, Development, & Accountability!

If we can remember the four keys, they will guide us to reach peak performance. In my experience, if you do these four things well in any role, you will see your performance evolve and improve. In section three, we will cover these keys in depth with strategies, tools, and resources. Although these keys are the roadmap, or guide, for how to get to peak performance (how to successfully climb our mountain), we need to first prepare for the climb.

Marcus Buckingham uses the analogy of altitude sickness in his book.[10] I want to apply it a little differently in this book. For anyone who has climbed mountains, you may have experienced altitude sickness. For me, altitude sickness is a very serious thing. When I change altitude (like going to Colorado), I get lightheaded, nauseous, and usually have a slight fever. It takes me days to acclimate to the altitude sufficiently to enjoy the scenery.

To be blunt, altitude sickness sucks, and if you try to climb a mountain before you are ready – the results are *not* going to be good! Experienced individuals know you need to take time to acclimate, drink lots of water, avoid alcohol, eat carbs, sleep, and take medication. We need to prepare our minds and bodies to experience the effects of changes in altitude.

 Likewise, as we climb our performance mountain, we must be conscious of altitude sickness and prepare ourselves to experience the effects of evolving our performance. To perform at our best, we need to prepare ourselves for peak performance. If we aren't prepared with the right capabilities and tools, our results will suffer. Peak performers know to perform at your peak, you need individual insights with regular reflection, authenticity & accountability, constant communication, respectful relationships, powerful partnerships, trusted teams, grit & gratitude, the wisdom of well-being, and to be future-focused.

INDIVIDUAL INSIGHTS WITH REGULAR REFLECTION – WHY WHO WE ARE MATTERS?

> **Insight**: the capacity to gain an accurate and deep intuitive understanding of a person or thing; a deep understanding of a person or thing [11]
>
> **Reflection**: a fixing of the thoughts on something; careful consideration [12]

In order to meaningfully impact our performance, we always need to begin with understanding ourselves and understanding the landscape of our performance, the current state of our performance, and our mindset related to our performance. Self-awareness is so important that I have devoted the entire next chapter to this topic!

Part of this self-awareness is ensuring we carve out the time to reflect on our experiences, our challenges, our plans, and our lives. Each month, a member of our sales team shares insights from recent training on a particular sales competency. During one presentation, a team member shared their challenge with finding time for reflection, time to prepare for the next day, and time to ensure they work on what really matters most. He shared that, ultimately, he chose nine pm because it was a good time for him, and now his kids have learned this new practice as well. When his alarm goes off to reflect, his kids take advantage and they all "strike a reflection pose together." What an awesome way to incorporate this behavior into a family practice!

Whether we take time to reflect on our expectations, our goals, our short or long-term plans, our progress, our development, or the results we have achieved, this reflection is truly a determining factor in our ultimate success and ability to reach peak performance. We must prepare to incorporate time for reflection on our experiences. This reflection can be on our own or with others, but we must ensure that we create the space and time for it to occur. We must remain open to the insights and changes which are necessary to evolving our performance. As a result, you will notice throughout the book, I have included 'Reflection' sections for you to take time and consider the questions and concepts in order to translate them into insights for yourself.

AUTHENTICITY & ACCOUNTABILITY
– WHY WE NEED IT?

We are social creatures, and it is not until we are able to truly embody our authentic Self that we become able to connect deeply with the people we love.[13]

Dr. Nicole LePera, in How to Do the Work

I will repeatedly address this topic throughout this book. I am knowingly doing so because these topics are so important reinforcing them is essential. I know from years of training employees that I often must repeat the same topic, different ways, before it ultimately clicks. Our mindsets and our level of authenticity and accountability are critical for preparing us to reach peak performance.

Much of what we do to reach peak performance requires us to approach challenging situations with a mindset of personal accountability. How we respond and what we do with our experiences is directly impacted by how we think about them. In other words, the greater our level of personal accountability, the greater our happiness and success.

To really be engaged in the conversations and self-work necessary to reach peak performance, we must get comfortable being our authentic selves. If we are wearing an alternative personality, style, or approach, we will fail to embrace the things about us which can and will contribute to our success and peak performance. We can achieve more in life than we even realize is possible, but first we must believe in ourselves.

To be authentic, we must be prepared to embrace our vulnerability. Yes, I know this is painful, hard, and complicated. I know showing our weaknesses is incredibly challenging. I also know this is the path to peak performance. You may not be ready yet to share yourself with the world, your boss, your family, or others, and I completely understand. What I ask is that you be prepared to, at least, be vulnerable with yourself. Be true to yourself as you read this book and consider your true self. Not the person you wish you were or the person you would like to be, but the person you are today.

COMMUNICATION WITH CONNECTION – WHY ARE CONVERSATIONS CRITICAL?

Excellent communication and frequent conversations are fundamental components that are foundational and necessary to evolving performance. This concept is important enough that I will state it again:

Constant Communication and Conversations are Critical!

In his book Everyone Communicates, Few Connect, John Maxwell says, "The first time you say something, it's heard. The second time, it's recognized, and the third time it's learned." [14]

If we want to improve our performance, we must ensure our communication facilitates the needed understanding by being both frequent and effective

The Frequency Issue – Constant, Consistent, and Clear

The topic of performance management systems has been well researched, and many examples exist highlighting the ineffectiveness of traditional performance management reviews. These once-a-year assessments designed to improve an employee's performance have consistently proven to not only fail to improve performance but, in some cases, actually negatively impact performance.[15]

By only discussing performance once–a–year, we fail to capture important information, internalize it, and take meaningful action on it. When I first heard of Adobe's HR Leader "throwing out the performance review," I reveled at the story![16] Now, many organizations have statistical evidence showing the positive impact of frequent conversations on performance versus performance reviews. We now know we must communicate often if we want to change behavior and performance results.

You might be tempted to think this applies only to the workplace, where formal reviews and annual goal setting have prevented or hindered better performance discussions. However, the other roles we play have the same challenges and maybe, in some cases, it's even worse. In our families and marriages, we often assume (a terrible practice!) that others know what they "should" and "should not" be doing. (Note: Should statements are always a red flag that something is likely wrong!) In fact, I've seen relationships (including in my life) go on for years without really addressing some of the fundamental elements of performance and, as result, cause pain, suffering, frustration, and anger.

We must be constant and consistent in our communication. By frequently communicating and having conversations regarding performance, we create a consistent experience and a better opportunity to adjust and improve as challenges occur. We must understand ourselves, learn from our experiences, and talk about them in the context of our roles with those we serve to reach peak performance. The only way we achieve these outcomes is by communicating frequently so we can reach peak performance.

The Effectiveness Issue – Connection, Capability, Results

I could write an entire book on the importance of good conversations and communication, and how they impact your life. If you struggle, I encourage you to read the many books on building strong communication skills, one favorite of mine is *Crucial*

Conversations.[17] We must be good communicators if we are going to reach peak performance. This doesn't mean we talk constantly or have to be professional speakers, but it does mean we have to communicate with intention and purpose.

We may talk about the weather, a sports game, our children's funny story – but are we having conversations about what really, truly matters for us to be evolving our performance? Even if we have conversations on critical topics, are they frequent enough to be impacting our performance? If they are frequent and on what matters, are we connecting during these communications to make them effective and productive? I would venture a guess that the answer in many cases is "no."

Connection with friends, family, pets, the divine, etc. is as necessary as food and water. Humans are not built to function autonomously we are built to oscillate between connection and autonomy and back again.[18]

Emily & Amelia Nagoski, in Burnout

If you struggle with connection, John Maxwell's book *Everyone Communicates, Few Connect* is a fantastic resource. In his book, Maxwell emphasizes the key to communication is connection, and to succeed you must learn how to connect with those you communicate. When leaders, speakers, coaches, and even strangers take time to connect in their communication, I remember it, I believe in it, and I frequently take action on it. I feel connected and therefore, make changes in my life which bring value.

Many years ago, I learned to create effective communications using Tim Pollard's Oratium method and if you have never heard of it – you must check them out! He taught me the critical element of any communication: always starting with the need or problem of our audience and the action we want them to take as a result of the communication. Taking the time to consider the issue of the person or people you are communicating with and what you want them to do afterwards dramatically changes how and what you communicate. The effectiveness of myself and our team increased significantly once we learned to take this pause before starting a communication.

If you are fortunate enough to work for a manager or organization which effectively applies agile performance management with frequent and effective performance conversations, consider yourself lucky. Take full advantage of those conversations. In my review, few organizations are doing effective performance conversations today. For those that are not, hopefully the principles in this book will provide a guide for incorporating more frequent and effective conversations in your life.

RESPECTFUL RELATIONSHIPS – HOW DO WE TREAT EACH OTHER?

When we enter into performance conversations our level of respect for the person is frequently the determining factor in the conversations' productivity and effectiveness. Recently, as conflict grows in our communities, the word "respect" became increasingly important to me both personally and professionally. All the workplace issues with harassment and discrimination, the increase in conflict due to different viewpoints, and the challenges brought by limited perspectives and personal biases, require us to return to the fundamental concept of *respect*. Evolving to peak performance requires us to respectfully interact with one another. Our performance means very little if we fail to meet the needs of those we serve. Frequently, we may fail to demonstrate respect in our behaviors and interactions.

> **Respect** is due regard for the feelings, wishes, rights, or traditions of others.[19]

For me, respect means we accept the other person for who they are – even if they are different from me and especially when I don't agree with them. I want to be very clear; I am not saying we must respect every person's beliefs. In fact, I personally do not respect some beliefs. I do not respect the belief women are inferior to men, I do not respect the belief some races are better than others, and I do not respect the belief violence is the answer. I can, however, speak respectfully to the person holding those beliefs. I do not have to respond to disrespect with disrespect. In fact, I can be respectful even when I disagree or am frustrated with the other person.

One particular mentor of mine holds very different views to my own. This mentor is a great person, with tremendous experience and capabilities, who always treated me with respect. We would get into extremely energized debates about topics with which we disagreed, or rather with which we were exploring our differences. In many cases, we found the basis of our belief was similar but the path we thought necessary to reach the outcome was quite different. I enjoyed those discussions immensely; I grew from the experience. His perspectives caused me to think differently about my own. Neither of us truly believed we would change the other's core opinion or belief, but we could understand more about our own beliefs by understanding those of others.

When it comes to conflict and interpersonal interactions – the respect we demonstrate is critical to developing meaningful relationships. At Experitec, we developed Respectful Workplace workshops to create clarity, encourage, support, and foster our culture of respect. For obviously disrespectful behaviors most people quickly understand what not to do – discrimination, violence, sexual harassment, bullying, and the like. However, many behaviors are grey and challenging to understand. They aren't sure, and hesitate to say whether a particular action is respectful or what we should do in a specific situation.

I facilitated this workshop for another company's leadership team. One leader asked me, "What about when someone wants to wear a MAGA (Make America Great Again) hat or a BLM (Black Lives Matter) hat? What do we do?" This question initially stumped me because I had not encountered or considered this example previously. Others suggested creating a policy against all hats or against any political messaging. After reflecting, I returned to the core concept of demonstrating respect between those involved. If I want to work in a respectful environment (which most employees do) and I want others to feel they can work in a respectful environment – then I must choose to demonstrate respect for those I work with. Therefore, individuals can wear what they want (assuming it is safe to do so) and when asked to change because of the negative impact on others they work with, they will do so willingly to foster the respectful culture.

This played out frequently during COVID. Whether you believed in the efficacy of masks or not, wearing a mask is required and respectful of those you are interacting with. Therefore, in most cases, people were willing to put on the required mask when with others and in public places, regardless of their personal beliefs.

Conflict, alternative opinions, and different experiences all contribute to better outcomes in our businesses, homes, and communities. However, we must maintain a level of respect in all our interactions to ensure conversations remain productive, effective, and have the desired impact.

Reflection: *Consider your own behaviors and interactions with others. Are you respectful? How do you ensure you remain respectful? Do you share when you feel others are being disrespectful? How can respect help you to have more meaningful conversations with less negative conflict?*

PERFORMANCE PARTNERSHIPS – WHY WHO WE ASSOCIATE WITH MATTERS?

Everyone can't possibly know and experience everything in this world, and we weren't meant to. Rather, we are each a uniquely different person with our own skillsets, strengths, personalities, and entirely different life experiences. If, when we think about our performance, we think only of ourselves, we will miss a major element of what the greatest performers do best – learn from others!

I could spend every minute of every hour of everyday reading, learning, and attempting to accomplish everything, and I would never come even close to achieving that objective. As a child, I attempted to read every book in the library starting at A… it didn't work! Even the most capable, successful, and accomplished people in the world can't possibly be successful at everything. The best performers know that developing partnerships and finding opportunities to learn, connect, and interact with others is critical to evolving performance.

"You are the average of the five people you spend the most time with."

Jim Rohn

I learned this quote in a Cy Wakeman training I did a number of years ago around Reality Based Rules of the Workplace. I realized who I choose to listen to, spend time with, and surround myself with is extremely important. I never really thought about how the people around us impact our beliefs and our lives. For example, if I surround myself with people focused on achieving positive results, improving the world, becoming better human beings, caring about others, and generally living a great life – I am going to be much more likely to do the same. Alternatively, if I am surrounded by people who judge others, always blame someone else, find something wrong even on the best day, and are generally living a miserable life – what happens? You guessed it – I am going to be judging, blaming, and complaining too!

I've experienced the impact of being on a team of people who are all interested in pushing boundaries, growing, learning, improving, and developing. The team of employees I work with every day are all focused on success and achieving positive results. We accept when we inevitably stumble, make a mistake, or just plain fail. We help each other brush off, get back up, learn the lesson, and move on to be successful the next time. These relationships are powerful – we keep each other lifted up, we keep each other motivated, and we keep each other learning and growing.

Think about these partnerships as the village at the base of your performance mountain. Who is going to be part of your village that helps you prepare, providing support and resources? Businesses need to create workplace villages – the community of resources to support employees in their performance journey. Our village provides us the coaching, advice, suggestions, and techniques to reach our peak performance. We must find ways to create our villages. In the digital world, we now have the ability to build villages for ourselves with anyone, anywhere in the world.

Over the last year I set a goal to build and expand my network of connections. Both due to COVID and due to small children and working full time, I don't have a lot of time to attend happy hours or events. However, I was able to find meet-up groups I could connect with virtually. I attended new events and actively engaged in discussions with people during those events. These connections even helped me find my way to writing this book and supported me during my journey!

Take this step – find your village!

Reflection: As you embark on your performance journey – consider who you are surrounded with each day. Are you surrounded with people who will inspire you, challenge you, and support you in improving your performance? If not, what could you do to make this change in your life?

TRUSTED TEAMS – WHY IS A FOUNDATION OF TRUST ESSENTIAL?

Our militaries know one absolutely critical element to succeeding in battle – we only want to go into battle with people we trust! When the worst, most challenging situations occur, we want to be on teams with high trust and strong relationships. Although respect and partnerships are valuable – trust is essential. The one thing everyone immediately notices when things get tough is the difference of a team with trust.

My teams went through a particularly challenging 'security event' during the writing of this book. One Saturday afternoon, I was making good progress on my book when I got a message that would disrupt the next few months of my life, cause significant challenges for our business, and forever alter my appreciation of cybersecurity awareness. When I got the text "Much worse than we originally thought" from my IT Manager, a trusted and close friend of mine (as well as my employee), I knew it was serious.

The details of the event itself – although interesting and unbelievable – are irrelevant to this book. However, the interaction of our teams, the communication, the collaboration, and, most importantly, the trust demonstrated under tremendous pressure is definitely worth sharing. Our teams worked around the clock to address the event and the subsequent activities to contain, remediate, and return to normal business. The stress was high, the pressure was extreme, and the decisions required in short periods of time were made and carried with significant burden. Here's the thing though – no matter how difficult what we went through was, because of our culture, our people, our workplace – things got better!

Our teams have high trust; they are friends, and they have good relationships with each other. Many had not yet returned to the office or seen each other since the start of COVID. As we returned (due to the challenges), people were hugging friends they hadn't seen in a year. They were joyous to be together. And everyone was ready to dig in and solve the challenges and problems in front of us.

At a leadership level, we maintained a high level of transparency, continuous communication, and provided relevant data as frequently as we could to employees. We made decisions focused on our people and what was in their best interest. At an employee level, we trusted our teams, managers, and functional leaders to make the appropriate decisions regarding our work processes and activities. And most importantly, our IT Team – they were amazing. Their trust was so high they worked together seamlessly. Everyone had everyone's backs and, even with working 18-to-20-hour days, they were laughing with each other. Everyone in the whole company came together in a way that is only possible when you have built the trust needed for such collaboration.

When you have trust – when you know you can count on people – you don't have to ask twice, you don't have to go meet with someone else, and you don't have to question whether someone is telling you the truth. You focus on the problem, know who can take on which tasks, and divide up and conquer whatever needs to be done. I am confident that despite this tremendous challenge, working long hours, and making personal sacrifices for the business, our organization and employees will come out of it more engaged, more committed, and more connected than ever before! And let me tell you – that is saying a lot because we were already an exceptional workplace!

I use this work example because I think it is so incredibly powerful, but the concepts apply in every setting. Challenges outside our control are going to happen in our lives and we aren't going to be able to stop them. However, we can come together, connect, and build trust so that when those challenges happen, we work together to solve them.

Teams must build and maintain high levels of trust!

GRIT & GRATITUDE – WHY DO WE NEED BOTH?

One day I was looking for a lost book my son desperately wanted to read about *popcorn*. (The book was not actually lost. Rather, my grandmother hid the book somewhere and couldn't remember where she hid it. Myself, my husband, both my parents, my sister, and my grandmother scoured the house for the book. The next morning my daughter Ella walked up to my husband with the book in her hands – we still have no idea where she found it!) While looking for the book I opened a drawer and found a little decorated box. On top of the box were stickers of the words "I can tackle anything!" Inside the box are fish and a little tackle box and pole.

The box was clearly handmade by someone and long forgotten. The message, on the other hand, is one worth spending time on.

When we are bombarded with the popcorn of challenges which inevitably get in the way of our performance – how can we stay the course? Believing in our ability to tackle and overcome any challenge we encounter is called grit or resilience.

> **Grit:** courage and resolve; strength of character[20]
>
> **Resilience:** the capacity to recover quickly from difficulties; toughness[21]

Duckworth, author of *Grit*, has conducted extensive research on what contributes to success. The result of her research was grit. She even developed a grit scale so you can assess your grittiness! The combination of passion and the desire to persevere in the face of obstacles is the skill of grit or resilience.

Grit is defined by Angela Duckworth "as the passion and perseverance for long term goals. One way to think about grit is to consider what grit isn't. Grit isn't talent. Grit isn't how intensely, for the moment, you want something. Instead, grit is about having what some research calls an 'ultimate concern' – a goal you care about so much that it organizes and gives meaning to almost everything you do. And grit is holding steadfast to that goal. Even when you fall down. Even when you screw up. Even when progress toward that goal is halting or slow."[22]

Throughout our lives we develop the ability to either push forward or give up in the face of challenges. I've had interns face this dilemma – it's the moment when they are first challenged, they make their first mistake, or they realize they screwed up big time. So, how do they respond? Do they give up? Do they try something else? They each respond differently, and I can tell a lot by how they respond.

You see, I am a really tough manager. If you ask any of my employees, they will tell you I probably made them cry (or close to it) at one point or another because of how I pushed them. Consequently, all of my (current) employees are exceptionally gritty, and I view that grittiness as a benefit to our team and customers. As a result of this grit, they persevere when others would give up. They achieve more than they first realized was possible. Grittiness is necessary preparation for reaching peak performance.

I wonder who made the box I found, why they made it, and who they made it for. I put the box at the front of my desk while working on this book as a reminder. I hope to use it with my kids – so they know they can tackle anything; they just have to persevere with grit and resilience. I frequently tell my son when it's hard we just keep trying, because in our house "We do hard things!" (Thank you Glennon Doyle!) and we try, try, try again! Now when I get frustrated, he likes to tell me "Mom we do hard things, just try, try, try again!"

Gratitude balances out some of the grittiness required for peak performance. In order to persevere through challenges and struggles we need something to help offset the intensity created by grit and resilience. Gratitude serves this purpose. What do I mean by gratitude? I mean our appreciation for the experiences in our lives and their purpose in helping shape us for the future.

> **Gratitude** is the quality of being thankful; readiness to show appreciation for and to return kindness.[23]

My gratitude practice started after encountering health challenges at Christmas one year (I'll share the full story later in the book). The time I spent struggling with my health transformed my appreciation for a practice of gratitude. I was struggling so much that I started a gratitude journal to help me stay positive. Each day I would write in the journal. Some days it was hard to find three things to be grateful for (especially when the pain was at its highest), but this taught me to look for the small things to be grateful for in my life.

According to Angela Duckworth's Character Lab, "When you feel gratitude, you feel a sense of abundance. When you express gratitude – especially when it's heartfelt – you strengthen your relationship with others[24]

This practice lasted over a year and created a lasting habit (and likely transformed my brain!) where now I am constantly looking for the things I am and can be grateful for. I could have wasted that opportunity and learned nothing and improved nothing, and my performance would have remained the same. Instead, I chose to grow and evolve my performance. This challenge helped me grow and appreciate how to reach peak performance.

Recently, I was doing yoga with my mom and sister outside on the patio while my kids were playing in the yard. The topic of the day for yoga was "Gratitude." While doing yoga, each of my three kids took their turn coming to do a pose next to me, sit by me, or even climb on me! The instructor said, "Focus on your gratitude, tune out everything else going on." Ha! I thought, how can I tune everything out when I have kids climbing on me? But you know what? My kids are one of the things in this world I am the most grateful for! What a great reminder in the middle of gratitude practice to have them so engaged and demonstrating their desire to be close to me!

During the pandemic, I stumbled upon the concept of a "Pandemic of Positivity," which identified four strategies for spreading positivity (especially during times of challenge).[25]

* Spread Connection – Let people know you are thinking of them, and they are meaningful to you.

* Spread Help – Offer help where you can and ask for it if you need it.

* Spread Optimism – If the cost of being wrong is low, let yourself believe things will turn out right.

* Spread Gratitude – Say thanks & really mean it!

 Research shows when people share gratitude for 21 days it improves mental health, increases happiness and feelings of social connection. Given recent challenges with being socially isolated, engaging in this challenge will have a positive impact on our company, communities, and social circles. Join the challenge: Send a two-minute email praising or thanking one person for 21 days straight. You might be surprised by the impact this has not only on others but on your own happiness and well-being.

Experitec adopted a "21 Days of Gratitude Challenge" to spread gratitude throughout our company and communities. I participated in this challenge and have to say – when you show gratitude frequently, you feel the difference! We need to include gratitude in our preparation for peak performance. We must be grateful for our progress, our challenges, our opportunities, and all our experiences. Our gratitude helps us build grit to get through the challenges, learning, and growth necessary to evolve our performance.

THIS WISDOM OF WELL-BEING – WHY DOES IT MATTER?

This past year I had a personal breakthrough on the topic of well-being and how to relate it to peak performance. I wrote the following article on my website explaining my breakthrough and I am including it here to highlight why we don't always recognize well-being as important. But the sooner we acquire the wisdom to appreciate its value and how it applies to us – the better we can perform at our peak.

Last week Gallup®[2] hosted a Learning Series for Gallup®-Certified Coaches with a number of the sessions focused on the topic of Well-being in the Workplace and when coaching with strengths. These thought-provoking sessions caused me to reflect heavily on my own past with the term "well-being" and my more recent challenges. They provided insights for me to finally begin to really grasp the concepts, what they require, and ultimately what they mean for me specifically.

I personally struggled for years to intellectually understand and make sense of the terms "well-being" and "work-life balance." Just ask the employees who work with me how many times we had in depth discussions (read: debates and even arguments) around this topic. A few years ago, my team created materials on "well-being" to better train our managers on its importance, our philosophy, the policies, and the tools/resources available to them as Managers to leverage with their teams. Despite creating and sharing this training, I struggled tremendously with the content and concepts. Why did I struggle so much?

My Struggle with Well-Being & Work-Life Balance

Well – my biggest challenge is – I LOVE working, I mean really truly LOVE working! I know it sounds crazy to some, but I love the sense of accomplishment, I love coaching employees, I love using technology, and I love creating an extraordinary employee experience. Therefore, why in the world did I need to do anything other than work? I mean, don't get me wrong, I also love being outdoors, taking vacations, and reading every kind of book imaginable, but because I enjoy work, I didn't understand the term "balance" and I didn't understand why "well-being" meant somehow achieving some superior state of being meeting social, community, financial, health, and career needs.

Before having my son in March of 2016, my personal values (what I deemed most important to me) did not include family – rather my focus was on excellence, results, learning, growing, etc. At the time, I truly believed having children would not change me. After the birth of my son (and more recently my twin daughters), I realize now that statement was only partially true. While I am still passionate about working, I still love it and it gives me tremendous satisfaction, I also adore my children and love the time I spend with them.

From Well-Being to Mindset to Work-Life Blending

While working on the well-being training, I was personally going through a tremendous struggle with a significant health issue. I struggled to see how life could ever be completely balanced as I was challenged daily to keep up with work and have the energy to spend time with my son and husband. I argued *"How could anyone ever really 'achieve' "well-being?"* I felt it was *impossible and unrealistic*. Then through research and significant self-reflection, I discovered **the power of mindset and the ability to improve one's state of being despite one's circumstances.** After a brief hospitalization just before Christmas undergoing tremendous challenges, I realized I could find joy, happiness, and contentment even in the midst of significant struggle. I pondered...if this is possible, then why should we focus on some abstract concept of "well-being" and an even more ridiculous concept of "balance." After this experience, I began referring to "work-life balance" as "work-life blending," which meant finding the right blend of the two and accomplishing them in parallel. I got quite good at doing this (with only one child) and advancing my career while reserving time for family (with tremendous support/involvement of my husband).

From Work-Life Blending to Survival

In 2019, I had twin girls that came with a whole new set of challenges (as I am sure you can imagine). As a female leader, I was juggling nursing twins and meetings, desperately trying to get into the office – and well-being was nonexistent…there was only survival. And balance well – it consisted of getting maybe two (sometimes one), three hour stretches of sleep at night! I learned how to pump milk while conducting trainings and in leadership meetings. Extra time – for friends, church, hobbies, etc. – just did not exist. Even "work-life blending" became ridiculous – I had no intentional blend of anything. I was simply doing my best not to completely disappoint at work while keeping my babies fed (who as a side note due to a health condition, FPIES, could not tolerate formula, so I had no choice but to keep feeding them myself). Don't get me wrong, I would do it all over again in a heartbeat. The choices and the life I struggled through was for my children who I love and adore and for my career which I also love and adore. I might be easier on myself and set more realistic expectations given the limitations so as not to disappoint myself, but it was absolutely what was required at the time.

Enter the 2020 COVID pandemic. You all know the story – working remotely, juggling kids, figuring out childcare, isolation, exhaustion, etc. etc. etc. Interestingly, although I miss interactions with people, going to fun outings (zoo, etc.), and traveling, I have actually had better well-being during the pandemic. I've gotten more sleep at night working from home (not needing to "get ready" and drive to work). I've actually accomplished more at work than I have in prior years. My teams became even more effective. I've developed closer relationships with my family and most especially my children. I've been able to see my girls grow up in a way I might otherwise never have. And I even re-established friendships with my two best friends from high school having regularly zoom video calls to catch up. Once again, don't get me wrong this last year was HARD but in the end despite the pain and challenges there are some silver linings.

All this brings me to last week and how I have finally started to grasp these concepts which have consistently proved difficult. I recently completed my Workhuman Professional Certification. Part of this certification is Workhuman's "The Charter of Workplace Rights" which include nine rights of a human workplace (amazing and I highly recommend you check the full list out). The right that stood out to me on this topic in particular was:

From Work-Life Blending to Work-Life Harmony

Finally, a term that makes sense and resonates with me personally - "work-life harmony" which is defined as:

"Work-life harmony is about how people respond to the constant fluctuations of work and personal priorities. It's about how much or how little these areas of life are integrated and, most importantly, how each one enriches each other.

Work-life harmony means all the various aspects of people's lives work in concert to create a sense of fulfillment. Everyone's version of work-life harmony is unique since people have different priorities, responsibilities, and values. What is consistent is the right for employees to achieve both personal and professional goals in a way that is fulfilling to them." -Workhuman[26]

What a fantastic explanation of what I have been struggling to wrap my mind around for years. I have always felt well-being was unique to the individual and I think this explanation is perfect. I truly want to have a life experience that creates this work-life harmony. Beyond my own life, my personal purpose is to help people have the best life experience possible and have our business contribute positively to that experience. Work-life harmony fits perfectly with my mission and purpose. For me, work-life harmony does not mean working less, rather it means intentionally getting the most out of my day/time to create results at work while also intentionally focusing on my children and husband while with them. I am very much "in progress" on working on my "work-life harmony" and recognize this is likely an ongoing process rather than a future state of achievement. I believe this is where "well-being" can play an important and meaningful role.

By paying attention to our current well-being and the various contributors that may be at play in impacting our overall well-being, we can identify strategies or make changes to move towards work-life harmony. Elements of well-being serve not as a destination, where you have 'achieved' success in all five areas, but rather a process for self-reflection and the tools to take action to improve. - Jessica's Breakthrough Insight

In my current life circumstance, my ability to reach some perfect "well-being" destination seems impossible. However, creating harmony through self-reflection, considering my current and desired state of well-being, and identifying small changes seems much more achievable.

Work-Life Harmony leveraging Strengths

Finally, as many Gallup®[3] coaches shared during the sessions this week, our individual strengths can play a major role and have a tremendous impact on our well-being. Even as a certified Gallup® Strengths Coach, I had not previously considered (even for myself), how my strengths might be impacting my well-being. My top five Gallup® strengths are Communication®, Maximizer®, Ideation®, Input®, and Strategic®.

With Communication® as my number one strength, being remote can be a big challenge for me. As a leader while I do have regular meetings with team members, I don't get as much of the casual conversation and interesting discussions. At some point during this past year, I began writing articles, insights, and now my own blog posts. This writing, I now realize, is my means of remedying my well-being using my Communication® strength in the written form. Even if only a handful of people read these posts/articles, they are meaningful and impactful for my own sense of well-being and harmony. Simply put, when I write, I feel more fulfilled and better as a result.

I intend to take this concept back to my employees and look at their strengths in the context of well-being and both coach and brainstorm ideas to help them achieve their appropriate work-

---

[3] CliftonStrengths® and the CliftonStrengths 34 Themes of Talent are trademarks of Gallup, Inc. Gallup's content is Copyrighted by Gallup. Used with permission. All rights reserved.

life harmony. I encourage everyone to consider how they might use their strengths in the context of well-being to achieve better work-life harmony.

As you see from my article, I only recently acquired the wisdom of well-being and how we can incorporate its' concepts into our lives. In the next chapter, I'll highlight how the challenges we experience can help us find even greater well-being in our lives today. Don't wait, don't question – instead, learn and talk about your well-being now so you get the full benefits of your peak performance by caring for your personal and unique needs.

VIGOR AND VULNERABILITY – HOW VULNERABILITY IS TRULY A STRENGTH?

Without acknowledging your emotions, there is no compassion or empathy for yourself or another, no possibility of forgiveness, understanding, or acceptance.[27]

From Brave Naked Truth, by Trish Leichty, M.D.

Imagine for a moment you have a bag you carry with you everywhere you go for collecting rocks. Each time you feel vulnerable – due to fear, anger, insecurity, frustration, or any other emotion, and if you don't resolve the issue, you must add a rock to the bag. That bag continues to expand each time you add a new rock to it, and you continue carrying the bag with you everywhere you go. The bag keeps getting heavier and heavier as you add rocks, trying to bury, ignore, or reject anything that makes you feel vulnerable.

As a result, you develop tremendous strength and vigor due to the weight of the rocks, but you are also forever burdened by the increasing weight which prevents you from going where you want to go. In fact, the bag gets so big you can barely move or make any progress on your life path. The path you want (and know you need) to go down in order to reach peace, success, happiness, and a positive future is so bumpy and challenging you can't even imagine taking that path while carrying your rocks.

Instead, you look for other paths to get you to the same destination. You try many different paths, but no matter where you look or what path you try, none of them lead you to the freedom of peace, success, and happiness. You return to the bumpy path – and try once again to go down it – but the bag gets in the way and makes it impossible to proceed. You are frustrated, exhausted, weighed down, and overwhelmed. You call out for help and guidance, "Please help me! I am so tired and just want to walk down this path!"

Like a bolt of lightning, help arrives. A voice which asks you, "Why are you carrying those rocks?" You think about it for a moment and can't answer the question. You realize no one ever told you that you had to keep carrying the bag. No one said you couldn't just put it down and walk away. You wonder why it never occurred to you before that you could just put the bag down and walk down the path to peace, success, and happiness.

Why does it take so long to realize we just have to put the bag down? Why does the path to peace appear as such a struggle to walk down? Why do we keep adding to and carrying the weight of our past experiences? Why do we look for other paths? Why do we struggle for so long before realizing we are the root of our own problems?

Vulnerability is hard... really hard. I am no expert on vulnerability, but I am an expert on struggling with my own vulnerability. During one of these struggles, the image of the above story became particularly vivid in my mind. I realized I was carrying a tremendous burden I didn't need to carry. My husband said one night, "Jessica is stronger than she knows." The next day, I realized

I really am strong and it's because I've endured tremendous challenges and struggles, and carried them for longer than I need to. I have a really hard time being seen as or appearing weak. I want to be as strong as a man. I don't want to own any of my woman-ness out of a fear that I will be seen as weaker or not as good as a man. I don't want to be unavailable due to my children, left out of events, cause drama, or be "too emotional." As a result, I hide these parts of myself and carry my vulnerabilities with me anywhere I don't feel safe enough to be myself. Luckily, I have great relationships with the people I work with, and sometimes I am able to drop the bag. But in my interactions with other people, I hold that bag tight.

I realized the fear of being seen as weak causes me to hide issues, not share challenges, hold back when I should speak up, doubt myself when I shouldn't, and significantly hinders my ability to have a trusting relationship with some people. I know in order to build trust you must be willing to be vulnerable. But in practice, I have struggled – a lot!

Depending on where you are in your journey, you may or may not, be aware of the bag you carry or your own challenges with vulnerability. However, I do know, without a doubt in my mind, that the path to peak performance (happiness, success, and peace) requires you to put down the bag, share your experience, find ways to connect, and move forward from these vulnerabilities. The strength we develop and can bring to the world and our own lives is tremendous if we can learn when to put the bag down!

I am stronger than I realized. I am not weak. I don't need to be afraid, worried, or concerned. I don't need to hide, keep private, or prevent my true Self from being seen. I can be who I am in all my glory (including my woman-ness) and bring tremendous value to this world. If one person fails to see it – the world will lead me in a direction where someone else will. If I can let the bag go – then I can see where my path takes me!

FUTURE FOCUSED – WHERE WE NEED TO FOCUS?

> *I can't change what's already happened, I don't know what will happen, I can only impact my present experience to improve my future self.*

Frequently, conversations and discussions regarding performance are focused on the past – who did what, when, and to whom? We provide "feedback," giving commentary that is primarily focused on what happened in the past rather than what will help us in the future. This type of feedback is problematic. We become defensive and, frequently, the feedback isn't actionable because it's so far in the past we have moved on. We have failed to discuss the feedback or provide context for how to meaningfully apply the feedback to evolve our performance for the future.

In the workplace, when employees receive this feedback (typically in the form of a performance review with ratings or rankings) they tend to focus on the negative, become defensive, and disengage. Research shows high performers actually become less engaged as a result of traditional performance reviews.[28] This challenge also exists outside the workplace. Anyone who has ever tried to give their spouse feedback on chores will likely be able to quickly call to mind the reaction and unproductive conversations that followed.

When we store up all our frustrations and issues and dump them on someone at once, it's overwhelming and not particularly useful to their future performance. Instead, we must purposely consider how the information we provide is going to evolve a person's performance. What do you hope to accomplish by providing this input? Alternatively, when we get feedback, we can ask – what would you like me to do differently in the future? How can we come to an agreement, so we don't have to repeat this interaction?

Furthermore, this input is best received in the moment it is happening when a person can translate it immediately into action. When someone is struggling, they want to know now, not three days from now! The only moment we can possibly impact is the one we are currently in. If we avoid feedback and input in the present, we can never positively impact our futures. In fact, when we do avoid feedback or even ignore the feedback, we eliminate the possibility of a different outcome in the future.

Instead, we must choose to impact ourselves (positively or negatively) in the present so that we can improve our future. We must receive the information and process the experience through reflection, learning, and self-growth. Then we can evolve our performance to improve our future. When we give and receive feedback regarding performance, we need to be thinking about how this will create a better future.

Frequently, I find myself asking before I ever give feedback or coaching to an employee, or anyone for that matter, "What do you hope to accomplish by sharing this? What outcome are you hoping to achieve?" I find when I ask this question, it completely changes the nature of what I am about to share and how I go about sharing it. This simple pause and question have saved me from numerous marital or family arguments!

Reflection: As I wrap up this chapter of preparation for peak performance, I ask you to consider how you might prepare yourself for the journey to peak performance? What will you do to ready yourself to have the performance conversations needed to reach peak performance?

Always remember, the past is over, the future is full of opportunity, and the present is where we experience what helps us evolve our performance. Try to stay present and enjoy the experience in the moment.

CHAPTER THREE
Performance
Starts with You

Where should I start to reach Peak Performance?

> **Key Insight:**
>
> I must understand myself and my current
> mindset to reach peak performance.

What would you change if you could change one thing (and only one thing) in this world to improve your life, your performance, your business, or your personal circumstances? What is that one thing you would change? Did you say yourself? Your performance? Your mindset? Or were you focused externally?

Our typical approach to performance is trying to perfect our circumstances. We look for the perfect role, the perfect company, the perfect working environment, the perfect tools, the perfect information, the perfect relationships, the perfect home, the perfect life. But, when we believe peak performance is the result of finding and perfecting our circumstances, we will undoubtedly fail. Rather, we must look inward and recognize our performance is purely the result of our own efforts.

> *We are the root of our problems,*
> *and we are the only thing that can solve them.*

Before anyone starts to climb a mountain, they assess their readiness (they must have the strengths and capabilities), ensure they have the equipment (or tools), and identify a guide (or map) for their journey. Likewise, before we begin reviewing the guide and tools (Four Keys to Peak Performance), we must start with assessing our own readiness – the one thing in this world we can always influence. Understanding our readiness to embark on our journey of evolving our performance is essential for reaching peak performance.

One major challenge with understanding ourselves is appreciating the difference between who we think we are, based on our cultural identities, and who we truly are. When we identify with a particular group, we tend to adopt the characteristics of that group. Our behaviors, our growth, our development, and everything we do becomes tied up in an identity which may or may not reflect who we are or who we want to be.

Instead, we must separate from our identities (past and present) and learn more about ourselves. For example, for a long time I thought I was not athletic, coordinated, or able to play sports. I developed an identity as a "non-sporty girl." When I took that self-imposed identity down, I learned I love playing some sports – like basketball and pickleball – and I'm actually quite good. I will never be an Olympian, but my self-imposed identity was limiting my ability to learn more about myself and what I could achieve. You've likely encountered similar examples such as "I'm not a math person," "I am no artist," or "I can't dance," where people develop an identity and believe they aren't or can't do something.

Similarly, when we identify with a group, we adopt the beliefs of the group without considering if some of the beliefs may not apply to us. We think of ourselves as "Republican" therefore we must be pro-life, pro-gun, pro-Trump. Or we think of ourselves as "Democrat" and, therefore, we must be pro-choice, anti-gun, and liberal. However, we don't have to be these identities. We can hold multiple identities at once. We don't have to fit into *one* identity. Even more importantly, our identity can and ought to change over time. I am more than one identity and it's changed throughout my life – from daughter, to lawyer, to employee, to spouse, to mother, to leader, to writer, and hopefully much more. I am more than the groups I choose to engage or participate in.

> *Who I am, the unique person, the only one in the whole world who is me, this is the person we want to learn about!*

As a result, our performance always starts by looking inward to create self-awareness – taking the time to truly understand ourselves, honestly recognize our current performance capabilities, and reflect on how our mindset is impacting our performance and results.

HOW DO WE LEARN ABOUT OURSELVES AND OUR CAPABILITIES?

If we are not our identity – as defined by our current experiences and groups – what are we? Who are we separate from our environment or culture? Who are we if not our identity? This sounds like the opening of a philosophical discussion and, although interesting, that is not my primary objective.

Rather, I ask you to consider the possibility there is more to who you are than you have learned thus far, and there is more to who you can be in the future. However, the core elements of your consciousness, spirit, personality, nature, character, or whatever you wish to call it are your foundation. Frequently, we fail to spend time understanding ourselves and learning about our strengths, values, interests, beliefs, and capabilities. We quickly move on to what we are going to "do" without first understanding "who" we are.

We struggle because self-reflection, self-assessment, and self-awareness fall outside the traditional categories of education we study in school like math, science, technology, and literature. We didn't receive bonus points or top grades for learning about ourselves and reflecting on our capabilities. Most people (with very few exceptions) don't encounter this type of self-learning until adulthood and, frequently, not until it is encountered in the workplace or maybe a church or religious program.

Despite a long education, I never spent significant time on self-awareness or self-assessment. Over the past ten years, I have taken many assessments, used different tools, and gained better insights about myself and those I work with. Although this effort has helped tremendously, the biggest insight I've gained is that I am still learning, growing, and discovering new things about myself and adjusting, changing, and improving as I move through my life.

I invite you to consider how you might engage in greater self-awareness and reflection. Identify what works best for you and leave behind anything which fails to serve you. We are each different and, therefore, must find our own path to discovery. Each of these elements of self-reflection provide an opportunity to generate greater self-awareness and understanding. This is a life-long journey as we continue to expand, grow, and change throughout our lives. Therefore, even if you have encountered these concepts before, I encourage you to revisit them.

OUR STRENGTHS – THE SECRET TO SUCCESS

Actually, strengths are not really a secret, but I've found most people have either never encountered a tool to learn more about their strengths or failed to apply the tool effectively. By far, the most valuable tool I use in both my professional and personal life has been Gallup®[4] CliftonStrengths® assessment. I believe so strongly in its application and usefulness that my whole family has taken the assessment, and five years ago I became a Gallup® Certified Strengths Coach. I've even had two of my employees also get certified!

I stumbled upon the assessment as a result of reading *First Break All the Rules,* but it took me years to finally take the assessment. (Occasionally, I reflect on time lost and where my performance might be today if I had only taken it sooner – I encourage you not to wait!) What is this magical assessment I believe in so strongly? The assessment provides you a tool for unpacking your true nature and talents – your innate abilities which make you uniquely you.

What is the CliftonStrengths® assessment?

Why was the assessment created and who created it? Don Clifton, an American psychologist, educator, author, researcher, and entrepreneur, created this assessment after significant research. Clifton asked: "What would happen if we studied what is right with people rather than focusing on what is wrong with them?" For Clifton, this wasn't just a slogan or campaign but rather what you might say was a life mission. The CliftonStrengths® assessment is a tool that has been around for 20+ years providing tremendous value to those who use it and apply it successfully.

---

[4] CliftonStrengths® and the CliftonStrengths 34 Themes of Talent are trademarks of Gallup, Inc. Gallup's content is Copyrighted by Gallup. Used with permission. All rights reserved.

The CliftonStrengths®[5] assessment is a web-based talent assessment tool to help you discover what you do best through your innate talents. The primary application is in the workplace, but it has been used for understanding individuals in a variety of roles – parents, children, churches, community groups.

To take the assessment there are a couple different ways to purchase a code, either directly through Gallup® website (Gallup.com) or by purchasing a StrengthsFinder book (I recommend the 2.0 version). If you purchase the book, there is a code in the back to take the assessment. If you purchase a used copy, you'll want to verify the code hasn't already been used. Purchasing online gives you the option to buy a code for either Top 5 CliftonStrengths® or CliftonStrengths® 34. There are 34 talent themes so you can choose to see your Top 5, or you can see your full sequence of 34 talent themes. No matter which option you choose, the outcome of the assessment is a unique combination of talent themes which makes each of us a unique human being.

The assessment is timed, takes about an hour to complete, and consists of 177 paired statements from which you choose the one that fits you best. You'll want to complete the assessment when you won't be interrupted and can complete it in one sitting. Depending on which version of the assessment you buy (either Top 5 CliftonStrengths® or CliftonStrengths® 34), you receive at least two reports, one Signature Themes Report and one Strengths Insight Guide. The reports serve as guides to help you discover and understand what it is that you do well.

The reports provide you a list of talents in the order of which they best describe how you most naturally think, feel, and behave. There are currently over 25 million people who have taken CliftonStrengths®! And only 1 in 33 million people have

---

[5] CliftonStrengths® and the CliftonStrengths 34 Themes of Talent are trademarks of Gallup, Inc. Gallup's content is Copyrighted by Gallup. Used with permission. All rights reserved.

the same top five talents in the same order. Our talents manifest differently based upon our unique combination – which provides each individual insights into their way of thinking, feeling, and behaving.

Talents are the best way to understand the things you have the natural ability to do best. We all have talents, but we may not have focused on transforming our talents into strengths. Our talents (a natural way of thinking, feeling, or behaving) can be transformed into strengths (the ability to consistently provide near-perfect performance) by investing (time spent practicing, developing your skills, and building your knowledge base) in our talents.

Our talents don't typically change over time – in fact, many tell the story of Don Clifton taking the assessment repeatedly trying to get a different result for his top strength of Significance. He was never successful at tricking his own assessment! How appropriate given that people with high Significance are driven to make a meaningful impact on the world around them – and obviously, Don Clifton was successful!

(Note: For fun you can try to search for your strengths twin at https://releasingstrengths.com)

I am going to share a bit of my experience working with the CliftonStrengths®[6] assessment and how it has made a significant difference in my life. The best place to start is usually at the beginning, and my start with strengths was quite the experience! Next, I'll fast-forward a few years to when I became a Gallup® Certified Strengths Coach and I was finally able to walk through strengths training to not just understand my talents and strengths but also learn how to apply them to improve my results, and

---

ultimately apply them to coach others! I hope my experience will provide some insight into how it may be helpful and useful for you in developing greater self-awareness in your life. For me, strengths are essential to living an exceptional life!

What if I don't like my results or understand a talent?

When I first received the results from the CliftonStrengths® assessment, my reaction was frustrated, angry, pissed off, disappointed, confused, and probably more. Before the assessment, I read the descriptions of all 34 talent themes and thought I knew myself well enough that I could self-select my top five (or at least some of my top five) talents. When I saw the results, I did not accurately pick my top five – not even close. I don't remember exactly what I thought my top five should have been, but I do remember I couldn't comprehend how Achiever® wasn't one of my top five strengths. To add insult to injury, my second talent is Maximizer®. You might be thinking the exact same thing I was "What the heck is Maximizer®[7]?" I struggled and even thought, "That's not me!"

As we all know, first impressions are often completely wrong and, in the case of receiving my first strengths report, that was certainly the case. I didn't have any background on strengths or anyone to help me interpret or understand the results in the report. I wasn't really sure what to do with them or even how to understand them.

Learning about our talents is a lifelong journey – we must explore, receive coaching, and reflect on our talents to turn them into strengths. Like I mentioned, I struggled with my talents at first – I still sometimes struggle with them. But, by creating self-awareness and reflecting on how they manifest for me over time, I

---

[7] CliftonStrengths® and the CliftonStrengths 34 Themes of Talent are trademarks of Gallup, Inc. Gallup's content is Copyrighted by Gallup. Used with permission. All rights reserved.

have come to understand, recognize, own, and even enjoy my Maximizer® talent. In fact, Maximizer®[8] is and always has been very much a part of who I am, even as a child. I've always wanted to make things bigger, better, greater, and more. I push the boundaries on just about everything trying to achieve excellence. I'll buy five of the same thing to make sure I find the best of something. For better or worse, I am very much a Maximizer®.

> **Maximizer®:** People exceptionally talented in the Maximizer® theme focus on strengths as a way to stimulate personal and group excellence. They seek to transform something strong into something superb.
>
> **Achiever®:** People exceptionally talented in the Achiever theme work hard and possess a great deal of stamina. They take immense satisfaction in being busy and productive.
>
> **Communication®:** People exceptionally talented in the Communication theme generally find it easy to put their thoughts into words. They are good conversationalists and presenters.
>
> **Deliberative®:** People exceptionally talented in the Deliberative theme are best described by the serious care they take in making decisions or choices. They anticipate obstacles.

---

[8] CliftonStrengths® and the CliftonStrengths 34 Themes of Talent are trademarks of Gallup, Inc. Gallup's content is Copyrighted by Gallup. Used with permission. All rights reserved.

How does this assessment compare to other assessments?

Many are familiar with other personality assessments like DISC or Myers-Briggs. I had more experience with both before taking the CliftonStrengths®[9] Assessment. A Gallup® instructor used the following analogy, which has always stuck with me, "If other personality assessments help you to get in the neighborhood of your personality, CliftonStrengths® helps you to describe the furniture in your house." In other words, CliftonStrengths® hits closer to home – it's much more detailed in describing your uniqueness.

Which report should I choose – Top 5 or Full 34?

Even if you purchase the full CliftonStrengths® 34 to see the sequence of all 34 talents, I recommend focusing on your Top 5, which are the talents that come most naturally to you. I worked with only my top 5 talents for two years before unlocking my full 34. Our greatest potential for success lies in those top 5 talents, so spending time there first is logical because it will provide the greatest return. I've found a lot of insights and actions can be taken when only looking at your top 5 talents. The biggest risk in the full 34 is becoming distracted looking at the bottom of the list rather than the top!

What does it mean if I don't have a particular talent?

The assessment provides you with the talents you demonstrate the strongest at the top. However, we actively use many, if not all, of the talents in our top 10! Which, for me, meant that Achiever®[10] not being in the top 5 did not mean I didn't possess it or use it! Rather, I am happy to share when I unlocked my full 34 talents, Achiever® was my #6 talent. For three years I was bothered by

---

[9] CliftonStrengths® and the CliftonStrengths 34 Themes of Talent are trademarks of Gallup, Inc. Gallup's content is Copyrighted by Gallup. Used with permission. All rights reserved.

Achiever® not being in my top 5 and ironically, I did have it – it was just a little less significant than my first five talents.

I also learned how we can use different talents to achieve the same outcome or result. For me, I lack a lot of relationship building talents, therefore, I use my Communication® talent to build relationships. You can always look at your talents to determine which ones might help you achieve a result.

How do talents manifest as weaknesses?

A key concept I gained significant insight into is how our talents are also most likely the source of our weaknesses. In fact, what is often seen as our weaknesses are simply our talents misapplied. Gallup® uses the concept of balconies and basements; our talents can either be used to help us perform at our best (balcony) or when our talents are overused or underdeveloped, they can actually manifest as weaknesses (basement). A focus on strengths does not mean ignoring our weaknesses. Rather, we must be very self-aware of our weaknesses and identify strategies to actively manage around them.

I have certainly been stuck in the basement of my strengths! For example, because of my Maximizer® talent I do things like order too much food for a family event, spend way too much time on small details, and obsess about how a specific PowerPoint slide looks when it really doesn't matter (but damn it, it drives me insane, so I have to fix it!). And I might (but certainly never have... wink wink) bought way too many of something because I am not sure which one is going to be the best and I want to make sure I have the best!

These weaknesses or behaviors are most likely going to frustrate ourselves and others. My Maximizer®[11] is a talent, but it can frustrate those closest to me and even myself sometimes. As a

---

[11] CliftonStrengths® and the CliftonStrengths 34 Themes of Talent are trademarks of Gallup, Inc. Gallup's content is Copyrighted by Gallup. Used with permission. All rights reserved.

Maximizer®, I want things to be great, but the truth is... not everything in life needs to be great. We must look at our talents to help us identify when we are in our basements rather than our balconies! I want to be on the balcony with the best view, rather than the basement!

How can our talents impact our relationships?

One of my employees, Jamie, and I used to get into conflict a lot. She would get frustrated when she provided me with something (a presentation, document, drafted email) and I would *always* edit and revise it. I literally can't and couldn't help myself – if something is good, I want to find every little way to make it even better. She used to think that when I made changes it was because I thought she hadn't done a good enough job. Therefore, she stopped wanting to start working on something because she knew I would change it.

After learning about my Maximizer® strength, we had a breakthrough where she finally understood I wasn't saying her work was bad, inadequate, and certainly not wrong. If I was improving something she had done, then it meant her work was good and I wanted to make it even better – I wanted to make it great. This breakthrough significantly improved our working relationship. She is a fantastic executer which meant she could get things started and then give them to me to maximize and finish. We have become the most amazing partners as a result of this insight.

Another major breakthrough with leveraging strengths occurred when I read the report of one of my fellow leaders. I struggled in my interactions and working with this individual because I didn't understand his response. I would present on a topic, and he would frequently "require more time to consider." I took this as an indicator that I had not presented effectively enough. But one of his top strengths is "Deliberative®[12]," which means he

---

[12] CliftonStrengths® and the CliftonStrengths 34 Themes of Talent are trademarks of Gallup, Inc. Gallup's content is Copyrighted by Gallup. Used with permission. All rights reserved.

requires time to think through decisions. Once I understood his strengths, it finally clicked why we struggled so much and why my approach had not worked for him. I either needed to prepare him in advance so he could consider the topic beforehand and be prepared to make a decision or give him time to reflect prior to making the decision.

I'll elaborate further on understanding the strengths of those we work with in the section on Feedback. However, learning about how we can shape our approach and techniques to better build relationships with others is an example of tremendous self-awareness.

Why are CliftonStrengths®[13] so powerful?

As a Gallup® Certified Strengths Coach for many years, I have performed numerous sessions with hundreds of people on strengths and seen the impact that learning your strengths can have on your relationships, results, and life. After six years of applying the insights from my strengths to my work and personal life, I know the benefits can be life-altering. By understanding who we are and what comes naturally, we can focus on our talents and turn them into strengths where we can occasionally achieve near perfect performance. And who wouldn't want to strive for near perfect performance?

Our talents form the foundation for reaching peak performance. Fully knowing ourselves and our talents provides us the greatest opportunity to reach peak performance in all the roles we perform. Our strengths or talents can get us started (and are certainly the best way to get started) on the journey of self-awareness but we must also consider additional components of who we are and our personal capabilities.

---

[13] CliftonStrengths® and the CliftonStrengths 34 Themes of Talent are trademarks of Gallup, Inc. Gallup's content is Copyrighted by Gallup. Used with permission. All rights reserved.

Reflection: *What are the things I do most naturally? When I lose track of time and I am in the flow of work, what am I doing? How do my talents help me be successful? How might my talents get in the way of my success? How do talents impact my relationships with others?*

HOW DO OUR VALUES, INTERESTS, AND CAPABILITIES ALSO CREATE SELF-AWARENESS?

Our Values and Interests

Our strengths provide clues or a starting point for what we value or are interested in – often they are related. However, understanding what is truly most important in our lives is critical to understanding ourselves and what we need. Unlike our talents, our values and interests change throughout our lives. We must revisit these regularly and consider how they have changed as our lives have changed.

For me, before I had children, some of my values looked very different than they do today, and some remain unchanged. I swore my values would never change even when I had children. Honestly, things did change but what makes me most passionate and what I value most has not changed, and I have found different ways to incorporate these values into my life in my interactions with my children.

Likewise, understanding our interests helps us identify our areas of passion, purpose, and possible opportunities of focus or growth. By gauging how our strengths relate and can be applied to interests we can leverage who we are and find ways to be successful at what we do each day in our roles.

Our Capabilities: Competencies, Skills, & Knowledge

We also need to consider our current capabilities. By capability I am referring to our knowledge (what we have learned or know), skills (what we can do or execute), and competencies (how we are able to perform). I treat these separately because they truly mean different things and are acquired in different ways.

Knowledge is what we know – it is knowing the formula, the law, the steps to perform, the products you sell, the ingredients in a recipe, how to drive a car. Knowledge must be acquired in order to perform a particular activity in a particular role. I had to attend law school and pass the Bar Exam in order to demonstrate I had the knowledge necessary to practice law. I still must do research to acquire knowledge when I am going to perform an activity I have not performed recently. Likewise, in order to cook a particular recipe, you must have knowledge of the ingredients required to make that recipe.

Skills are how you execute – how you write, enter data, use Microsoft, cook, clean, drive a car, and otherwise complete your work or daily activities. We must learn different skills (the steps required) to perform activities in our role. As an attorney, I had to learn how to conduct legal research, how to write legal documents, and how to review legal contracts. As a cook, we must learn how to execute the steps of a recipe – sauté the onions, whip the dressing, combine the ingredients.

Competencies are how we perform – our interpersonal abilities, level of accountability, communication, planning, and organizing. Competencies apply to any role or function and help to articulate or look at what needed to improve our performance. To be a successful attorney, I needed to develop competencies in communication, writing, planning, and organizing. To be a successful cook, we must learn planning (to have the ingredients), organizing (to execute steps at the right time) and attention to detail (to not miss a critical step or use a tbsp instead of tsp). (What? You've never mixed-up TBSP and TSP? Details are definitely not my thing!)

Any assessment of our capabilities represents a single point in time, and both can and should change dramatically over our lives. While strengths and talents are who we are – capabilities are what we do with who we are. Our competencies can support different skills and even the acquisition of knowledge. Any job or role we perform requires some combination of all three to reach peak performance.

Reflection: *What are your values & interests? What knowledge do you have today with respect to your roles? Are you missing information you need to learn? What skills do you have in the roles you perform? Are there skills you still need to learn and master? What competencies do you need in order to perform your roles well? How proficient are you with the competencies?*

WHERE ARE WE TODAY IN OUR CURRENT PERFORMANCE?

I am not a gambler, but I am willing to bet you'd really rather skip over this section and move onto how you can be better! Most of us don't want to take the time to do the hard and challenging work of acknowledging where we are falling short, but it is necessary before we start on the path to peak performance.

I'll start with a very personal (and vulnerable) story. When I first started working, I actually thought I was the 'bomb diggity' – spellcheck doesn't think that is a real word but I think it fits perfectly! I thought I was pretty great. I truly believed I knew what I was doing, that I could learn what I didn't, and I could do just about anything. I wasn't necessarily wrong, but this mindset left me closed off to greater self-insight, to external input, and the ability to internalize those insights to improve. As a result, I remember distinctly early in my career responding to performance feedback and insights with rejection, denial, frustration, and, as Brené Brown aptly calls them, many "shame storms."[29]

To truly impact your performance, you must acknowledge the vulnerability around your performance. Brené Brown's many books on this topic provide tremendous insights and actions for addressing these challenges much better than anything I will cover here. However, I do want to address that, for many of us, given how much we care about our performance in the roles we are performing, when we question that performance (or worse, others question that performance), it can be a huge source of shame and vulnerability.

For example, I want to be the most amazing mother in the world (hear my Maximizer®[14]). Anytime my mom, sister, or anyone questions my performance or capability in this role, I immediately fall into a shame spiral of denial, anger, frustration, and sometimes even blame. My natural instinct is to close myself off, and reject whatever I am hearing given how painful it feels. However, in order to truly evolve, we have to recognize these shame spirals, be willing to acknowledge our vulnerability, and move through it to get to our performance insights.

The self-awareness that comes from working through our vulnerabilities can help us leverage the strategies provided around the four keys. For me, starting with just acknowledging I don't have all the answers, but I have the capability to do tremendous things if I am open to receiving input on my performance. This doesn't mean I am open to input from everyone on this topic. Can you imagine if you had to take input from every person who has given you

---

[14] CliftonStrengths® and the CliftonStrengths 34 Themes of Talent are trademarks of Gallup, Inc. Gallup's content is Copyrighted by Gallup. Used with permission. All rights reserved.

parenting or marital advice? Much of which, by the way, is unhelpful and sometimes even inappropriate.

We don't have to listen to every person in every situation regarding our performance. We don't even need to listen to every expert – although they know more, they aren't in your role, your life, or living your specific circumstance. Experts certainly can provide tremendous insight and I highly recommend exploring experts who can provide insight on your performance to create self-awareness. However, you are the driver, and you are the one who can synthesize, digest, determine, and decide how to apply those insights in your specific role.

If you don't want to take this step yet, you can wait and come back to this at the beginning of section three as we dive into how we apply the four keys to peak performance in the roles we serve.

Reflection: As the driver, you must get started on this self-assessment of your performance capabilities. Are you growing? Are you honest with yourself on where you are in performing your roles? What are you doing to improve performance in each role? Are you even doing anything in some areas? Are you just hoping your marriage will get better or your children will become less difficult to deal with? Are you wishing your manager would notice your efforts and appreciate them?

I recommend taking a few minutes to reflect and capture your current performance. Capture what you are actively doing with respect to your performance in each role you serve. What are the things you are doing in the role that contribute to your performance?

After reflecting on what you are doing, reflect on how you are doing in that role – is your marriage the best it can be? Do you feel good about your parenting? Are you rocking results at your workplace? Are you leading in a way others should emulate? Be honest – this is just for you. The first step is recognizing where we are today.

Consider whether you are using your strengths? Are you living by your values? Are you pursuing your interests? Do you have all the necessary knowledge, skills, and competencies or are you missing some capabilities?

Then, take a moment and capture where you want to be. What does peak performance look like to you in each role you are performing? If you are comfortable, this is a great time to close your eyes and visualize what you look like when achieving peak performance? How does it feel? What are you doing and what are you not doing?

WHAT IS OUR PERFORMANCE MINDSET?

Whether we know it or not, we each have a performance mindset – the way we think about and approach our performance in a role. This mindset might be different in different roles – for example I may be very open to growth, feedback, and expectation-setting in the workplace but struggle with the same concepts in my marriage. Our performance mindset, the way we think about our performance, has the most significant impact on how effectively we apply the four keys to reach peak performance. In fact, this section, if applied successfully, has the greatest opportunity to help you reach peak performance.

What is mindset?

According to the Cambridge Dictionary, **mindset** is "a person's way of thinking and their opinions." [30] Another way to say this is your mindset is a set of beliefs that shape how you make sense of the world and yourself. Your mindset influences how you think, feel, and behave in any given situation. [31]

Our mindsets are the way we think, feel, and behave. They are based upon what we believe, which comes from where we exist (our environment), and are impacted by our experiences. To impact our performance, knowing **what** we need to do is not enough. We must **know** it, **feel** it, and **embody** it to evolve our performance. Frequently we know what we need to do, but we lack the beliefs, environment, and experience to feel and embody what is required to evolve to peak performance.

Our mindsets are shaped from the moment of birth through our lives as a result of every experience and interaction we have along the way. Our mindsets can be shaped to bring us greater value, but they can also cause us to sink into failure and inadequacy. They have the power to create tremendous results in our lives or destroy our happiness and success. Mindsets are critical to our performance and the path to an exceptional life. With a performance-based mindset, we will reach peak performance.

I've grown a lot in my understanding of mindset, from not truly understanding what it was or recognizing its impact on my life to incorporating mindset into all my life practices. If you have never encountered these concepts before – you are not alone. I, too, was blown away by their impact when I first encountered them in books like *Reality Based Leadership*, *The Untethered Soul*, *Before Happiness*, *Mindset: The New Psychology of Success*, and more!

Recently, my sister asked me about a weekend we spent together as a family. She texted me, "Was this weekend good or bad?" I pondered her question for a moment before quickly answering, "Mostly good." But, after reflecting, I realized I really should have answered, "Neither, but it was a valuable and wonderful experience with both happy and sad moments."

When we categorize events in our lives as good or bad, we are limiting how we choose to think about and respond to these experiences. When I reflect on my life – I love living. I love experiencing life. I enjoy so much of it on purpose by choosing to love each moment and each event and each experience. I want to continue to experience all of it – my family, work, praying, healing, socializing, writing – and I want to experience the happy, the sad, the frustrating, and all the emotions because that is what truly creates growth and makes me love living life even more.

Likewise, when we think about our performance and, more specifically, our experiences performing – we need a mindset emphasizing choice and opportunity over categorization and limitation. For example, we require a mindset emphasizing the ability to believe in what is possible, push boundaries, learn, and grow from every experience, especially our failures and heartbreaks. Rather than a mindset which categorizes each choice as good or bad, which limits our beliefs and prevents or eliminates opportunities for growth.

Our Beliefs

Our mindset begins with our beliefs about ourselves and what is possible in our lives. Knowing we **could** be successful matters very little if we don't believe we **will** be successful. One of my favorite quotes of all times by Cy Wakeman is:

"Whether you believe something to be possible or impossible, either way you'll be right!"

Cy Wakeman

What if the only limiting factor in our lives is how we choose to think about and respond to the experiences we have in life? What if our ability to be happy, have more time, and experience success and happiness is only determined by our willingness to believe it is possible? I believe God gave us the power to choose – to choose for ourselves what to believe and what to pursue. Which means we can *choose* to believe in ourselves and our abilities, and that all we want in life is truly possible. And, when we choose, *truly* choose – not pay lip service but truly mean it – and choose to believe in the possibility of what we seek, then maybe we can have all that we pursue. Maybe we really will get back more time! Maybe we will be successful and happy!

I've found, for most people, our beliefs are rooted in our life experiences – our religious upbringing, the challenges we've faced, the people we've encountered, and the lessons we've learned. Our beliefs are shaped by our experiences in life, and they create the lens through which we see the world. Our beliefs are not static. They grow, evolve, and change over time and with more experience.

How did I come to my beliefs?
What challenges shaped my beliefs?
Who did I encounter and what lessons did I learn?

A few years ago, I went through a significant health challenge. For months, I was having chronic idiopathic urticaria (hives that keep coming back with no known cause) and angioedema (swelling/throat closing). I had seen numerous doctors, tried many medications, and was even getting monthly injections. Despite my efforts, no one could give me an answer. No one could tell me why my body was having such serious reactions. I struggled to work, struggled to care for my son, and struggled each day wondering if that day I would get hives.

In 2018, a week before Christmas, after a night of no sleep due to hives on literally every inch of my body itching uncontrollably, burning, swelling, and bruising, I ended up at Barnes Jewish Hospital emergency room. My hands and feet were turning purple, hives were all over my body, and I was struggling to breathe. The doctors quickly administered epinephrine and high doses of steroids which helped alleviate my symptoms. They called in specialists and took biopsies but could not figure out what was wrong with me.

They sent me home with lots of steroids (which have awful side effects) and some EpiPens. For a few days I couldn't even get out of bed. A few days later I discovered I was pregnant, a few days after that I learned I would miscarry the pregnancy, and then on Christmas Eve/Day I miscarried.

I share this story because it was during this time, I had the most transformative experience of my life. This experience forever changed my mindset and my performance. I had always measured my performance by what I did and accomplished each day – the tasks, activities, and general busy-ness. Then, I was stopped dead in my tracks by my health issues. These issues caused me to question my performance – I couldn't go to work, I had to cancel an employee training, I couldn't wrap presents for my son, get ready for Christmas, or help my husband with anything! I went through serious pain and soul searching, and through the process I discovered my value, self-worth, capabilities, and my performance are not tied directly to the "things I get done" but rather what I choose to do with my experiences to create an exceptional life.

In my role as mom, I couldn't wrap all the presents, but I could be there with my son. I could laugh with my son, drink hot chocolate with my son, and be a great mom to my son, even if it were different than I imagined. I may have not been at 100%, but so long as I am alive, I can be there and make a difference for my children. In my role as leader, I couldn't execute and direct the work on my own, but that allowed those who work with me to grow and take on more. I could still coach them, and I got to see how they handled having to step up and accomplish more in their roles.

> *My value, self-worth, capabilities, and my performance are not tied directly to the "things I get done" but rather what I choose to do with my experiences to create an exceptional life.*

We need to think about our performance in this way. We are always going to perform – sometimes better, sometimes worse, sometimes one way, sometimes another way – and none are wrong or bad. They are all just our performance experience on that day, in that situation. What we want to focus on is how we cultivate our beliefs to evolve our performance and get the most out of each experience.

We are always going to make mistakes, have sick days, screw up, and mess up. We can't prevent these things from happening. What we can do is believe in our ability to respond in a way that allows us to learn, enhance, and evolve our performance in new and different ways. We must cultivate beliefs based upon our experiences to help us to make better choices in the future.

Reflection: *What on your list of challenges and struggles has shaped you and your beliefs? What has fundamentally helped to create and craft how you think about and see the world today? What of these beliefs serves you? What gets in the way of where you would like to be?*

Our Environment

The context of our lives and our environment includes our daily interactions, places, situations, relationships, and internal dialogue. Our environment has tremendous influence over our performance mindset. What we choose to include in our environment impacts how we perform and interact every day. When our environment includes powerful partnerships, trusted teams, goal setting, and cultures of accountability, our performance is positively impacted. Likewise, when our environment includes blaming, complaining, excuse-making, reacting, and negative relationships, our performance is undoubtedly negatively impacted.

We may *know* evolving our performance through growth and development is necessary, but unless we *feel* the need to evolve our performance, we are unlikely to take action. We must know it and feel it in order to see it! What we know and what we feel can often be in conflict with each other. We may know we are smart but not feel smart, we may know we are capable but not feel capable, we may know we can be successful but not feel we will be successful.

The biggest challenge with our environments negatively impacting our performance is the excess noise we fill them with. What is noise? "Noise is anything that distorts your positive reality and distracts you from harnessing your multiple intelligences that chart a path toward your goals."[32] Simply, noise is all the "stuff" that gets in the way of what matters to us. Noise is both internal and external. External noise includes the pop-up news alerts, emails, texts, phone calls, social media, and everything else which is being blasted at us every single day. Internal noise is our thoughts – getting stuck on worry, fear, shame, avoidance, and self-doubt.

All this "information" becomes noise because we can't differentiate the noise (useless information and self-talk) from the signal (valuable information and self-awareness).[33] The trouble with all the noise is it prevents us from solving the problems or issues which really matter, from focusing on our families, from achieving our goals, and from enjoying our lives. The noise prevents us from identifying valuable actions for moving forward. The noise prevents us from taking what we know and feeling we will do it.

In his book *Before Happiness*, Shawn Achor provides useful strategies for reducing the noise to better identify the signal. I encourage you to read Achor's book and consider how you can reduce your level of negative self-talk and worry, as well as limit the streams of data you take in each day.

When we incorporate valuable strategies into our lives, we cultivate healthy environments supporting our growth, self-awareness, and insights. By creating an environment with people, resources, and strategies supporting our goals and objectives, we increase the probability of achieving those objectives. When we move from knowing success is possible to feeling we can be successful – we are evolving our performance.

Reflection: *Consider your current practices – does your environment reflect what matters most to you? Do you reserve your mental energy and focus for the things you want to achieve most? Do you manage your emotions, so they do not take your mental energy and focus away from what you are trying to accomplish?*

Our Experiences

Our performance is truly the result of our experiences and how we choose to respond, learn, and grow from those experiences. Each day, our mindsets impact how we translate our experiences into meaningful results. Whether we engage, resist, or translate the experiences to help us evolve, our performance is determined by our mindset. We may know we can be successful and feel we will be successful – now we must **embody** this success through our experience.

My parents recently purchased a new house on a lake. It has a waterfall from a small pond at the top of the hill to a small pond at the bottom of the hill. I spent time working on this book looking out the window at the pond filled with Japanese Koi Fish. As I reflected on performance mindsets, I discovered the waterfall was a useful analogy. Just as we watch the water flow down the rocks of a waterfall, we should watch our experiences and performance. Let go of what does not serve or benefit us and continue on our journey through life, down the waterfall.

Leave the moments that cause us to get stuck or unable to evolve behind and continue on, always moving forward – sometimes fast, sometimes slow, but always forward. We must never attempt to go back upstream by trying to change or redo an experience. Rather, we must observe these experiences, take them for what they are – an experience on a specific day – learn from them when possible, and then continue on in our lives.

When we take this approach to our performance, we can experience more peace as we grow and evolve. I want to be clear – I am in no way saying evolving our performance is easy. Rather, we will likely have to experience pain, frustration, anger, and a host of emotions to reach peak performance. However, we must accept those experiences for what they are – opportunities to learn and grow. We want to fully experience them, process them, and then let them pass as we take what is valuable and leave behind what is not.

When we hold on to these experiences, we get wrapped up in them and expend unnecessary energy trying to fight against the experience (trying to go back up stream). Ultimately, fighting is wasted energy, which is better applied processing, learning, and growing from the experience. We can never change what has already happened. At best, we can make good decisions regarding what we do next based upon the experience we had.

For example, when in a conflict with another person, like your boss or spouse, and they criticize you in some way, you are likely to experience an emotion – denial, anger, frustration. You can't force the other person into taking it back or having never said it, no matter how much you would like to. Even if they say they didn't mean it, you still felt the emotion during the experience. If, instead, we choose to see the experience for exactly what it is (someone is criticizing me), acknowledge how it makes us feel (I feel angry because they don't understand how hard I work), and separate ourselves from the experience (okay, I experienced that), what is the next best thing we can do? We move ourselves through the experience rather than resisting it.

Our tendency to resist is not limited to negative experiences. In fact, we have similar reactions to positive experiences. I have seen this happen with many employees when they get recognized for their work and immediately begin denying their success, explaining it away as luck, due to the team, or another external factor. Some may see this as a humble approach to performance, but when we feel this response internally, it is not humility but rather self-doubt and insecurity. When we feel these emotions and respond with resistance, we fail to see the experience for what it can be – an experience to evolve our performance. We must separate ourselves from the experience, acknowledge it, and determine what we will do as we move ourselves through the experience.

Once we achieve this level of self-awareness – we are better prepared to begin the process of evaluating our next step in evolving our performance and results. We are not going to evolve and reach peak performance if we are "stuck" resisting and avoiding the experiences we have – both good and bad. We must move from knowing to feeling to embodying through our experiences to build the capabilities necessary to evolve our performance.

I want this book to be very practical so let me break this down in the simplest way I can. Every time you experience anything, and you can start very small if you want, I want you to stop and watch the experience like you are watching a television show. (This exercise is incredibly powerful when you want to get the most out of spending time with your family and create magical moments.)

Magical "Lifetime Movie" Moments: Look at a moment as if you are watching a television show (think Lifetime Movie), imagine the music in the background, imagine the plot, and imagine how it would all appear to a casual observer.

As you watch the experience, acknowledge what you are feeling, seeing, hearing, and experiencing. Try doing this in situations which are not highly charged first – this will help to prepare you for the more difficult life experiences. Once you've taken this step – then you are ready to apply the four keys to determine how you can learn, grow, and evolve your performance in each role to reach peak performance.

In 2020, we all experienced so much – pain, joy, change, frustration, exhaustion, sadness, confusion, and more. The events happened so quickly that I think it was hard for many of us to process these experiences while we were experiencing them. I know for me personally, I am still working through the events of 2020 and how they have forever impacted me, my life, my family, my workplace, my community, and the world. I hope the next section can help you get "unstuck" and stop fighting to move back upstream to the way things were. Then you can begin to process and translate the experiences into growth, which can help you reach peak performance.

The next section is going to bring you back to the experiences we lived through in 2020. I encourage you to reflect on your experiences as you read this next section. How did you respond in the moment? Did you resist? Did you avoid? Or did you observe, reflect, and grow? Are you prepared to approach your path to peak performance with a mindset of growth?

Section Two
LESSONS LEARNED THROUGH CHALLENGING TIMES

How do challenging times help us learn critical lessons about peak performance?

Key Insight:

The challenges we faced in 2020 impacted how we work, connect, live, relate, share, serve, perform, and communicate creating valuable lessons. If we learn and grow from these lessons, they will continue to positively impact our performance.

The global COVID-19 pandemic significantly impacted and changed many facets of our daily lives. What exactly changed as a result of the COVID-19 pandemic and why are these changes so challenging and different from other significant events in history? Writing this section shortly after 2020 came to an end feels like announcing the sky is blue and grass is green. Pointing out the extremely obvious and putting into words what is intuitively apparent to every human being working and living on the planet in the year 2020 at best seems redundant, and at worst seems tortuous.

However, taking time to articulate and truly appreciate the changes humans experienced both honors how those changes impacted everyone and how they can help to shape a completely new world. A world where what used to take many years was achieved in record time. If we learn the lessons from the challenges we faced, we can acquire wisdom which has previously taken an entire lifetime to develop.

This new world makes possible things that, up until now, have eluded most people – having exceptional experiences at work and in life. The challenges we face provide opportunities for learning and growth, both as individuals and as a society, while simultaneously making a better future more possible than ever before. If we are willing to learn from the lessons we experienced, we will grow into having life experiences beyond what we previously believed possible.

In 2021 shortly after the roll-out of the vaccine, I was on a business call with two people out of New York that I have never met before, discussing getting approval for an article our business wrote and wanted to share. I was chatting with one of the individuals and apologizing for my scratchy voice because I lost my voice earlier in the week due to a cold. I mentioned sending my kids back to school and that we've been sick ever since. The person responded with empathy and expressed how strange it is going to be to get sick this year. After quarantining and separating for so much of last year, most people stayed healthier than in years prior. This year we are going to be back together, and those pesky cold viruses are going to be throwing snot parties! What this silly small talk made abundantly clear was the opportunity for people everywhere to relate to the pandemic experience.

Everyone can connect and relate through our shared experience with the pandemic. Unless you were a baby or a child too young to remember – everyone else on earth can share and connect with this experience. The world has been forever altered as a result of such a significant experience and the tremendous challenges everyone on earth experienced together. The challenges we faced represent a unique opportunity as one of the only shared experiences every person on earth can identify with in one way or another at the same moment in time!

Therefore, sharing our experiences is absolutely essential to garnering the benefits available from such a transformative event. We must understand the challenges we faced, how they impacted each of us differently, and what we can learn from these shared experiences. The wisdom we gain from this understanding is what will allow us to reach peak performance earlier than anyone who came before us. We have a tremendous opportunity, so let's make the most of it!

This next section is meant to highlight how the challenges with our workplaces, technology, families, social interactions, politics, and economy have impacted how we work, communicate, relate, connect, serve, share, perform, and live. Each of the challenges can teach us valuable lessons for the future and we will miss a significant opportunity if we don't learn and find ways to apply them.

As mentioned in the prior chapter, we must connect with and process our lived experience in order to discern the lessons and garner the benefits. Furthermore, if we want to accomplish the greatest growth, we must consider the lived experiences of others and the lessons they have learned as a result of their lived experiences. By connecting with each other and sharing our lived experiences, we can begin to truly improve our performance and, maybe, hopefully, change the world for the better.

CHAPTER FOUR
Our Workplaces
& Technology

How was our work, performance, and communication challenged?

OUR WORKPLACES – HOW WE WORK

I'm starting with workplaces and the changes we experienced in how we work because, in some ways, they are the most obvious. The challenges faced by workplaces vary dramatically based on the work environment, from essential businesses (grocery stores, manufacturing, transportation, medical, etc.), to schools and daycares, service industries, and to other non-essential businesses. I will try to touch on the impacts, but I acknowledge my experience is limited, so many of my comments are based on speculation or reading other experiences. Despite this, I still think it is important to touch on as much as we can to really discuss how we have been transformed as a society.

Regardless of the type of workplace, every company had to change how they approach safety; how they communicate and interact with co-workers, suppliers, and customers; and how they leverage technology to conduct business in new and different ways. Every workplace had to reconsider and implement completely new safety protocols, and leaders were faced with difficult decisions regarding how to protect employees and customers while still conducting business.

On top of those challenges, many individuals had intense and varying beliefs that conflicted with those safety measures. Essential workers were faced with customers who were willing to hurt them rather than wear a mask. Those who feared the virus and wore masks were sometimes coughed on or harassed by others who disagreed. The stress and challenges for everyone were significant when deciding how to be safe during a global pandemic.

Communications and interactions in the workplace changed dramatically. My team went from only having face-to-face meetings to completely virtual (as did many). We discovered we could actually turn cameras on and have good conversations and collaboration even though we weren't in the same room. What we missed was the casual interactions when we would pass co-workers informally in the office. My organization is a sales and services company in the manufacturing sector, and when you can't go to a customer site, look at their issues and talk about their systems, selling and providing services becomes extremely difficult. We had to pivot how we interact with our customers, discuss their challenges, and provide them services.

For those still in the workplace, they were forced to remain socially distanced, could not meet in an office, and had to remain masked. I was never in this situation, but I heard stories about how difficult it was to take an all-day meeting wearing a mask.

The medical professionals would likely scoff at this last statement as they are used to having to wear masks while performing their everyday functions. Beyond that, medical professionals were faced with the greatest exposure, highest risk, and having to care for those who were truly suffering from the effects of COVID-19. Doctors chose to self-isolate from their families (some for as long as a whole year) to protect them. Hospitals were nearly overwhelmed, and the stress was likely incomprehensible for those of us who did not experience it personally.

Teachers (God bless our teachers!) had to find ways to keep children's attention virtually and continue to educate them. I have three children, and communicating in the same room with them (sometimes even right next to them) can be a challenge, let alone over a computer or device. Teachers also had to find ways to follow up with students, chat with them, and support them all virtually.

Reflection: *Our experiences in our workplaces (all quite different) have truly changed how we view work. We were forced, in many instances, to improve skillsets we had never considered. When you reflect on your experience in the workplace, consider what you felt and what you still feel about your experience.*

Are you holding on to the past approach to work, desperately hoping to return to "normal"? Are you able to separate yourself from your experience and observe it objectively? When you do so, what do you see? Can you let go of the experience and begin to look at how you have improved, grown, and what is possible in the future? Do you need to look at your performance and find ways to improve and grow in order to keep up?

Have you considered the experiences of others – what they have been through and how it has changed them? Keep this last part in mind as you interact with others and talk about your experiences. They are likely to be very different and, as a result, we may all be approaching the future quite differently.

OUR TECHNOLOGY – HOW WE PERFORM AND COMMUNICATE

As a result of the challenges faced in 2020, the world dramatically changed and leveraged how it uses technology in all facets of our lives. The world has changed so dramatically that many, including myself, believe the world will never be the same again. We must understand the impact of technology – good and bad – and how it will continue to play an ongoing critical function in our lives and alter performance in the roles we serve.

We knew technology was going to ramp up, but we had no idea how essential it would become so quickly. To perform our roles, we were forced to use technology more heavily than ever before. Much of the technology already existed, but our desire and capacity, or propensity, to leverage the existing technology was limited. We preferred to hold a meeting in person or to visit with friends and relatives face to face (even if only once a year) rather than use video. Obviously, the virtual video meeting capability was essential to communication and collaboration. Most tragically, for those who were in ICUs battling the virus, many could only connect with and see their families (some for the very last time) via video. Thankfully, nurses with tremendous compassion (truly one of the most noble professions, and I would know since my sister is a nurse!) began using their own personal phones to FaceTime and video call family members of hospitalized patients. They knew, for some, this would be the last chance to say goodbye before their family member ultimately succumbed to the deadly effects of the virus.

Many families were separated – some with essential workers protecting their family from the virus, some due to living facility requirements, others due to an inability to travel safely. Whatever the reason, without technology, many may not have seen their families or those they love without the use of video technology. My grandmother celebrated her 90th birthday over Zoom with her grandchildren, great grandchildren, son, nieces, nephew, and friends all dialed in on video. Although it was not the same as being together – we could at least see one another on such a big celebration day!

My workplace had already been using video conferencing for purposes of interviewing candidates for the past ten years. We had not, however, conducted virtual meetings on a regular basis. During the first days of remote work, cameras were not turned on. Everyone would dial in, but we wouldn't see one and others faces. A few weeks in, I knew this needed to change and I made it standard practice to always have my camera on during meetings (as did our full leadership team). Once I did it, my team started to do it as well. No one cared how you looked, it was being able to actually look at you and see facial expressions that mattered most. Without this technology, we would have been significantly challenged to work successfully in a remote environment for a full year.

Our businesses also had to find ways to leverage technology to accomplish things we had done very differently before. The most significant example of a major shift I saw was in the shopping arena. Our ability to "shop" virtually existed prior to COVID – Amazon was already a daily event in my life. My son used to express profound disappointment on days we did not receive an Amazon package and sometimes, in shock, state that they must not be delivering today!

However, the ability to get any restaurant direct to our doors did not exist. In fact, my family lives in an area where, at best, all I could get before COVID was a pizza! Grocery delivery did exist prior to COVID – we began using this service when my twins were born. When nursing and caring for twin babies (and a 3-year-old) around the clock, a trip to a grocery store became a luxury. In fact, we developed a relationship with our grocery delivery person as he has now been delivering groceries to us for nearly two years!

Although this technology existed, I think most still went to the store – going to the store can in fact be quite enjoyable! During COVID, the wait times for deliveries skyrocketed due to the number of people using this service. Then we saw wine shops, Target, Sam's, pharmacies – you name it – begin to be available by delivery. I am not sure there is anything I can't get via delivery anymore. The technology that made all of this possible has transformed these industries. I imagine these businesses had to change a lot of their practices in order to be able to sell and serve in this new way.

You know what the biggest impact of all this new technology can be? The ability to get time back! I reflected the other day on how much time must have been spent taking kids to the store for new shoes and clothes. I am able to order them right to my house and instead spend that time hiking, walking, or playing with my kids! Maybe those moments were also enjoyable, but now I can choose which moments I want to have versus which moments I must have. I've never had to battle three kids under four in a grocery store –

and frankly I am truly glad I could avoid that experience! Instead, I can intentionally create experiences that bring value and meaning to my life.

My experience, as highlighted above, was primarily positive. However, I am sure others have had more challenging experiences. I am sure the many doctors who experienced transforming how they saw patients and made diagnoses were challenged. The essential workers who had to change how they provided food from restaurants and their ability to get tips as a result probably struggled. And likely many other examples I have not personally experienced.

During President Biden's first address to the nation after 100 days in office, he stated we will experience more technological change in the next ten years than we have experienced in the last fifty years.[34] Let that sink in for a moment. The world of technology is going to progress at five times its previous rate. The change people used to face slowly over 50 years will be compacted into the space of only ten years. We will be going through what prior generations experienced over lifetimes in just decades. We can approach this change with fear and resistance, or we can appreciate how the benefits can actually improve our lives.

Reflection: *When reflecting on your use of technology, how do you feel about your ability to leverage this technology? How have you felt during this experience of using new technology? How do you feel about technology continuing to change? What can you do to learn and improve your performance as you process your experiences with technology?*

CHAPTER FIVE
Our Lives
& Relationships

*What challenges impacted
our families and relationships?*

Lessons Learned

How we live

Our life experience directly impacts our work
experience and vice versa. We must take care of
our family dynamics and treat it with the same
attention we give our work and careers.

How we connect

We have more ways to connect than ever before
and we must always connect. The more isolated
we become, the greater our struggle.

OUR CHILDREN AND FAMILY DYNAMICS
– HOW WE LIVE

For many, our families were at least as disrupted as our workplaces. In the beginning, we were all trapped at home under the Stay-at-Home orders with our families – whether those were roommate families, spouses, children, or people we consciously chose to quarantine with together. Depending on your country, you likely experienced varying degrees of lockdown over the year based upon government decisions and virus transmission rates. When limited to being with family you are far more motivated (positively or negatively) to make that time as meaningful and valuable as possible.

In some cases, I am sure these interactions caused much pain. I've seen the reports on increases in domestic violence and child abuse in the home due to more time at home, as well as an increase in the use of drugs and alcohol. For others, given their roles in essential businesses or the medical fields, they had even less time with families as they carried many of our societal burdens. In other cases, it forced those of us with work that pulled us away from family to be with our family more and realize the value of that time. Whatever the impact, the time during COVID inevitably impacted your family dynamic, how you interact with your children, and how you see your family role in the future.

Many families were forced to make difficult decisions about family and work. Conversations about who would watch the children, how they would be cared for, and for many families who would be doing the virtual schooling! (Important Lesson from the pandemic – young children were not meant for virtual school!) These decisions were not easy for anyone, everyone struggled with what to do. Including employers who needed to keep businesses running but also wanted to support employees during a particularly difficult time.

From a personal perspective, I know the struggle families faced deciding what to do with children, careers, and family responsibilities. My family was blessed with options that many other families did not have. However, my husband and I did have repeated conversations about whether he should take more time off or if I should. Ultimately, my husband and I chose for him to be the one to take the extra required time off to care for children. He used the FFCRA Extended Family Medical Leave Act to take the time required to care for our children when schools were closed, as we had no childcare alternatives.

My sister, one of the many women who left the workforce due to COVID, agreed to take my son Wyatt along with her two girls and do preschool in her home. My parents, recently retired, were gracious enough to watch my twin girls so that our family could stay together, and we could see one another. We became entirely isolated from the external world but remained together as an extended family unit. Those decisions were not made easily. My sister did not want to leave her job as a pediatric nurse practitioner. My parents, especially my mom – an amazing unpaid worker who already raised three outstanding daughters, were not particularly excited about taking care of babies once again.

I watched my employees in the workforce struggle too, juggling children on their laps while taking work calls and performing work long after their children went to bed. The line between our work and our home life, which had already become blurred with technology, all but disappeared during COVID. Even now, as we begin to return to some version of normal, the line that used to exist just doesn't exist the same way anymore. We've experienced our family more fully and our work was incorporated into our family life in a new and different way.

Trying to separate our work from our life is virtually impossible. No, I am going to go even further than that – it is absolutely impossible! No matter where you work or what you do, the two are inextricably linked together. When one suffers, so does the other. When one is out of harmony, so is the other. Businesses are starting to realize this correlation and the need to pay attention to employee well-being. They are finally beginning to consider work practices that respect not just the employee's work experience, but also the employee's life experience. Employees are not machines – we are people, and we must all be treated as people first.

We all want to live great lives – ideally, even exceptional lives – but the challenge is, unless we are having an exceptional experience in both work and life, we inevitably have poor experiences in both. Challenges at work impact our lives, and challenges in our life impact our work. One inevitably impacts the other – a great experience at work impacts our life positively, and a great life impacts our work positively.

Reflection: *As you reflect on your experience with your family, spouse, children, and friends – how did those experiences make you feel? How did you respond to those experiences? How have those experiences changed how you view your family life?*

How can you continue to create the positive experiences? How can you let go of the experiences that bring frustration and negativity? As you reflect on your experiences, have you considered your performance and what you could learn, grow, and improve? Once again, have you considered the experiences of others? Have you considered what they have been through and how it has changed them?

Keep this last part in mind as you interact with others and talk about your experiences. They are likely to be very different and, as a result, we may all be approaching the future quite differently. (Note: I think this is critically important for all leaders who may not be taking into consideration the experiences of people with life situations differently from them. Leaders, more than anyone, must think about this topic and truly learn about the experiences of their stakeholders to help make good decisions about the future.)

OUR SOCIAL INTERACTIONS – HOW WE CONNECT

Social distancing, by definition, changed how people interact.

Social Distancing also called 'physical distancing,' means keeping a safe space between yourself and other people who are not from your household. The practice of maintaining a greater than usual physical distance from other people or of avoiding direct contact with people or objects in public places during the outbreak of a contagious disease to minimize exposure and reduce the transmission of infection.[35]

Humans require social interactions.[36] These interactions are necessary to our health, well-being, and life satisfaction. As we were required to stay apart, to be separate, to not interact face-to-face, the frequency and quality of these social interactions changed significantly. Humans are creative and we began identifying alternative means for having social interaction. However, the level of interaction, particularly amongst those who did not already know one another, was dramatically reduced, if not eliminated entirely.

I remember taking a walk one day on a path near my home with my kids. We passed others as we walked and smiled, saying, "Hi," "Isn't it beautiful," and "How are you?" My son *loves* to say hi and talk to new people. I commented on how good it felt just to interact with someone else outside my limited circle – to have that casual smile and see one in return. I've always made it a point in my life to try to smile and say something kind to those I interact with. You never know what another person is going through and what a difference a little bit of kindness might bring to another person. These interactions are important – and they were certainly missing.

One day on another walk, we came upon some painted rocks with sayings on them like "This too shall pass," "Smile," and "Be happy." I can't tell you the joy those rocks brought my son but, honestly, they brought me tremendous joy as well. I felt a little less alone, I loved seeing those rocks on our walks. My son and I painted more rocks and placed them around the neighborhood as well – the smallest joy and connection means so much more when we are isolated and separated.

I think this is why providing food when someone is going through a challenging time or personal crisis is so powerful. When I had my twins – I remember how much people bringing me food meant to me. I felt cared for, I felt loved, I felt supported. My mother started a charity years ago called "Meals Do Matter" where individuals come together to make freezer meals that are ready to go for anyone who needs them. Anyone in the church can grab a meal and bring it to anyone who is in need of a meal. I think the meal is helpful (certainly needed in some cases) but I also think the gesture and the feeling of being cared about is equally important. The church says, "You matter to God, you matter to Us," and that is included with each meal. I think receiving this message – feeling like you matter to someone – helps build up that connection.

As a result of all the limitations, I began to seek out other opportunities to interact with new people. I'll admit I did not take those steps as soon as I should have. Rather, as time went on, I realized I needed to adapt further. I began interacting with some old high school friends more frequently. I also joined a number of *Meetup* groups to join and network with others. These interactions started to expand my circle well beyond what I ever would have done prior to COVID. I am not sure I would have taken the same steps if those groups had been in person rather than virtual. These steps led me to participate in the Voices of Women Summit on International Women's Day. After speaking, I heard another speaker, Keira Poulsen, talk about writing books. Her speech led me to contact her and begin the process of turning this book into a reality. And participating in her Spiritual Entrepreneur program introduced me to many other women authors and I am building amazing partnerships as a result.

Reflection: *In life, we require social connections. Without them, we are isolated, alone, and our experiences at work and home suffer. Think about your social experiences in the last year – what did you feel? What did you do? How did you connect? Have you considered how you can intentionally improve your capabilities with respect to building connections with others? What will you do to build on your experiences and ensure you are creating connections with others and learning from the experiences of others?*

CHAPTER SIX
Our Cultures and
Communities

How were our communities impacted?

Lesson Learned

What happens in the world isn't just "someone else's problem." Rather, it can, and eventually will, directly impact our lives. We must care about the world and the experiences of everyone in it, not just our own, and if we do, we can create change which will transform lives for centuries to come.

OUR COMMUNITIES, ECONOMY, AND POLITICS - HOW WE RELATE, SHARE, AND SERVE

If COVID-19 wasn't enough – how our economy was impacted and what transpired in the political world as a result certainly added to the transformation. The often-divisive response to the crisis left many struggling with what was real, true, and accurate. Medical professionals were conflicted on their advice and experience with drugs, treatments, and the severity of COVID. Even in the highest levels of government conflict was apparent in how to communicate, handle, and respond to the crisis. We ultimately saw a breakdown between federal, state, and local governments. Everyone became focused on convincing others of their polarizing view. Many of us were left wondering who to believe and what to do.

This confusion wasn't limited to the start of the pandemic – it continued throughout the entire year. At times I felt like a ping pong ball trying to keep up with the changes, the revisions, and the conflicting information. Even now, mid-2021, with a vaccine available, people remain confused – and many are hesitant to get a vaccine that is saving hundreds of thousands of lives. The distrust, conspiracy theories, and inability to create consistent messaging has ultimately cost (and may continue to cost) us many lives.

The pandemic significantly impacted the economy, and many jobs were lost. With bars closed and restaurants doing delivery, stores unable to have people shop, and sporting events cancelled – much of our economy was halted. Businesses had no choice but to let people go because there was no revenue to support their compensation. People were forced to shift to new roles and jobs, and a gig economy has exploded as a result with lots of drivers, deliveries, and shoppers. Despite this, many remain unemployed, especially women who left the workforce at a much higher rate than men. Over *two million* women left the workforce in 2020. Let that sink in for a moment. The long-term impact of that kind of exodus from the workforce can't even be comprehended yet.

From a more positive perspective, people also found new ways to serve each other. Neighbors got groceries for the elderly, those in need were met with support, and the government provided loans and unemployment. One of the most memorable experiences for me of giving was actually after the vaccine was produced. In the St. Louis area (where I live) getting a vaccine was extremely difficult in the beginning. In Missouri, rural communities had an abundance of vaccines, but the city and county had virtually nothing (when compared to the population). A Facebook group called "St. Louis and Eastern Missouri COVID-19 Vaccine Info"[37] was created by a kindhearted person. People would share when they found vaccines available so others could locate a vaccine. Hundreds and hundreds of people got their vaccine by joining this site.

Even more amazing, a group of people actually volunteered to find others who needed vaccines a place to go and register on their behalf. This group of people did amazing work helping those who struggle with technology, who weren't sure how to do it, and who had serious conditions requiring access to a vaccine. The group served each other, supported each other, and helped each other. Not because they were paid to do so or told to do so – but because they wanted to do so! What an amazing lesson for the future – what could be possible if we spent more time helping each other and less time fighting and disagreeing with each other!

When I was a boy and I would see scary things in the news, my mother would say to me, 'Look for the helpers. You will always find people who are helping.

Mr. Fred Rogers

In May 2020, the murder of George Floyd by a police officer kneeling on his neck in the middle of the street was recorded by numerous onlookers and body cameras. This murder shocked the nation. I remember when I first watched the video. I remember the emotion, the anger, the outrage, the frustration, and even the disbelief. I am a white woman. I have never been stopped by the police. I haven't had a speeding ticket since I was 18 years old (and believe me when I tell you it is not because I do not speed!). My life experience does not include these types of traumatic interactions with the police. I also went to law school. I know well the laws and how they can be misapplied and misconstrued. I know how you can believe someone *should* be guilty, but because of how the laws are written, it might be impossible to rule them guilty.

Following this event, Breonna Taylor's murder was also widely publicized. My reaction and feelings might have been even more intense when I learned the details of her death. Asleep in her own bed, police breaking down her door, shooting her in her own home. I can't imagine the same situation happening to someone in my neighborhood or who had a different color of skin. I couldn't imagine it – because I don't think I've ever seen it happen. I did know these types of incidents were occurring, but I did not realize the extent of the problem.

I think for many this was a huge realization – that in our world, really terrible things happen, and no one seems to care. The world needed to (and still needs to) change as a result of these major revelations. As I worked on this book, the jury in the Floyd trial of Officer Chauvin found him guilty on all three charges. I'm still in shock and amazed the jury convicted a police officer for their grievous behavior and I am grateful justice was finally done.

Our world was stuck at home, watching these terrible incidents unfold, and we were forced to reflect on our own experiences and, in some cases, privileges. Many people came together to protest, stand up, and say, "Black Lives Matter." I personally felt (and still feel) that I have more work to do to better understand the experience of others. I know I can't have every experience personally – the world is big – but I can seek to listen and learn from others. I can also then use my talents and strengths to support and improve the world. Seeing the seriousness of what others face with such intensity allows us to look at our own performance in the world and how learning about these events can shape what we do in our lives.

For example, I have worked hard to make sure my children understand that differences in people make us beautiful. But also, differences can make life more challenging for people. We must learn about people and their experiences and not judge them based upon their appearance. My son (who is five) attends a Montessori school with a rainbow of colors in the classroom. I don't have all the answers, but I recognize my own performance needs to grow in this area – how to talk about topics like racism and sexism and how to grow in how we approach them.

As if these events weren't enough, 2020 happened to be an election year and, oh holy moly, what an election year it was. I refuse to allow this book to become polarized and political the way our media and world has become. However, I think acknowledging the polarization and negativity in our politics is essential.

Every year, it appears we become more "them versus us" in how we talk and interact. Rather than talking about a topic to understand each other – we talk about topics to convince each other. Let me emphasize – there is a HUGE difference. When I talk about topics to understand, I am learning about your perspective, experience, data, and insights. When I am trying to convince, I am trying to tell you why you need to believe me (or more frequently believe whoever fed me the information I am arguing).

In Matthew McConaughey's new book *Greenlights* he shares a story which struck me. While in Africa he engaged in a conversation with two men who were sharing different opinions on a topic when Matthew decided to enter the discussion and agree with one of the men. They responded with "It is not about right or wrong. It is 'Do you understand?!'"[38]

They are not trying to win arguments of right or wrong. They are trying to understand each other. That's different. (Hey, America, we could learn from this.)

Matthew McConaughey, Greenlights

I am not sure when we started to believe social media posts and memes more than our family and friends. I am not sure why our media became so two-sided. I am not sure who decided it was necessary to begin acting the way we tell our children not to act. We don't allow them to argue, scream, talk over each other, and call each other names (or at least we shouldn't').

The behaviors we saw in 2020, and especially after the 2021 Capitol Riot, must lead us to figure out how to come together in a different way. How to listen more than we speak? How to consider we might be wrong? How to stay open-minded to the beliefs of others? How to keep learning and improving? And most importantly – HOW TO CHANGE! We must learn to be able to change what we think, what we do, and what we believe as we continue to learn and grow. I want a politician who changes his or her mind as he or she learns – I don't want someone with the same beliefs their whole life.

For example, the Jessica before dating a drug addict and the Jessica after leaving that abusive relationship are completely different people. The Jessica before children and the Jessica after becoming a mom to three amazing children are very different people – with totally different beliefs – because my experiences changed me for the better. My understanding after experiencing significantly traumatic health conditions has changed how I respond and see the world of healthcare. And I plan to continue to change my beliefs as I learn and grow and gain new experiences.

Our government must be about service – we pay them to serve the needs of the country, the greater good, and to invest in areas we cannot invest individually. Therefore, we need our government to be performing at peak performance.

In my trainings on Accountability, there is a section where I ask (rhetorically), "Who here agrees the government is productive, efficient, effective, and creates the best results possible?" How many people do you think raise their hands? Yes, you are right... absolutely no one ever agrees. In fact, I think the one thing most people agree on is the overall impression that government is not as effective as the private sector, that the performance of the government is inferior to businesses, and that the government has significant room for improvement.

I am not writing this to criticize or critique the government but simply to be honest about its current state. In order to grow we must start with acknowledging where we are. Frankly, the opportunity for improvement in our government excites me. If we can do things better, if we can improve performance, the results our government could achieve in the future are tremendously greater than we are experiencing today. We need to look at performance as essential to the future of our country. We must evolve everyone's performance and especially all those in government.

I highlight these events because I think they are part of what is shaping a new future. We can't ignore what is happening in the world at large and focus only on our small part in it. In order to change and improve the world, we must start by improving ourselves. If our performance does not appreciate the experiences of others in the world and those we interact with, we will miss the opportunity to truly grow. Furthermore, we can choose to change, and it all starts with changing ourselves and evolving our performance in the world.

Reflection: As you reflect on your experience with these events, how did you perceive them? What did you feel when they occurred and what do you still feel now? Can you separate yourself from those feelings so you can process and move beyond them?

What is your part in what is transpiring in the world and how can you improve yourself in response to what is occurring? Have you taken the time to consider the perspective and experience of others? (Let me be clear here – I am not suggesting you debate or try to convince others of your perspective. Have you asked and simply listened to the experience of those who may think or see things differently?)

Can you see how each of our experiences are interrelated and how our decisions impact one and other? Are you open to considering your experience and whether your response is beneficial to you, your family, your community, and the world?

CAN YOU SEE A BETTER WORLD?

We currently live in a time of hostility, division, and partisanship. People would rather draw lines and throw stones than engage in conversation and try to find solutions together. In this climate, cooperation may seem like the best we can hope for between people. But that's selling ourselves short. We can do better. Cooperation is unity for the sake of unity. Cooperation says "Let's just get along or else nothing will get done." Collaboration is unity for the sake of shared vision. Collaboration says, "Let's work together because this has to be done."[39]

John C. Maxwell, in Change your World

Do you feel that weird, uncomfortable feeling – the feeling that is somewhere between good and bad? Like when you see a child dance with complete joy and abandon while also remaining totally oblivious to the judgement of those watching. It makes you smile, but somewhat uncomfortably. This is the place where we exist in the "in between." The space and time that exists between the challenged, overwhelmed, frustrated, concerned, hesitant, unhappy, and hurting world. And the moment where we feel excitement, potential, opportunity, possibility, hope, happiness, and can see a better world.

What if we are actually at one of those truly unique points in time? One of those moments in our history where we are right on the precipice of a tremendously exciting, new, and better world? What if we are right between what was and what can and will be? What if, around the corner, lies a future we have only dreamed to be possible?

I believe in what some would characterize as impossible or unbelievable. I believe in the possibility of achieving the impossible. I believe we *can* change the world. I believe in God's ability and desire to do so. I believe we can advance as human beings to the next level in our evolutionary process. I believe we are at the beginning of the Exceptional Live R-Evolution. And I'm sure my beliefs will cause some to call me a dreamer. But then I'd be in the company of greatness, like Martin Luther King Jr., Abraham Lincoln, and Mother Teresa.

I believe we can change the world by changing our workplaces, homes, and communities. I believe by changing how we think, live, and perform in our lives we can create a better future for everyone on this planet. I believe we can change our world to be a better place for everyone if we can change how we live and work. I believe we can achieve more in this world than we ever knew possible if we can collectively evolve and reach peak performance together. Just consider for a moment all the possibilities:

What if we could *curiously* recognize and enjoy our differences rather than judge?

What if we could *connect* and build meaningful relationships with anyone, anywhere?

What if we could *create* opportunity and growth for everyone?

What if we could *change* how we respond to failures and mistakes in order to improve?

What if we could *craft* how we interact in ways that build community rather than conflict?

What if we could *care* about everyone, everywhere?

What if we could *consider* positive results over negative perceptions?

What if we could *challenge* everyone to learn, grow, and develop needed capabilities?

What if we could *cure* hatred, disease, evil, and disconnection?

What if we could *cross* into new ways of thinking and living?

What if we could *celebrate* the world's success at reaching peak performance together?

Why have I spent all this time talking about the past in a book focused on how to create an exceptional future? I believe our experiences over the past year have created the transformation necessary to make a better future possible. These experiences, often challenging, both positive and negative, are what will allow us to reconsider how we live and work creating the possibility of an exceptional life. The lessons around connecting, working, performing, living, relating, sharing, serving, and communicating can all contribute to how we reach peak performance.

After reflecting on your lived experiences and the experiences of others, we can begin to look at how we evolve to reach peak performance in the future. As we evolve into this new world, transformed by our experiences, anyone, in any role, in any business, in any community, and in any family, can choose how they want to live and work in the future. The key is in evolving to reach peak performance.

Section Three

THE FOUR KEYS TO PEAK PERFORMANCE

*What will guide us on our journey
to peak performance?*

> *One day, I saw my son run right into a wall. I
> said to him, "Ouch, that must have hurt! Watch
> out for walls – they usually don't move!"*

One day, I saw my son run right into a wall. I said to him, "Ouch, that must have hurt! Watch out for walls – they usually don't move!" I have talked a lot about what is changing and what we have to be prepared for as a result. This topic may make some uncomfortable or concerned with how they can possibly improve when everything is constantly changing. I'd like to point out here that, although a lot will change, the walls are going to stay the same. The wallpaper, decoration, furniture, lights, and more may change, but the walls are rarely going to move and, if they do move, they won't move quickly.

In the last section, I highlighted the challenges and lessons we have learned from everything that has been changing. We took the time to evaluate where we are as individuals in the midst of all this change. For many people, change can be an extremely difficult and challenging topic to consider, let alone experience. Many people struggle with experiencing change because, naturally, it is harder to change than remain the same. Remaining the same is easier because we don't have to expend effort or energy, but easier does not mean positive, better, or ideal. Rather, change being hard means we must go through some effort to adjust our current state of being – physically or emotionally. How we approach change and respond to our environment when we encounter an opportunity for change has a significant impact on the outcomes in our lives.

Like the walls, the framework for our lives will generally stay the same, but there are various doors to enter or opportunities we can choose in our lives. The Keys to Peak Performance will unlock doors that we may have treated as walls in the past – areas we could change, but simply did not have the key to unlock the opportunity! The keys are our guide to navigate an ever-changing world as we progress up the mountain path on our journey to peak performance.

While all four keys are necessary for peak performance, one key has a bigger impact than the others. The concepts provided in the Accountability key directly apply and relate to the other three keys. Everything we do in life begins and ends with our Mindset and Personal Accountability. When I train on the four keys, I spend one day on the three keys of expectations, feedback, development, and agile performance management. Whereas I spend a whole day on just Mindset and Personal Accountability. I have witnessed throughout my career the impact of mindsets on our outcomes and results. If you get nothing else out of this book – make sure to spend the time on Mindset & Accountability!

The next section is our guide for navigating our performance mountain and directing us on our journey. The keys will unlock our true potential, new opportunities, and strategies that will help us to reach peak performance. We will cover each of the four Keys to Peak Performance in much more detail. I've used these four keys and the concepts provided for many years and have seen how they positively impact performance in the workplace. I only recently recognized how applicable these elements are to the many roles we perform in our lives. I've tried to incorporate examples from a variety of roles we perform to highlight the concepts. The last section will then provide greater detail and examples specific to the different roles we perform.

CHAPTER SEVEN
Setting Expectations

How to set and exceed clear expectations?

> **Key Insight:**
>
> Establishing clear expectations for myself and those I interact with in the roles I perform is foundational to reaching my peak performance.

Beginning with expectations is similar to being born. Just like we can't skip this step-in life, we must start with expectations before progressing to the other keys of peak performance. Think of expectations like a new baby. At first glance, their functioning seems incredibly simple – eat, sleep, poop, and cry. But take a closer look and you will witness the baby's extraordinarily complicated development – the tremendous learning and growth in capabilities occurring at an unbelievable speed.

Expectations initially appear to be the most simple and straightforward (like a baby at birth), however, upon closer examination, the work required to establish basic clarity is significantly more complicated and difficult than it first appears (like the development of a baby).

I'll admit, early in my career as a manager, I thought I was extremely clear in my expectations of those who worked for me – and I was very wrong. Anyone who believes expectations are easy, simple, or straightforward does not understand what it truly means to establish clear expectations. They have overlooked the complexity created by different people with different perspectives, different experiences, and different approaches to communication. These differences make creating clarity in expectations quite difficult and requires each person to put in significant time and effort.

HOW DO EXPECTATIONS RELATE TO PERFORMANCE?

Before we begin evolving to reach peak performance, we must understand what is expected in the roles we perform. This begins with identifying who we are serving or performing the role for, and what others require of us in our performance. At first blush, the expectations appear obvious. As a parent, we must feed our children, and as an employee, I must complete my work – but the complexities of these expectations are almost infinite. For example, making decisions about feeding children can include:

* what to feed my children (organic or junk food; fast food or homecooked)

* when to feed my children (when they are hungry or at mealtimes)

* how to feed my children (snacks or full meals)

* where to feed my children (at the table or in front of the iPad/TV)

Likewise, the same complexities apply to employees in the workplace – what work to do, when to do the work, how to do the work, where to do the work, and even why to do the work (beyond a paycheck!). Typically, we assume expectations are clear and simple and, therefore, think discussing them is unnecessary. Even in the workplace, where expectations are probably more likely to be discussed, we spend very little time discussing and reviewing those expectations.

However, before we can understand our performance in any role, we must first define the expectations of our performance in that role. We can't begin to understand or measure how we are performing, look for opportunities to improve, or hold ourselves accountable for achieving results unless we fully understand the expectations for our performance. We can create these for ourselves or with others, but peak performance is impossible without completing this step.

WHAT HAPPENS WITHOUT CLEAR EXPECTATIONS?

A quick Google search reveals the many comics, videos, and jokes made around unclear expectations. Why is it that everyone knows the challenges that occur from unclear expectations but still struggles to create them? Most don't realize how detrimental these challenges are to our businesses and lives. They appear comical, and therefore, many don't take seriously the inevitable impact on our results. Without clear expectations we may experience:

Frustration

The first reaction by almost everyone in a situation with unclear expectations is frustration. Everyone becomes frustrated, because *everyone* thinks *someone* is doing something, that *anyone* should be able to do, but *nobody* actually does it because *everybody* thinks *somebody* else is doing it! Who was supposed to do it – everyone, someone, anyone, nobody, everybody, or somebody? Ever experienced this before? If you find yourself frustrated with a situation and are unsure why – always start with expectations.

Comparison – Knowing when we excel

Without clear expectations, we have nothing with which to compare our day-to-day performance to understand how we are performing. At best, we compare ourselves with "common intuition" expectations but, like the example of feeding our children, each individual expectation is different. These differences fail to make clear which actions will result in positive outcomes. At worst, we do not even consider what is expected and how we compare to that expectation. When unable to compare our performance, we begin to struggle with self-worth, value, appreciation, and overall reinforcement of our performance. We will talk more about the criticality of recognition in the next section, but without clear expectations we may never feel recognized because the bar for performance has not been set. You can't jump over a bar that doesn't even exist!

Misalignment with Others

Greatness can also not be achieved when we are misaligned with others. A significant challenge when expectations are unclear is misalignment on what is required and what is being delivered. Our constituents will be challenged to recognize or appreciate our efforts if we were misaligned on the expectations of our role. We will deliver but it may not be what was required, needed, or wanted.

Ultimately Conflict, Lots of Conflict

When expectations remain misaligned (even when the parties know they are misaligned) all roads lead to the same outcome – conflict. Until expectations are redefined and realigned, the conflict between parties will continue to grow. The simplest and most obvious example is little kids fighting over the same toy, yelling "Mine!" When we aren't clear, conflict occurs, and we tend to get loud and stubborn about our own perspective. By setting and aligning expectations, we can avoid all this unnecessary conflict.

Most importantly, without clear expectations of performance in our roles, we cannot ever reach peak performance and success in our roles.

HOW DO I SET AND ALIGN ON EXPECTATIONS?

When addressing the Expectations Key, I break it into two types of conversation: Performance and Impact. Both are necessary for reaching peak performance and we must ensure we are addressing both in any role we perform. Understanding the impact of roles is the first conversation. The next is focusing on our performance in the roles themselves. I find it helpful to look at each of these elements as steps to follow:

1. Define who your role is serving and why serving them is important.

2. Create Direction by setting Vision and Strategy.

3. Confirm your Values.

4. Define Outcomes of your Role and Goals to Achieve them.

5. Confirm what is required to perform your role.

6. Align and Commit.

The impact we make in our role helps clarify the expectations of the role.

For many years, I started by defining the expectations of a role using the outcome or result the role was meant to achieve rather than the impact of the role on others. I consistently noticed that people knew "what" they needed to accomplish (which is good and also critical to performing) but not really "why" they needed to accomplish it. When people don't know why "what" they are doing is important or matters, their commitment to achieving excellence while performing the role suffers.

> *When people don't know why "what" they are doing is important or matters, their commitment to achieving excellence while performing the role suffers.*

Ultimately, people know the steps they need to execute, but not how those steps make an impact (on others, the business, customers, the world). The impact of our work is what ultimately gives us the motivation to perform at our best and reach peak performance – our meaning. Without the impact, we are left feeling empty, unappreciated, and unvalued for our accomplishments. When people understand who they are impacting and why what they are doing is important, their results improve. This step, although relatively easy, is frequently overlooked.

"A clear and detailed understanding of the purpose of work, and of the values we should honor in deciding how to get it done. Our people don't need to be told what to do; they want to be told why."

Marcus Buckingham, in Nine Lies About Work

Take the employee who doesn't understand why making sure orders are on time is important to their customers. They know intuitively that deliveries being on time are important – but if they don't recognize the details, they may not appreciate the significance of their efforts. (The customer is a power company, and, without that product, the power plant could stop providing power during a heat wave or blizzard!) The importance of our efforts and our commitment to reaching peak performance is significantly impacted by our understanding of who our actions are impacting and why that matters to us as individuals.

What about in our homes? How do we appreciate the impact our choices make at home? Take a mother who is breastfeeding her baby. If the mother doesn't appreciate the impact of her sacrifice of sleep, time, and energy on the baby's long-term health and development, she may lack the commitment and desire to persevere and be successful. (Speaking very much from personal experience here as I breastfed my twin girls!)

> *A person in any role can always find someone they are serving.*

In all of these examples, by understanding our impact when performing the role, we can better identify the expectations we need to meet in the role. We appreciate who we are serving and can base our performance expectations on what is needed or required rather than simply what we believe is necessary.

Step 1: Define who your role is serving and why serving them is important.

Start by considering the role you perform and who you are performing that role in service of, such as children, a business, customers, your spouse, or parents. Take time and look closely – oftentimes we may overlook less obvious individuals who are also served by our role. These are important as they can influence and impact how we define our expectations.

For example, as a mother, my children are obviously served by my role. However, my husband is also served by my role as mother, and he has an interest in how the expectations of my role as mother are defined. Each family has expectations for parents and the roles of mother or father. In one family, the mother may be expected to stay home and care for children and the home, and the father expected to work. In another family, both parents may work, requiring the housework be divided differently. Or any other wonderfully unique combination of possibilities. A lack of clarity in expectations as it relates to parents and children is the cause of significant discord in many families. Ensuring you define who is impacted by your role in your specific family structure and circumstance is essential.

Reflection: Who benefits from you performing a particular role? Who would be upset if you failed to perform your role? Who do you want to recognize and acknowledge your work? Why does the work matter to you (if it does)? Who needs you to do what you do each and every day? These are the people you serve. They may be customers, clients, children, animals, organizations, groups, and even your family.

We must also define how serving in that role impacts those we serve. In other words, why does my performance matter? Why do I want to be an excellent mother? Why does my performance as an employee matter to my customers? The best way to answer these types of questions is to consider what happens if I do well and what happens if I do not do well.

In the first instance, if you perform your role well, what can you be proud of achieving? What will occur as a result and why does this matter to you? In the second case, if you chose not to perform your role at all, what would happen? What happens if you perform but not to your best? If you do not know the answer to these questions for your role, I recommend taking the time to ask the question of someone you interact with who performs the same role as you.

Creating clarity of expectations (what is required to perform) is multi-faceted.

Think of expectations like an onion – you must peel away each layer of what is required in order to deliver the necessary outcomes. Each layer adds more complexity, but also addresses necessary elements to consider, including:

1. Individual expectations: your specific role and responsibilities in it, what you are achieving

2. Team, Group, Family expectations: who does what, when and how; allocation of responsibilities; commitments

3. Expectations of the broader population (business, family, community)

Once we have confirmed the "who," we must confirm the "what." In order to define the "what," we can consider four different elements for providing context and clarity including:

*   Direction: Vision (where are we going) & Strategy (how are we getting there?)

*   Values: Who are we and what do we stand for?

*   Outcomes & Goals: What will the result of my contribution be long term and short term?

*   Roles & Responsibilities: What will I specifically do to contribute?

I like this framework for expectations, but if the specific words don't make sense to you, feel free to substitute in a way that suits your needs. If one particular element does not seem effective for your role – you can pick and choose those that do!

Step 2: Create Direction by setting a vision and strategy

Direction: "A guiding, governing, or motivating purpose"

> **Direction**: A course along which someone or something moves; the management or guidance of someone or something[40]

Expectations can be tricky, complicated, and (as we all know well) ever-changing. Therefore, by providing overarching guidance on where our performance is supposed to be leading directionally, we can gain confidence even when absolute clarity is lacking or impossible. Directional expectations help to guide and direct us toward more detailed and specific clarity. I've always used both vision and strategy as two key elements of setting direction.

Have you ever gone hiking in the woods and seen markers on the path (a colored sign, paint on a tree, a ribbon) which indicate you are going in the right direction? Consider the elements of our vision and strategy as our markers, helping us to know we are on track and moving in generally the right direction. They also provide the ability to ask ourselves if we have gotten too far off track – have we veered too far away from our vision and strategy?

Vision is about where we are going – as an individual, business, family, team, or community. What are we working towards and trying to achieve? For those with a Futuristic®[15] strength, defining a future vision may come easily, however, for others, defining a future vision can be challenging. Strategy is about how we are going to get there – the approach, the steps, the elements, the focus – which will help us achieve our vision.

---

[15] CliftonStrengths® and the CliftonStrengths 34 Themes of Talent are trademarks of Gallup, Inc. Gallup's content is Copyrighted by Gallup. Used with permission. All rights reserved.

Our workplaces have almost universally adopted the practice of defining a vision for the future of the business and a strategy for how the business will get there. In this case, our role is simply to learn and understand the vision and strategy so we can be clear on how our role will support and contribute to achieving them. In other contexts – like communities, organizations, families, or even us individually – a vision and strategy may not yet be created or defined. If one is, it may not provide the necessary clarity to bring value. In these cases, I encourage you to consider how you can ask questions, reflect, and establish this clarity for yourself and those you interact with.

This process is not exactly easy. I've seen many employees struggle to define their vision and strategy. I've seen workplaces define them but ineffectively apply, communicate, or explain them in ways their workforce can accomplish or achieve. All businesses, communities, and organizations need to go through this process.

Reflection: Consider those you want to impact in your role (customers, children, etc.). Imagine if you achieved everything you possibly wanted or believed was required – what would this look like? Where do you want to be in the future in order to achieve this impact? Where do we want to be, how do we want to be seen, what do we want to be doing or demonstrating?

Step 3: Confirm your Values

Values: "A person's principles or standards of behavior, one's judgement of what is important in life"

> **Values:** the regard that something is held to deserve; the importance, worth, or usefulness of something; a person's principles or standards of behavior; one's judgement of what is important is life[41]

Like direction, values provide a framework with which to gauge our thought processes, interactions, and decisions. Values help us identify who we are and what we are going to stand for. Values can be for you personally, your family, your workplace, your team, your community, or even your country. By identifying and living by a set of values, we confirm a structure for guiding our choices and influencing our performance.

Values can vary by person, role, team, or group. For example, the values in my workplace (driven, positive, collaborative) are different than the values I focus on within my family (connection, trust, joy, learning), and are also different than my values as a leader (trust, accountability, excellence). I live by these values in each area of my life and use them to help guide my decisions and behaviors.

Once you've identified your values you must consider them frequently in your decision making. Values must be incorporated into all our practices to truly make a difference in guiding our performance. At Experitec, we incorporate our values into everything, so employees are consistently thinking about and reflecting on their meaning, intention, and demonstration. With my kids, I speak often about what is most important to Mommy and try to ensure our family keeps those values top-of-mind!

Reflection: Consider your role and the environment where you perform the role – what are the values? I have used a variety of tools and exercises to help individuals identify their values. I've used card decks. I've used web-based tools. I've used Gallup®[16] resources. Any of them are useful and can provide you with a method for considering your values. What is important is to narrow it down to only a few values in each role you perform. If we value everything, then we truly value nothing. Consider your personal strengths, principles, and life experiences – how do these contribute to your values?

---

[16] CliftonStrengths® and the CliftonStrengths 34 Themes of Talent are trademarks of Gallup, Inc. Gallup's content is Copyrighted by Gallup. Used with permission. All rights reserved.

Step 4: Define Outcomes of Your Role and Goals to Achieve Them

Outcomes and Goals: Determining success and the steps to reach peak performance

> **Outcome**: a final product or end result; consequence; issue; a conclusion reached through a process of logical thinking[42]

We will shift from broader guides that help us with our performance expectations overall to greater detail and specificity with respect to the expectations in our specific role. I truly believe the best place to begin in getting more specific is with the question:

"What does success in this role look like?" or

"If I were performing this role perfectly, what would I ultimately achieve?"

In other words, what outcome or result occurs in the future if I am performing at peak performance? For example:

* As a parent, my children are happy, healthy, and meeting development milestones.

* As a spouse, my relationship is stable, committed, healthy, and continuing to grow.

* As an employee, I am exceeding performance targets and growing in my capabilities.

Take time to consider what success looks like in your specific role. Then write down the definition of what success in your role looks like for you specifically. What does it look like when you achieve the outcome? The more specific you define the outcome, the greater the probability you will achieve the result. Then, once you have clarity on where you want to end up (the results) then you must define what goals you want to set to get there.

Goal setting has been written about, trained on, and covered extensively by others. I've read countless books on goal setting, habits, tracking, and the methods and strategies for achieving them. I have even created many tools, worksheets, and workshops on goal setting. In all my research and experience, I think the most important part about goal setting is, quite frankly, just doing it. It is just taking the time to consider the goal and writing something (anything) down!

I am sure many would argue goals need to be SMART – specific, measurable, achievable, realistic, and time-bound, or some other set of requirements. However, I find the more complicated it is to identify and write a goal – the less likely we are to create them. Don't get me wrong, if you can get good at writing goals, this will certainly be helpful and beneficial. But for all those who struggle, I think we must start simple and build momentum.

The only critical thing you must do with your goals is to create them (come up with something) and write it down (where you can find it again). Even if you don't look at it, and even if it isn't perfect. I have consistently found that just writing down what we intend to accomplish significantly increases the likelihood that we will accomplish it. Once we've identified it clearly, we know what the goals are, and our brains can and will work on pursuing them!

Reflection: Consider what the outcome will be if you perform your role perfectly. What do you hope to achieve three, five, or ten years down the line as you work to reach peak performance? How will you know if you have been successful in your role? What goals are you going to create to help you reach that successful result?

Step 5: Confirm what is required to perform your role.

Roles & Responsibilities

> **Role**: the function assumed, or part played by a person or thing in a particular situation[43]
>
> **Responsibility**: the state or fact of being responsible, answerable, or accountable for something within one's power, control, or management[44]

As we funnel from the broad to the narrow, we must also get clear on the specific responsibilities or tasks we are expected to perform. I've seen this step often overlooked because it appears obvious and therefore must not be necessary. However, as a leader and manager I have repeatedly seen simple mistakes occur because the roles and responsibilities were either not clearly defined or uncommunicated.

Why is this so difficult? The complexity of our organizations, families, and communities are like a beautiful puzzle with hundreds or thousands of pieces. At the beginning, it can be hard to see how all the pieces fit together to create their purpose, or their vision. Identifying how each piece relates to one another (or fits together) is the only way to get to a completed puzzle. Ever worked on a puzzle where the pieces were so similar, they could look right even when they were put together incorrectly? We end up having to take things apart in order to put them back together the right way.

Roles and responsibilities are like the puzzle pieces. There are many ways they can go together, but only one way which creates the vision, the outcome, and the picture. We can't just assume everyone understands how the pieces fit together. And, we may have to try the same pieces many times before we figure out how they fit together correctly. We must look at all the roles and responsibilities required to achieve peak performance in our roles and work to figure out how they fit together.

Let's take the challenges in a new marriage before the inevitable discussions to clarify who has responsibility for which household tasks or chores. I'm sure no one has ever had the argument over who should load the dishwasher, do the laundry, or take out the trash! (I say dripping with sarcasm.) Let alone the details related to each. For example, my husband has very strong views on how the dishwasher should be loaded and I, on the other hand, have very specific views on who should take out the trash... anyone but me! Each relationship, role, and family are different and require a different degree of clarity. However, clarifying roles and responsibilities can save a lot of time you might otherwise have spent arguing, complaining, and disagreeing!

In the workplace, we use RASCI charts, or Role Matrixes, to identify the specific responsibilities we must perform (daily tasks and activities) and how those relate together in particular roles. We then determine who is capable of performing and who will be responsible and accountable for ensuring the roles and responsibilities are performed successfully.

If you do nothing else around setting expectations, you must clarify roles and responsibilities – who will be doing what and when! Don't make the mistake of leaving this open-ended or confusion and frustration which will inevitably ensue!

Reflection: *Start by considering the different elements for your specific role. Think about the outcomes and goals you defined for your role – what must you do each and every day in order to achieve those goals or outcomes? What do you have ownership for performing? What do you need to ensure you accomplish regularly as part of your role?*

Who do you need to discuss these roles and responsibilities within order to ensure they fit together with those of other individuals you work or perform with? What are you best suited to perform? What are others better suited to take responsibility for? Who will ultimately be responsible for ensuring a particular task or activity is accomplished?

Step 6: Align and Commit

Align, Re-Align, and then Align again

Align: to arrange in a straight line

Once we've identified what we believe to be our expectations, we must align our beliefs with those we interact with and serve when performing our role. To create full alignment, we must ensure we have the commitment of all those who are impacted.

Have you ever sat in Southwest Airlines First Class? Yes, Southwest does have a first class – it's the exit row! If you have, you have likely been asked something to the effect of, "Do you agree to perform these expectations in the event of an emergency?" They require you to provide a verbal affirmation of your commitment. Why do they do this? They know people are significantly more likely to act when they have given their verbal commitment.

Likewise, we need to ensure commitment to the expectations defined for the roles we are performing. If I haven't committed to do something, I am going to be much less likely to accomplish it than if I have said I will do it out loud to someone else (or in some cases even to myself).

Also, we must ensure that what we decide in terms of expectations stays aligned as things change, shift, and adjust. After the experience we had in 2020, it appears many expectations will be changing quite frequently in response to our changing environment. To ensure we understand when things change, how things are changing, and what needs to be changed or re-aligned – we must actively engage in conversations on these changes. We must be having constant clarifying conversations to ensure we are aligned on expectations. I can't count the number of times people thought they were aligned but were not.

As I previously mentioned, when I first started using these keys to set expectations with my employees, I had them complete Outcomes Responsibilities and Goals documents – defining their roles and what they were going to accomplish for the year. My employees and I talk almost daily about different projects and initiatives. I expected us to be easily aligned. We were not even close. Rather, what I thought was important wasn't even on their list and what they thought I wanted was not at all how I believed I described it. We had a lot of aligning to do and now we know this alignment must occur frequently or our alignment will most surely fade.

Re-aligning our expectations frequently is as important as setting the expectations to begin with. We've learned first-hand how quickly things can change – like with the pandemic – and we must ensure we are regularly touching base and realigning our expectations. Failure to re-align will inevitably cause us to end up in conflict! Issues and conflict will persist until expectations are addressed and aligned successfully – **do not** skip this step or key.

Reflection: Consider whether you have aligned the expectations of your role? Do you need to have further discussion to ensure you understand what is expected? Are you aligned with others on what you have defined you need to achieve? Are you committed to those expectations? Are others you work with committed to those expectations?

HOW DO WE MAKE EXPECTATIONS CLEAR, SO WE ARE ACCOUNTABLE FOR THEM?

I've provided a framework for creating or establishing expectations. Clarity, however, comes from being easily understood. We may believe simply stating our expectations is sufficient, but deep down we know it is not. How often have you set an expectation with someone and later discovered you were not operating under the same expectation?

Being clear in what we expect is definitely the hardest part of setting expectations. Being clear does not mean being simple, nor does it mean being complex. Being clear does not necessarily mean being brief in our communication nor being long in our communication. Rather, clarity must be based upon the people involved. We must understand who we are setting expectations with and determine how best to communicate these expectations in a way they will understand them, commit to them, and align on them.

Only once we have understood, committed to, and aligned on expectations can we possibly hold ourselves or others accountable to them. For example, I can say I want to be a great mom or a great leader but what does 'great' mean? How will I know if I am achieving this expectation? I can declare I want Experitec to be an Exceptional Workplace with high engagement, but how will I know if we are and when we do? By getting clear with our expectations, we are better able to identify both our successes to celebrate and failures to course correct. With clear expectations we create accountability for ensuring that we achieve the results and outcomes of our roles. Then, we can begin our journey up the performance mountain to reach peak performance.

WHY ARE EXPECTATIONS REALLY IMPORTANT RIGHT NOW?

As we have illustrated, expectation setting is foundational and critical in terms of performance. Although expectation setting is always important, in the digital world where the traditional boundaries have blurred, expectations have needed to change, as well as how frequently we set and revise them. As organizations transitioned almost overnight to a virtual remote workplace, schools closed and children began learning virtually, and traditional commerce was halted – inevitably, expectations were bound to change as well. All the roles we serve were impacted and required a re-alignment and communication regarding expectations.

The challenge was no one knew how significant the pandemic would be or how long it would ultimately last. Therefore, decisions related to the new environment had to be made with insufficient information. As technology continues to change the world we live in, expectations are going to continue to change at an ever-increasing rate! As those changes happen, we have to take the time to realign and clarify expectations for the roles we are serving, how they have changed, and how we need to perform differently as a result.

CHECKLIST:
WHAT DO I DO FIRST?

✓ Identify your constituents

✓ Discuss and consider their needs and how you will impact them

✓ Create direction for your role

✓ Identify your values and use them as a guide

✓ Define the outcome or results you want to achieve

✓ Create and set meaningful goals for achieving those outcomes

✓ Confirm your roles & responsibilities

✓ Have constant conversations to ensure clarity and alignment

CHAPTER EIGHT
Providing &
Receiving Feedback

How to receive and provide Feedback?

Key Insight:

We must fully understand ourselves,
find our source of motivation, and both seek out
and provide continuous feedback to reach peak
performance.

WHAT DO WE MEAN BY FEEDBACK?

Even if we know exactly what we should do, being motivated to do it and actually knowing how we are doing *at it* are both necessary for reaching peak performance. I struggled the most to name this particular key. At one point, I almost changed it to Motivation. Others might call it coaching (especially in the business context). I even considered caring and connecting. Ultimately, the feedback key is about all of these things. Feedback is about understanding people (ourselves and others), connecting with people, caring about people, and providing impactful perspectives and knowledge to help us improve and guide us on our journey evolving to peak performance.

We spent time on our personal preferences in the earlier chapters in this book, learning about our strengths, values, interests, beliefs, and capabilities. Oftentimes, better understanding ourselves allows us to better understand and interact with others. Which, of course, increases caring, connection, and motivation. As humans, we are hardwired to need caring, connecting, coaching, and motivating.

Feedback starts with connection – learning about ourselves and others in order to build connection and understanding between ourselves and those we serve. I call this type of conversation a preferences conversation. Connection is the foundation for building relationships and caring about the people we interact with. Building trust is critical to connecting, caring, and building the necessary relationships to make feedback effective. Once we've built caring relationships, then we can more effectively provide feedback and/or coaching to those we interact with daily.

WHY DO WE NEED TO LEARN ABOUT PERSONAL PREFERENCES FOR PEAK PERFORMANCE?

I like to think about a person's preferences as an iceberg. If you want to move the iceberg, you have to learn and understand what is below the surface. Similarly, if you want to grow, develop, or improve, you must learn about yourself and others, including what is below the surface.

As we mentioned in the earlier section on our personal preferences, learning about ourselves is not something that occurs  naturally. As a result, you can imagine that learning about others' personal preferences occurs even less frequently. Sure, we learn these things naturally to some degree over time – I know what frustrates my husband and I know when an employee is struggling – but we do not typically turn this knowledge into insights we can act upon. The first step is taking the time to understand our own capabilities, preferences, strengths, values, and interests. Once we better understand ourselves, we can receive feedback from others more easily. Strengths represent our best opportunity for self-awareness and insight. Therefore, they are a highly useful tool when receiving feedback from others. By understanding ourselves on this deeper level we can better interpret the feedback from others that relates to these challenges.

I have received feedback from people in the past that I need to listen more and argue less. My number one strength is Communication® – I think by talking, learn by talking, and process by writing. I love words, debates, and discussions. Which means I also spend more time talking than listening. Similarly, due to my Input®[17] strength, I tend to want massive amounts of information. Just ask my husband, who likes to joke, "Jessica always has at least three books in reach – even when sleeping." And he's right! I will read many books at once, research articles, learn new skills or about new technology all at once, and sometimes I am taking in so much information that I am not actually making progress on any one thing! I am always going to have these challenges, but I can be aware, appreciate, and internalize the feedback because I understand myself.

> **Input®:** People exceptionally talented in the Input theme have a need to collect and archive. They may accumulate information, ideas, artifacts or even relationships.

---

[17] CliftonStrengths® and the CliftonStrengths 34 Themes of Talent are trademarks of Gallup, Inc. Gallup's content is Copyrighted by Gallup. Used with permission. All rights reserved.

> People with strong **Input®** talents are inquisitive and always want to know more. They crave information. They might collect ideas, books, memorabilia, quotations, or facts. Whatever they collect, they do so because it interests them. They find many things interesting and have a natural curiosity. The world is exciting precisely because of its infinite variety and complexity. A few minutes spent surfing the internet may turn into hours once their curiosity takes off. They constantly acquire, compile and file things away. Their pursuits keep their minds fresh. They know that one day the information or things they've gathered will prove valuable.[45]

Strengths also provide us a language for giving those we have relationships with feedback and understanding specifically who they are as individuals. We each have different talents, and we react and respond differently based upon them. The nuances of coaching and managing each person is very different and I've learned I must adjust my approach accordingly.

For example, I have one employee with Achiever®[18] as number one – give her a list of what to do and she will plow through it. However, she can also ignore other critical focus areas which are less tactical. I have another employee with high Responsibility® – put her in charge and she will make sure the whole project gets completed. However, she can also overwhelm or push too hard when a softer approach is required. And another employee with Analytical® as her number one – give her a report, system, or process to get completed

---

[18] CliftonStrengths® and the CliftonStrengths 34 Themes of Talent are trademarks of Gallup, Inc. Gallup's content is Copyrighted by Gallup. Used with permission. All rights reserved.

and she will knock it out of the park! However, ask her to think about a challenge and she might overanalyze it until she can't act at all. We can't possibly be good at everything there is to accomplish in this world. Therefore, we must each pursue our own personal excellence and learn where we need to partner with others to achieve the greatest results. I love looking at my relationships as partnerships and how we can leverage each other to achieve more and increase our opportunity for success. Understanding our own preferences and the preferences of those we interact with in our workplaces, homes, and communities provides the foundation for good collaboration and communication regarding performance and expectations. We need this knowledge before we can truly give and receive feedback.

Reflection: How can you learn more about the preferences of those you interact with in your performance? What can you do differently by knowing the preferences of others better? How will this change how you interact and perform each day?

HOW DO WE BUILD A FOUNDATION OF TRUST?

Recently, I had a conversation with an employee from a very large corporation. He had been observing Experitec's culture and wanted to talk about his personal challenges with his company. He started the conversation with "I don't feel safe enough to share openly what I really think and feel about the company." I asked him why he felt this way and what he was concerned would happen if he shared his experience. He said that any critique or criticism of the company was likely to impact his growth, compensation, authority, and credibility in the company. The leaders he works for do not want to hear negative feedback or input and he doesn't trust them enough to share it anyway.

Learning about and understanding those we work, live, and interact with equips us with the knowledge and tools we need to build our relationships. However, these relationships remain shallow and can easily be destroyed if not built on a foundation of trust. The challenge is not unique to this particular employee or company – anytime a manager or leader fails to create a culture of trust – the ability to speak openly and address challenges is hindered.

Early in my career I was exposed to the teachings of Patrick Lencioni and his book *The Five Dysfunctions of a Team*.[46] Our Leadership Team hired a consultant from the Table Group to facilitate a series of sessions to help us improve our collaboration as a team and drive cohesive direction as an organization. Lencioni uses a pyramid to highlight the five dysfunctions of a team. At the base of the pyramid is a lack of trust. When you see dysfunction within and across teams, it can almost always be traced back to a lack of trust.

I like using the analogy of the pyramid when considering how we build relationships. Pyramids are incredibly strong structures – the Egyptian pyramids have existed for thousands of years. Pyramids, like relationships, must be built brick by brick, slowly over time. To build a strong pyramid, you have to start at the base building a strong foundation. Similarly, in our relationships, we must start by building trust before we can truly create connection, demonstrate caring, and provide motivation, coaching, and feedback.

Once I was working on improving a process and handoff between two teams. One team was resisting moving the handoff, which was strange because the change would help them and decrease their workload. The discussion moved around, and it took the full hour-long meeting before, near the end, it finally became apparent that the concern was truly a lack of trust. One team did not trust the other team (who is still quite new) to do the particular task effectively. The specific details are actually minor, but this example highlights how even the smallest lack of trust can impact our results and performance. When we don't trust others to do their part, we waste energy checking work and entirely duplicating the work.

Early in my career, before developing stronger management and coaching skills, I had an employee who made a lot of mistakes. As a result, I started double-checking every single thing she did, and ultimately, I did not trust her to successfully complete anything on her own. We became quite dysfunctional. As I hired additional team members, they grew concerned I would be a perpetual micromanager (which I definitely was in this instance). After much self-reflection, I recognized the need to ensure trust is developed so, as a Manager, I wouldn't need to have the same level of concern and involvement. More specifically, I wouldn't allow dysfunctional behavior to exist in our team and I wouldn't perpetuate it myself.

Creating a culture and team-based environment where members trust one another is critical to reaching peak performance. We can't all do everything (believe me, I tried)! We must share and work collectively leveraging the strengths of the team to reach peak performance. Therefore, we need to identify the activities and methods for building trust within our teams.

My father taught me from a very young age about what he called a "trust bank." He would tell me each time you demonstrate particular behaviors and your level of trustworthiness, you get a deposit in the bank. But, when you betray trust, you break the bank and have to start building the trust back all over again. (In case you are wondering, yes, this was very much related to my poor choices as a teenager!) The key is to maintain trust and allow it to slowly build overtime. You can't force trust. You can't convince someone to trust you. You must demonstrate through your actions their ability to trust you consistently over time. I call this earned trust.

When you first join a team, or even more so become a manager or leader for the first time, more likely than not your trust bank is empty. You must recognize it will take time for those you manage or work with to build the necessary trust with you to produce productive and effective relationships. But beware, more important than building trust is ensuring your actions never betray trust. And the quickest way to betray trust is while you are building a relationship.

Recently, I was having a coaching conversation with an employee (I have one every three weeks with all my employees). These conversations span from tactical (project updates) to development (how are they progressing) to personal (wellbeing, current state, etc.). This time, the conversation was quite personal. Many managers might view these conversations as a waste of precious business time. I, however, have grown to appreciate these conversations as the ones that matter most.

By talking about our lives, our challenges, and our experiences, we are able to actually connect with our employees (or others), and when we do this, we create the opportunity for building trust. We can demonstrate our humanness, our caring, our insights, and our confidence in the other person. By taking this time we begin to develop that trust, and we make our "deposits" in the trust bank.

Likewise, when we have opportunities to socialize, to share about our lives, to relate on our experiences, the trust within and across our teams grows as well. For example, in our high potential group (iLEAD), which we created six years ago, each time we got the group together we covered team building, strategic topics, but also had social or game-based activities in the evenings. This time was not just about having fun and being social, but also about building real relationships and trust. Our employees-built relationships and trust with the leadership team, which was actively involved in these activities.

When you know someone – know their family, what they think, who they are as a person – it is much easier to work together. You don't misread messages or second guess a person's intention. Rather, you pick up the phone, you call your friend, you reach out to your colleague, and you solve problems together! Fast-forward to today, many of the iLEADers are now leaders and managers – and friends! We work together with ease and enjoyment. We have fun when we see each other. Most importantly, we trust each other to make good decisions, to address issues, to (as one member put it) "call each other out when they are wrong," and to work for the benefit of the whole organization.

Being on teams with trust is a tremendous opportunity. Cultivating this trust with my team members is essential for my success as a manager. How do I do this successfully? What is the best way to build this trust? I have found, outside of time and interaction, the most important element to trust is authenticity – or the "quality of being genuine or real." By being authentically yourself, you allow others to be their authentic self. When we are authentic, trust naturally follows.

Before you can ever give feedback – take time to build trust!

Reflection: What is your level of trust with those you serve and perform? What can you do to add to your trust bank? Who do you need to build trust with before giving them difficult feedback? How can you incorporate more opportunities for interactions which build trusting relationships?

WHY DO WE NEED TO SEEK OUT AND GIVE FEEDBACK TO REACH PEAK PERFORMANCE?

Ask anyone "If someone you worked with had an issue with you (you were driving them crazy), would you want to know?" and virtually everyone will say yes to this question. Although we all want to receive feedback, we often struggle to ask for that feedback proactively and respond in a way that encourages others to continue to provide feedback. This struggle stems from the need for approval or the innate human need to belong. We all want to experience feeling accepted, well liked, and connected with others. However, if we place greater emphasis on others' approval than our path to peak performance, we will do it at the expense and sacrifice of our progress and performance. We can develop relationships based upon respect, kindness, and a mutual desire for both parties to improve rather than a need to be similar or the same. We can be our authentic selves and stay open to input and feedback helping us to improve performance and be successful in achieving results.

The challenge we experience is the feeling of "I want to belong" therefore "how do I belong?" without needing to change myself to experience the approval of others. The first step in this process is determining who you want to belong with – who are the people who will accept you, who will respect you, and who will provide you the appropriate and effective feedback and information to help you improve? I am not suggesting this group will always agree with you and never challenge you. Rather, this group should be able to provide you with truthful feedback intended to help you to evolve rather than cause shame or a sense of isolation.

Likewise, consider who you can provide feedback to and still allow that individual to remain their authentic self. We are not always in a position where providing individual feedback is going to be effective. In some cases, it is better not to provide feedback. For example, before you have developed a relationship and a degree of trust with an individual, it will be difficult to articulate and share feedback with that person. If I have just met you, don't know much about you or your experience, my input or suggestions are not going to carry much weight. Therefore, providing feedback in those instances might actually be more detrimental than helpful.

Additionally, when there is a high-power differential, such as between a manager and employee, until that trust is built an employee is likely not in a position to provide their manager with meaningful feedback. I know from my own experience with employees that they had significant discomfort being honest and direct with me until we had developed a trusting relationship where I was open to receiving that feedback. If you have a manager or boss, be cautious with providing feedback unless asked and only once the trust exists.

Peak performance means we are in the flow, we are at our best, and we are knocking it out of the park! We can't possibly do this without some sort of audience. We need someone to see what we are doing and help us to identify growth opportunities, challenges, and, most importantly, reinforce what we are doing well. Without this input we would have little need to interact with others. Rather, we depend upon our interactions with others and the feedback they provide to help us achieve the results we want and reach peak performance.

THE IMPORTANCE OF POSITIVITY – 6 TO 1 OR MORE!

We all have egos, and these egos can hold us hostage when receiving any form of feedback – positive or negative. Anytime we get feedback we respond with an emotion – it's natural, it can't be prevented. We will feel something inside – either good or bad. What is important is the frequency of the types of feedback we receive (and even more importantly we *give* to others) and how we respond when we receive it. I will dive deeper into how our mindsets and emotional response to negative feedback impacts us later, but for now let's focus on the positive!

Research shows our brains require a minimum of three positives to every one negative piece of feedback.[47] What does this mean? In order to appropriately respond to constructive or negative feedback we need to have received three times as many positives to every negative and that is just to bring us back to neutral. In fact, research has shown those with the happiest marriages and most productive teams have closer to a 6 to 1 ratio of positive to negative.[48] I'm sure you are thinking – that's crazy, how can I do that? This must be the result of the "everyone gets a trophy culture." But let me tell you – it's not!

Biologically, our brains are hardwired to pay more attention to the negative. Way back when we were created, we needed to respond to threats in our environment (negatives) and our brains were wired to do so. When we perceive a threat, we respond with adrenaline, energy, and alertness as if we were facing a predator. Ever seen a deer respond when they hear or perceive someone close? They either freeze or take off running as fast as they can. Essentially our brains are doing the same thing to us, only because there are so few external threats our brains have chosen to turn inward.

Most of us have food, shelter, and safety, therefore, our brains look for other threats or negatives in our environment. We see this happen in our internal thoughts and emotions. When someone shares a critical piece of feedback – we tense up, we get adrenaline, and we transition to a freeze, fight, or flight mode. I like how Brené Brown says this in her books when she feels this response coming. She says, "Don't puff up, don't shrink, stand your sacred ground."[49] Our bodies are always going to respond how they are programmed to. However, we can choose what we do to prepare and what we do after we experience this response.

Whenever I'm faced with a vulnerable situation, I get deliberate with my intentions by repeating this to myself: "Don't shrink. Don't puff up. stand your sacred ground." Saying this little mantra helps me remember not to get too small so other people are comfortable and not throw up my armor as a way to protect myself.

Brene Brown, in Daring Greatly

The best way to prepare is having built up positives. When I receive that critical feedback from my co-worker, I'm much less inclined to react negatively if the same person has provided me significant positive feedback in the past. I know they aren't attacking me or trying to hurt me – rather I can be more neutral in my response, listen, and understand. If your team appreciates each other and gives each other positive cues regularly, then when an issue arises, the reaction to the feedback is less intense. This feedback is just another piece of information which will help us improve and evolve!

Likewise, if I have been praised or given positive feedback many times by my husband, when he asks me why I didn't empty the dishwasher I am much less likely to puff up and say, "You never see everything I do and always just criticize me!" Instead, I hear his input and go empty the dishwasher or simply explain why I have not yet done so. Let me tell you – this makes a HUGE difference in marriages. My husband and I started making it a point to thank each other for everything we do – "Thanks for getting the kids up," "Thanks for changing the diaper," "Thanks for cooking dinner," "Thanks for emptying the dishwasher" – it seems silly at first, but over time you will feel so much better, and your marriage will be better as result. (Bonus – kids pick up on this as well and begin saying thank you, which is awesome!) I can't recommend this enough!

Reflection: *How frequently are you giving those you serve positive feedback? Are you pointing out all the positive things your employees, children, and others do each day? Are you looking for opportunities to praise those you interact with? How could you do more?*

HOW SHOULD WE RESPOND TO POSITIVE FEEDBACK?

When we receive positive feedback, we need to internalize it and not brush it off. Frequently, we will downplay praise and imply our efforts were not significant or were merely what is to be expected. Instead, recognize what you are doing was just praised, and therefore is something you should strongly consider continuing to do! Praise equates to and creates reinforcement of behaviors we want to repeat.

During an interview with a potential new hire, she mentioned how important getting feedback is for her to understand how she is doing. She immediately tried to clarify the statement saying something to the effect of "I don't need to be recognized for everything, but I need to know when I'm doing well, or the critical feedback can be challenging." I agreed with her completely and the image came to mind of a person stuck in a riptide. We get into a negative feedback loop – negative feedback leads to worse performance which leads to more negative feedback and so on. I've seen employees get stuck in the current and it becomes extremely difficult to pull them out. However, if we provide significant positive feedback and recognize what people do well – it is much easier to avoid getting into the negative feedback loop to begin with!

Reflection: Anytime you receive positive feedback – praise, recognition, or appreciation – take note of the input. Consider what behaviors led to this response and which ones you want to be sure to incorporate moving forward. Acknowledge your performance and how you can continue doing the behaviors which are being recognized.

But what about when, inevitably, we do receive critical or constructive feedback (and trust me we want to!)?

HOW SHOULD WE RESPOND WHEN WE RECEIVE CONSTRUCTIVE OR CRITICAL FEEDBACK?

When the feedback is constructive – take a breath, listen, and experience the feedback. Ask questions if you aren't sure you understand. In fact, even if you do understand, start by asking questions. If nothing else, asking the questions gives you time to take a breath and shift into a productive mindset to receive the feedback. Then (in most cases) take a little time to process when possible. The time spent on processing helps us to really internalize what is being shared without trying to defend ourselves or argue with the input.

I once got feedback on my 'leadership persona' on social media – I was sharing things that were too personal and it was impacting my leadership persona. Whether I agreed with the feedback or not, I listened, asked a question to clarify it, and then thanked them for the input and said I would keep it in mind. Whether I agreed or disagreed with the feedback, this was important enough for the other person to share and therefore I should consider it.

Most of our major struggles with feedback relate back to one of our inner fears or insecurities. For me, this feedback highlighted some significant personal challenges I had over the prior years which, at times, rose to a pretty substantial level. I experienced severe postpartum depression after my twins, I was extremely depressed and anxious when I first got hives, and at the beginning of the pandemic I had some very dark moments and felt very alone. When I got the feedback, my internal response was to argue, but that was because the topic was sensitive for me. He was highlighting my personal struggles. The best thing I could do was to let go of the feedback and not hold onto it. (Which honestly, I didn't do for a while – I stewed and fretted over it for quite a while before I realized I just needed to let it go). My growth from this feedback came from learning to just let some input go – do what you can, then let it go and move on with your life in any way you choose to live it.

Ultimately, we can't experience and grow from feedback unless we can get past the emotion that we feel as a result of the feedback. If you continue to protect yourself entirely from feedback, you will never grow. The only thing you can do to prepare yourself for the emotions from challenging feedback and interactions is to create as much positivity as you can. Remember – you can provide yourself feedback too!

Seriously, I am sure you haven't considered this too much, but taking time to consciously acknowledge our own outcomes, results, and performance is critical. With my team, at the end of the year I often compile everything we accomplished on all our teams over the course of the year. Holy moly, this is a powerful process. Just seeing it all completed helps you to realize how successful you are being and how good you are doing. So often we just move onto the next thing that needs to be done without actually acknowledging all that has been accomplished.

Reflection: *Always provide yourself feedback – when you do something good, reflect on why it went well. When something feels like it did not go well – reflect on why it did not go well and what you could have done differently. Oftentimes, we can be our own best coach – there is no one to get defensive at, and we have to listen to ourselves if we choose to do so!*

CHECKLIST:
WHAT DO I DO FIRST?

✓ Learn about the preferences of yourself and others

✓ Build trusting relationships

✓ Prepare yourself for challenging feedback by focusing on positives

✓ Give yourself feedback whenever you can

✓ Choose whose feedback truly matters to you

✓ Listen to feedback and ask questions, lots of clarifying questions

CHAPTER NINE
Strengths-Based Development

*Why is development critical and
how do we do it successfully?*

Key Insight:

The only constant in this world is change.
Continuing to grow and develop is critical to our
ability to become better humans and reach peak
performance.

After five days of writing and working on this book, and then taking vacation off to spend extra time on it, I returned back to work on a Monday. When I returned, I was immediately hit with a multitude of issues. Some I had left behind, like a legal issue (contractor who went out of business on a building we were renovating) and a customer complaint issue (customer who was upset about our performance levels), and some which were new (a system outage caused by an air-conditioning unit failing, causing work to halt for almost an hour).

These issues were in addition to the day-to-day projects and activities I am always responsible for managing, as well as the email backlog which built up substantially during my three-day absence. Suffice it to say, my return that Monday was rough. My emotions started swirling and the dark thoughts (I am not proud of) began – maybe I should quit, who can I yell at, why do I have to deal with this, who can I blame?

Later that night, while talking to my sister and frustrated about the day, the outcomes, and everything that needed to be fixed, she made a comment which struck me. She was talking about her own progress, growth, and development, and commented on how much she has learned. And then she paused and said, "But you know what? I still have a lot to learn, and I need to keep learning a lot." My response was "Holy moly" – or something close to that – "You are right. This entire experience can't be about who did what wrong or how bad they are for letting it go wrong, or how frustrated I am with the fact that it did go wrong. Instead, what if we approach it as only an experience – an experience we can learn from that is the next opportunity for growth?"

What if we look at the challenges – the pain, the heart ache, the frustration, the anger, and all that came with the challenges we are facing – as simply a way to get better? Frequently, when experts talk about development, we think about training, tools, competencies, habits, etc. We tend to overcomplicate what actually is a pretty simple and straightforward concept. We are all meant to improve, grow, and develop. We know this because we are physically growing and developing from the moment we are born. Therefore, the development key is truly just about how we respond and how we create experiences which help us to improve, grow, and develop in our capabilities, to evolve in our performance.

In my example with the system failure, we learned so much about our process, our security access, our building, our work practices, how we make decisions about access, and how we monitor our equipment. We learned so much from this single challenge and, as a result, can make improvements which will dramatically reduce future risk. Personally, through these challenges, I'm learning how to deal with frustrating customers, how to manage through other people, and, once again, the importance of seeing everything as an opportunity to learn and grow.

WHAT IS THE DIFFERENCE BETWEEN PERFORMANCE AND DEVELOPMENT?

As we begin to talk further about development, I think it's important to address the difference between performance and development. I've often had people struggle with this difference. For me, performance is what we do and what I am currently capable of doing – I can be demonstrating peak performance in a current role, but when my role changes, I will have to start over again. Development is what helps us get prepared for those role changes and the growth required to reach peak performance. Before we climb our performance mountain, development is the work we do at the gym on the rock wall to get ready, get stronger, and be prepared for challenges we will face. Development provides us the tools and resources to help us be successful.

We must perform, but we often have the choice of whether to develop. I can move through life, executing and performing in the same ways I always have. I can approach the same problems with the same mindset and beliefs. But, to really get the benefits of development (preparation for performance or growth through performance) we must either learn from the experiences we have or create experiences which will help us learn. Learning from and creating meaningful experiences doesn't sound particularly hard in theory, but in practice we often struggle.

WHY DO WE OFTEN STRUGGLE WITH GROWTH AND DEVELOPMENT, AND WHY IS IT CRITICAL?

True freedom is very close –
it's just on the other side of your walls.

Michael Singer, in The Untethered Soul

Why do we build walls? What am I talking about? I am talking about the walls that resist change, resist feedback, resist learning, resist and repel what we are experiencing – what is in front of us. We build walls for protection. We want to keep ourselves safe from the possible pain or potential injury that comes with simply living and engaging in the world. However, we are not as fragile as our sensitive minds believe us to be. We must get beyond our walls in order to do the hard work of learning and growing. While we are safely locked behind or within our walls, we are missing all the beautiful views.

We have long known as a society that one of the most effective means of torturing a person is to leave them alone – with themselves and their thoughts. This knowledge is why prisons use "the hole" to punish prisoners. When we close ourselves off to experiences, we are figuratively and literally torturing ourselves. We are so busy trying to control everything in our lives to stay "safe" that we end up cutting ourselves off from the valuable experiences in life. This torture of never fully living, growing, and experiencing our lives is what prevents our growth and development.

What walls have you built? What is protecting you from really engaging, living, and experiencing life? For me, I have been afraid of getting hurt. I was once hurt so deeply, betrayed so badly, I have feared rejection, criticism, and exclusion for years. Even writing this book, I fear the potential response – that no one will buy it, no one will read it, or, if they do read it, they won't find it valuable. Or worse, they'll actually criticize it. These fears – my walls – could and would prevent me from writing a book at all if I let them. Instead, I have chosen to take the risk of a great reward – the growth that will come from writing this book.

If we want the great rewards in life (exceptional experiences), we have to be willing to take the risks to create them. We need to know when we are getting in our own way. We need to recognize we are more prepared than we realize to deal with the challenges of life. And the fewer challenges we face, the less opportunity we have to experience, learn, and grow from them. The less we will evolve.

Reflection: Consider what is getting in your way of development. What are the walls you have built, and do you really need them? Are they helping or hurting your growth and development? I will talk more in the next chapter about the principles we can use to change our mindsets in order to reach peak performance. But for now, getting beyond these walls in order to have the experiences in life which allow us to learn, and grow is absolutely essential to our future.

Even if we believe we have reached peak performance in our current role – if we are going to keep up with the massive rate of change, we are going to have to keep developing. Unlike mountains, our lives are going to keep changing at an ever-increasing rate and there is little we can do to prevent this impact. We know roles are going to completely change in the workplace – by some estimates, 85% of roles that exist today will not exist by 2030.[50] In fact, those in school right now are going to primarily fill jobs that don't even exist today![51] Experts predict we will have significantly more jobs throughout our careers as roles are transformed and changed.

With the half-life of a learned skill just five years – meaning much of what we learned 10 years ago is obsolete and half of what we learned five years ago is irrelevant – we all need to become life-long learners, prepared to transform throughout our lives.[52]

Jeff Schwartz, in Work Disrupted

Even the technology I am using in 2021 is completely different than what I was using in 2019! I was watching the Microsoft Ignite conference and they introduced some of the virtual reality which is currently being used and some that is just on the horizon. We are going to be transforming how we interact, how we travel, how we work, and how we live. The skills required to live in this newly transformed world are going to be significant. The quicker we remove our walls in order to see the view and the need for development, the better off we will be in the future.

Even how we parent today compared to twenty years ago has already changed significantly. We are faced with different challenges (iPad use, remote schooling) than parents were in the past. Our lives are filled with complex and challenging experiences which are only likely to increase.

Our greatest opportunity for the future is to lean into these experiences so we can develop and grow our capabilities. Growth and development are no longer optional – we are going to have to pursue vigorous learning for the rest of our lives if we want to keep up and be successful. For those of us with strengths around learning, this will come naturally. For others, we will have to find ways to make learning fun, interesting, and relevant.

HOW DO WE DEVELOP THROUGH EXPERIENCE, EDUCATION, AND EXPOSURE?

I want to emphasize the importance of experience, because I don't believe growth truly happens in a classroom, and research often confirms this. You may have heard of the Adult Learning Model – of the 70 - 20 - 10 Rule, which states that 10% of our learning comes from education, 20% comes from exposure to other people, and 70% comes from our experience. Most development programs in the business world (and in our education system) have this completely backwards. We spend the bulk of our time on education – developing training programs, materials, information, work processes, and policies. We read books, watch videos, and attend training events to learn new skills and capabilities. Frequently, however, we fail to translate this information and education into experiences which bring true growth and development.

Take a moment and reflect on the times in your life where you grew the most, where you learned more and improved more than any other time. For most of us, when we do this exercise, we think of a particular experience or situation which forced us to grow. When I posed this question at a leadership conference, I held in 2015 with CEOs and Senior Leaders, the answers I got were overwhelmingly focused on experiences – taking over leadership for an office, acquiring a new business or selling new products, and being forced to run a new business unit or department. When we take time to think about our lives, we realize most of the lessons that have stuck with us weren't in a classroom, but in the experiences, we have had that helped shape us as individuals.

Likewise, our children need to learn with a greater focus on their experiences. My children attend a Montessori school where the focus is on self-led learning with boundaries. The children choose the focus of their learning each day and then they experience learning that skill. They move freely about the room, selecting tasks to accomplish and experience. Occasionally, the teachers encourage them to embrace the more 'challenging' work, so they are stretched even when the work is hard.

When my husband and I first visited, we were amazed at how quiet and peaceful the classroom was with such small children. The teacher said to me, "When you allow children to choose, and they know the limits of those choices, conflict is reduced significantly, and they thrive in their growth and development." The children also work with and help one and other – the older children helping the younger children learn. This allows the older children to solidify what they have learned by showing the younger children how it is to be done. My son Wyatt loves to help other children and comes home very excited to share what he has helped another student learn. I have seen my children grow very quickly in all their skills by using this experience and exposure-based method.

In the business world, in our attempt to streamline and create absolute efficiency by establishing step-by-step written instructions or videos to train people, we have completely forgotten the value of experience and exposure. I have learned a tremendous amount from observing other leaders demonstrating leadership. The compassion and empathy they demonstrate in interacting with employees has helped me develop similar skills. The absolute accountability they show when taking responsibility for poor business results has grown my commitment to demonstrate the same. Simply watching others perform and demonstrate capabilities has shown me what they look like (rather than simply reading them in a book).

I am not sure why, in our businesses and schools, we have chosen to instead focus heavily on the "telling" and "training" rather than the "experiencing" and "exposing." As we approach our own development to evolve and reach peak performance in our roles, we must be conscious of incorporating experiences and exposures which will help us develop and grow faster. We must also consider purposely creating experiences and identifying opportunities for exposure. Occasionally, we get lucky with these situations occurring naturally, but most of the time we must actually seek out these opportunities. In the roles we serve at home, this can be even more difficult as opportunities to see others parent or interact with their spouses are significantly less common (more on this in the last section).

Reflection: *As you consider your own development, think about how you can incorporate more experience and exposure into capabilities you are trying to develop. Identify who might be someone you could ask or learn from. Look for opportunities to experience challenges – this won't be easy as naturally we want to shy away from potential failure – but the reward (growth) will be great!*

UNDERSTANDING THE GROWTH MINDSET AND CULTIVATING AN APPROACH TO GROWTH

Carol Dweck introduced the concept of a fixed versus a growth mindset.[53] As I have previously mentioned and will likely continue to mention, I am a firm believer in the power of our mindsets. The difference between a fixed and a growth mindset is all in how we approach the challenges in our lives. When we hit a roadblock – do we rise to the challenge, even if there is a chance we could fail, or do we shy away to ensure we never risk failure? Do we put on our armor or build a wall to protect ourselves?

While writing this book, one day I was watching my twin girls who were not quite two years old yet at the time. They decided (despite many toys available) that their primary objective would be dressing and undressing themselves repeatedly. I am not exaggerating when I say they probably took things off and on twenty to thirty times! In the beginning, they would get frustrated every few minutes – yelling and getting angry. Anytime I would offer to help they would scream at the top of their lungs "I do it!!!!!" They instinctively knew they needed to keep practicing over and over and over and over again in order to master the skill.

We do this throughout our lives. We have to repeat skill sets and behaviors many times in order to achieve proficiency and many more times to develop expertise. If we allow ourselves to stay in a growth mindset and keep trying new ways to grow and improve, we will evolve and achieve amazing results. However, frequently we get frustrated when a task is hard. We decide it must not be useful, or it is slowing us down so it must not be beneficial before we even really get started. Initially, as children, we didn't have this tendency – so somewhere along the way we learn it's easier to give up and it's easier to be successful at one thing then fail trying new things.

As we get older, our brains begin to develop stronger neuropathways – this is a benefit because it allows us to respond more quickly to situations, to know what will happen and what we should do as a result, and to complete our work and lives with greater ease. The challenge is that sometimes these neuropathways lose their relevancy in a new environment. We become so comfortable with our standard mode of operating we fail to continue to grow and experience new and better ways of operating.

For example, many people learned to execute their jobs successfully without the use of email. They may have been the best at their role – but with the advent of email, the speed at which a response was required changed dramatically. Rather than sending letters or quotes through the mail and waiting days for a response while you move on to something else, we send a quote and in an hour the customer might come back wanting a change. The skillsets required to manage a day of activities where changes are occurring, and requests are coming in all day long are quite different from the offices of the past.

We must decide which pathways we want to reinforce and which pathways we want to continually challenge so we can keep improving our capabilities. In the new world with super computers, the skills and pathways associated with learning, growing, adapting, agility, grit, resilience, and performance are far more important than any single bit of knowledge or capability.

Science and technology will continue to grow and change the world in the process – we must grow our minds and neuropathways in parallel. And we must know – we are *absolutely* going to fail, it is going to hurt sometimes, and we are going to feel like giving up. This is where our mindset and accountability come in and play a critical role, which we will talk more about in the next chapter.

Reflection: *Do you have a fixed or a growth mindset? What do you need to do to change in your practices so you can stay growth minded? How can you help those you perform with or lead also be growth minded?*

THE DIFFERENCE BETWEEN DEVELOPMENT AND CAREER

If we are going to have multiple different careers in our lives, we are going to need to be developing skill sets for our next career while still performing our current role. Development means growth in our skills and capabilities, transforming our talents into strengths, and applying them in ways that improve performance. Alternatively, career conversations are about what is coming next, what is it we want in the future, and what we will be required to do in future careers. We must be "future proofing" our careers by continuing to develop capabilities which will help us be successful in new roles in the future.

This growth has been a focus in my life for a few years now. I recognize many of the simpler tasks I perform in HR will ultimately (hopefully because they suck) be automated! I started really learning the space between technology design, learning, and adoption. I want to be prepared to understand how to quickly design a technological solution, implement it, learn how to use it, and help others quickly and effectively adopt that new technology. I recognize we won't have time to spend years transforming business systems but, rather, will need to keep adapting and improving quickly. This career space will be critical in the future, and I hope by leaning into it and developing new skills and understanding, I will be better equipped in the future.

Likewise, we must regularly consider the future of our skillsets (not our particular job or career). Consider how the capabilities you are developing can translate into different roles or jobs or titles and bring value in the future. Consider which capabilities you need to keep developing in order to be prepared for subsequent career opportunities when they arise.

I have seen on many occasions when an employee has been working on their growth and development and regularly developing new skills and capabilities, so when an opportunity arises, they are ready and prepared to raise their hand. Most of the time when someone is prepared and raises their hand, I am ecstatic as a leader! Be ready for the opportunity you never saw coming. Don't assume because your company is small and there isn't a career ladder or an obvious position available for you to move into that one won't open up. Frequently, just as someone is ready for a new opportunity, one becomes available.

Which means we must consider the best way to be prepared – how do we choose where to focus, and how do we choose what to develop and work on? As an organization, we have used the analogy of the rock wall for years. Dr. Beverly Kaye wrote the book *Help Them Grow or Watch Them Go* many years ago and used the analogy of a rock wall in lieu of a career ladder.[54] We conducted her fantastic training on career development and actually created a physical rock wall in our main classroom. This rock wall is meant to remind us of our development and the many opportunities available for growth.

We think of each hand hold on the rock wall as a different skill or competency we choose to grow. Dr. Kaye talks about the many directions we can move throughout our career and specifically that "up is not the only way." I've seen employees take steps back given personal circumstances, including my husband when we had babies and needed more time for family. I've seen employees successfully change roles, moving laterally to completely different jobs. I've seen employees expand their capabilities through a unique project opportunity. I've even seen employees leave the organization to find their next successful opportunity.

As you move throughout your career, the rock wall can be a great reminder of the many ways and options you have for growth. You can zoom in and focus on your growth in skills, competencies, and knowledge on specific topics, or you can zoom out and look at the wall of opportunity available to you in your workplace, homes, and communities.

HOW DOES STRENGTHS-BASED DEVELOPMENT IMPROVE OUR ABILITY TO LEARN AND GROW?

Frequently, when we do competency assessments in the workplace, which can provide employees valuable insights on their current capabilities, they backfire. The natural reaction from most people is to respond to any negative input or weakness or "area for improvement" by arguing or disagreeing with the assessment.

> *We must stop focusing on what is wrong with people and trying to "fix" them. The more we focus development on weaknesses the less opportunity we have to see them grow to their full potential.*

Our sales force took a sales competency assessment which provided them with a detailed report on how they scored against particular sales competencies and skills. The natural reaction to these results (as described by some of my salespeople) was anger, frustration, disbelief, and rejection of anything suggested by the person providing the results. They saw the assessment as saying they were lacking in something, rather than seeing it as the opportunity to be more of something!

Unfortunately, this reaction is not helpful to producing meaningful improvement in performance and development in competencies. However, if a person can take their ego out of their results long enough to learn the details surrounding the competency, they will find there is room for improvement. The challenge is in framing our development as opportunity to become better, rather than an exercise in fixing something that is broken.

Think about a cup of water. If we want to see our cup be full and subsequently realize that it isn't, we will feel "lack." But if instead we approach learning about what the size of our cup truly is and what opportunity we have to fill our cup further, we create a mindset of "abundance." Simply, we have more capacity to grow rather than think we are missing something we should have. When we feel capable and realize we can be capable of even more, this realization is incredibly motivating. Whereas, when we feel inadequate like we aren't measuring up to what we should be, we are incredibly de-motivated to take action.

The thrill of life is not about who we are but about who we are in the process of becoming. [55]

David Eagleman, in Livewired

Take, for another example, a car. Fixing or repairing a broken transmission is quite different than suping up the car with additional horsepower, faster wheels, and a fancy interior. When we feel like we are being fixed, we tend to resist the change. However, when we feel we are being enhanced, improved, and made into greater versions of ourselves, we tend to feel more excitement and have greater energy pursuing the challenge. Therefore, when we need to address growth in competency or skills (which we all can and need to do), if we focus on the opportunity and what that can mean for us, we are far more likely to be successful.

Furthermore, when coaching the person to achieve this positive outcome, a strengths-based approach is far more impactful. Gallup®[19], using their research on strengths, advocates the use of a strengths-based approach to development rather than the traditional approach[56]. What does that mean? We are all fairly familiar with the traditional approach to development, which is to assess an individual against a series of competencies, identify what they don't do well (their weaknesses), and then direct them to focus all their energy and effort on improving those weaknesses. But we know this doesn't work, and it certainly doesn't help people reach near perfect performance!

I like to use the analogy of a star to explain strengths-based development. Think of your strengths as the tips of the star and your weaknesses as the dips in the star. When we focus on our weaknesses, as in traditional development, it takes a significant amount of effort and energy. So much effort and energy that if we are able to improve, we, at best, only become well-rounded! Whereas, with strengths-based development, we focus on the tips, our strengths, and how we can improve them to make us even stronger performers, and even bigger stars at our performance!

---

[19] CliftonStrengths® and the CliftonStrengths 34 Themes of Talent are trademarks of Gallup, Inc. Gallup's content is Copyrighted by Gallup. Used with permission. All rights reserved.

Skills and competency development is still required. We still need to get better at what we are doing each day. The path of how we grow our capabilities (skills and competencies) should depend on our particular strengths. For example, when it comes to managing people, I use my Communication® talent; another manager might leverage their Developer® or Individualization® talents. We each have to grow to be able to successfully coach and develop employees, but how we do it can differ.

We don't ignore our weaknesses. Rather, our weaknesses are frequently just our strengths misapplied. In other words, our strengths, when we overuse them or underuse them, tend to be the source of our weaknesses. (Just as I shared in an earlier chapter how my Communication®[20] can be a weakness when I talk too much and don't listen enough!)

I am going to use the analogy of a professional athlete to help explain further why strengths-based development is so powerful. If you take any professional athlete or Olympian, they are most literally the best in the world at their particular craft. Take, for example, Michael Jordan (he was my Grandpa Zimmermann's favorite player growing up!). He was frequently referred to as the best basketball player in the world. Why was Michael able to become (arguably at the time) the best in the world?

First and foremost, he had the necessary strengths – he had the height, the body, the coordination, the drive, and the desire. Then, in order to become the best in the world, Michael had to work every day to hone and perfect his natural talents into strengths. He used to watch his own performance and marvel at his capabilities. Imagine if you were to swap Michael to be the best in the world at figure skating or gymnastics – he would likely not be as successful! Michael leveraged what came most naturally to him and therefore, he could achieve near perfect performance.

"Some people want it to happen, some wish it would happen, others make it happen."

Michael Jordan

As you begin to approach your growth and development, start with your strengths – start with what you have the opportunity to be best in the world at doing! While I've worked on developing my strengths and coached others who are developing their strengths, I have found repeatedly that we act based on our talents. Therefore, we must leverage that which comes most naturally and work to perfect it in order to learn and grow more effectively.

Development should almost always be focused on the future rather than the past. Likewise, the approach to careers, business, organizations, and even parenting of the past do not have to (and likely will not) dictate our future. In businesses, people used to graduate from school, get a job, work that job (sometimes their whole career), and if they switched companies, they certainly weren't switching occupations. Based upon the rate at which change is occurring, we must begin preparing to have many careers in our lives including holding multiple completely different jobs or occupations.

Reflection: What capabilities do you need to develop in order to be prepared for the future? What opportunities exist which you can identify for growth? How can you focus on your strengths and apply them to help you achieve your goals?

CHECKLIST:
WHAT DO I DO FIRST?

✓ You must consider both your current performance and your future development

✓ Focus on creating and learning from experiences

✓ Take time to be exposed to others and learn from the best

✓ Apply what you do best to achieve the greatest results

✓ Stay growth minded in all that you do

✓ Look at the full rock-wall of opportunities to grow and develop

✓ Acknowledge your growth and progress

CHAPTER TEN
Mindset of
Accountability

*Why is a mindset of accountability essential for
reaching peak performance?*

> **Key Insight:**
>
> The single greatest factor in reaching peak
> performance for extraordinary work and life
> experiences, being happy and successful is
> cultivating a mindset of high personal
> accountability.

In the last section on the Development Key, we talked about
getting prepared to climb the mountain by developing capabilities
on the rock wall. If development is about strengthening our bodies
(capabilities) to be able to climb the mountain successfully,
accountability is about preparing and strengthening our minds. I've
heard stories of individuals who have climbed Mount Everest and
how, frequently, the greatest challenge is the mindset of the
individuals during the climb. Many a life has been lost on the

mountain due to people making the decision to move forward when they should have turned around. They allowed their desire and emotion to overcome their minds with serious consequences.

We'd like to believe the situations in our lives are not quite as serious as those climbing Mount Everest and, in the short-term, they likely are not. However, the long-term consequences of failing to develop a mindset of personal accountability in our lives can actually be just as serious. Our mindset and how it impacts us influences everything in our lives including how long we live, how healthy we are, how much we accomplish, how happy we are in our lives, how successful we are (or feel we are), our relationships, our marriages, our families, and ultimately our results.

I've spent years learning about mindset and the ever-growing neuroscience research that continues to expand our understanding of our brains and how they work. I've even considered going back to school to become a neuroscientist because I love it so much. Through this research and innate love of the topic, I have come to appreciate how significant a role our minds play in our lives. In fact, as a result of this understanding I found my personal purpose in life: To help others live and experience the best life possible (an exceptional life) and to help workplaces be a part of it, such that when a person looks back on their life they think, "I lived a great life, and my company was a part of it."

Given the intensity and conviction of my knowledge on the Accountability Mindset Key, I want to emphasize that this key will have the biggest impact on your ability to reach peak performance and have an exceptional life. Our schools and education teach us so much (believe me, I know – I have been through college, graduate school, and law school) and yet they fail to teach one of the most useful topics or at least if they did, I missed it! We learn calculus and long division (or, at least, we did before calculators), the history of the world (as written by those who won the wars), and much more. And yet, we don't learn about the power of our mindset.

The resources available on this topic and researchers providing insights and data to support what I share here are significant. I hope this section provides a foundation for your mindset and accountability. Just as we strengthen and prepare our capabilities for performance, we must strengthen and prepare our mindset to help us evolve and reach peak performance.

WHY ARE MINDSETS AND PERSONAL ACCOUNTABILITY IMPORTANT?

I start every training I do with employees on accountability with these questions:

What are the stressors you are experiencing in your life?

What are the things that frustrate you at work and in life?

Everyone takes a few minutes to get up the courage to begin sharing and then the examples of stressors flow easily – too much to do, not enough time, difficult customers, unclear expectations, poor communications, natural disasters, politics, illness, disease, etc. Quickly, the list of examples (or rather excuses) for frustrating and distracting things grows! I've done accountability training for six years – I've never once had to change my slide on why the world is stressful – the same examples happen over and over again.

Cy Wakeman brilliantly says that your circumstances are not the reason you can't succeed; they are the reality in which you must succeed.[57]

It is not our circumstances which make us unhappy, it is how we choose to think about our circumstances which causes our suffering. Suffering is a choice. We all face challenging circumstances – really tough and difficult things happen in our lives. The challenges we experience and subsequent pain that occurs is not avoidable. The suffering we put ourselves through, however, is completely optional. We have the ability to choose how to think about and respond to these circumstances and can, therefore, eliminate our suffering.

Our thoughts, if left to their own devices, tend to focus on and find the problems. As mentioned earlier, we are biologically wired to pay more attention to the negatives in our environments, therefore our minds naturally go to these problems. And our minds, if we let them, will always find more problems. You might be thinking: Why is this a bad thing? Isn't it good to identify problems so we can solve them? Yes, solving problems can be a good thing, however, many problems are not solvable and focusing on or suffering from our challenges is not necessary or helpful.

In order to avoid this suffering, many people believe they can (and actually try to) control what happens in their lives. Naturally, we don't want to experience suffering. We want to stay comfortable in a familiar space and try to remove the pain we experience as a result of the challenges in our lives. We try to control things and believe we can "fix" everything that isn't working or meeting our needs – or, even worse, meeting our wants and expectations. We begin to think if we can be who we need to be and control what we look like, what we say, what we do, or control what others do and say, then maybe we can avoid suffering. And when we inevitably fail – we try to quickly fix whatever isn't working and start the cycle over.

The problem with this approach is we don't control the universe and we never will. Challenges will keep coming at us and *we* are the ones who get to decide how to respond and whether we *choose* to suffer as a result of those challenges. In fact, when you think about your life and the world in general, much of what occurs is simply an experience and the facts of that experience. Illness, natural disasters, market crashes, car accidents, and so on are all just experiences happening in the world. We don't control or decide what happens in our lives. However, we can control and decide what to think about them and how to respond to them. Simply – we can change our mindsets.

> **Mindset** – A set of beliefs or a way of thinking that determines one's behavior, outlook, and mental attitude.[58]

When I talk about mindsets in the workplace, I always make the point that this is not about categorizing people as good or bad – those who are good and think correctly and those who are bad and think incorrectly. Rather, the tendency to ride the waves of the up and downs in our lives is simply the human condition. We naturally tend to react to our circumstances. When things are good, it is because we are good, when things are bad, we have an excuse for why it is bad. For example:

* A good year with bonuses = I got a bonus; I did a great job and deserve it!

* Health issues, childcare, and behavior issues = It's not my fault, my health and kids are preventing me from achieving results.

* Strong economy, business up = This is good; it must be I am doing an exceptional job!

* Pandemic occurs, economy crashes = The pandemic and economy are ruining everything; I can't be happy or successful!

* Good health, lost weight, feel good = I am awesome and am so great at staying healthy!

We react to the waves and, when down, we allow ourselves to believe there was nothing we could do – it was caused by our circumstances. And, as we know from earlier, our brains are hardwired to be addicted to the negatives in our environment, or the "noise" that distracts us from what brings value.

Our environments are filled with opportunities to focus on the negative. Even though for most of us, our actual physical survival is not at stake, our minds tend to gravitate towards this external negative noise and create an internal dialogue so severe it feels as if our survival is actually at stake. As if the external noise we suffer isn't enough, this internal dialogue of worry, fear, and doubt causes us to endlessly suffer. We tell ourselves things like "I'll never be successful," "My kids will be behind because of my failures," or "I will never get ahead and get it all done." The more we tell ourselves these things, the more they become our reality.

Our mindset is what determines our level of happiness. The more time we spend below the line focusing on the negative noise, the worse it becomes. And this is the human condition – everyone, everywhere, experiences this in their lives. My father once argued with me about this fact. He said, "No way – I don't do that! I don't think that way!" To which I said, "When was the last time you talked about how you couldn't wait for retirement?"

When we get frustrated, we think about quitting, about winning the lottery, moving on, going away, and we begin to argue with our reality. And even though this is the human condition, we can impact both the frequency we find ourselves in this state and how quickly we can move beyond it. If we can cultivate a mindset of high personal accountability, we will be able to spend less time below the line (in our negative thoughts), and when we do fall below the line, we can get ourselves out of the hole more quickly. Most importantly, we'll be happier, more successful, and achieve better results!

Reflection: *When have you gotten stuck in this mindset? How have you ridden the waves in the past – above and below the line of accountability? How are you suffering because your mind is focused on the negative? How are you focused on what needs to change rather than on changing yourself?*

HOW DO I IDENTIFY MY MINDSET OR MY CONSCIOUSNESS?

I think many of us struggle to know what our 'mindset' really is and separate our mindset from our thoughts. To help you understand, I want you to take a moment and pick a song (Baby Shark, Twinkle Twinkle). Take any song you want and sing it all the way through three times. Don't read ahead until you do!

Now, what were you thinking about as you sang the song?

Be honest – I know you were thinking something.

Maybe – this is stupid?

Maybe – this is relaxing?

Maybe – this is fun?

I can guarantee you were thinking about something else. I've done this exercise with hundreds of employees, and everyone is always thinking something! Those are your thoughts – you *can* actually think about more than one thing at once! The real you, through your consciousness or your mindset, is the one observing and experiencing those thoughts. You are not your thoughts, and you don't have to allow your thoughts to shape who you are, what you think, what you say, or what you do.

WHY DO PEOPLE IN THE SAME CIRCUMSTANCES THINK AND FEEL SO DIFFERENTLY?

Everything we think and feel is based upon the lens through which we see the world. How we choose to see the world greatly impacts our reality and results. Each of us has our own unique life experience, set of beliefs, and backgrounds which have created our lens. If we look through a lens that is highly accountable, we will see our ability to influence our fate and future. If we look through a lens that lacks accountability, we will see our inability to create change and believe we are a victim of our circumstances with nothing that can change them.

I want to be clear, objective facts exist. We have challenging circumstances occur in our lives which we cannot control. However, how we *choose* to respond to these circumstances is a choice. We (our consciousness) get to decide which thoughts we believe, which response we select, and which approach we choose to take. We get to choose how we look at our lives and see what is happening in them.

We know this is a choice because our brains receive 11 million pieces of information every second from our environment. But our brains can only process 40 bits per second.[59] Which means our brains are actively making choices about what to pay attention to and what to ignore. Our reality is truly a choice that our brains are making every single second of our lives. What we choose to focus on shapes how each of us perceives and interprets our world.

HOW DO WE THRIVE RATHER THAN JUST SURVIVE?

Through our mindsets, we have the innate ability to not just survive in this world but to actually thrive. The first step is to accept what is, let go of what was, and believe in what can be next! The pandemic certainly demonstrated the challenges of trying to cling to a reality which no longer exists. When we do this, we experience unnecessary pain trying to recreate our old reality rather than moving into the new reality. We get to choose between two very different paths with two very different results.

We can be worried, scared, anxious, judging, angry, or stuck, which will all lead to a lack of accountability, being overwhelmed with information, seeing only challenges and limitations, and choosing anger, fear, frustration, worry, and anxiety. Or we can have a growth mindset. We can learn new things, prepare, look for ways to help, stay calm in chaos, have confidence, be resilient, limit the noise, focus on what matters, looking for growth and learning, choosing positivity, peace, and happiness.

HOW DO OUR THOUGHTS IMPACT OUR MINDSET AND RESULTS?

One way to think about how our thoughts impact our lives is to think of them like wildflowers. At first, wildflowers are beautiful – there are a few here and there, with beautiful colors lighting up nature's canvas. But left to their own devices, wildflowers spread – popping up anywhere their seed lands and growing ever higher, ultimately taking over your gardens and tree beds. The flowers get taller and taller until they are as high as your hip, and you can't even pass through them.

Likewise, our thoughts start out as a useful tool, helping us process and understand our experiences. But over time, these thoughts can overtake our mind and expand as our brain thinks the same thoughts over and over and over again. Then the thoughts become overwhelming, to the point that they actually surpass the experience itself. They cast a shadow over the experience, preventing us from evolving, seeing, learning, and growing from the experience itself.

For example, when someone fails at something that matters to them, and they feel as though they failed to accomplish what they set out to accomplish, they begin thinking about all the reasons for the failure. They begin to think about why they shouldn't have failed, couldn't have failed, and why it wasn't their fault that they failed. Those thoughts go around and around and around in their minds until the person can only see their thoughts about the failure. They are no longer able to simply observe the experience as a single experience in their life (an experience that can provide growth and learning). Rather, they identify with their feelings about the experience – their failure becomes their identity. We become that failure and it becomes our shame. Our identity and thoughts are focused on how we feel about the experience, and we remain stuck and trapped in those thoughts and feelings.

I mentioned my employee Meldina earlier in this book, and this is where I want to tell her story. I love her story so much because the experience was so impactful to both of us at the time. Meldina was an intern who I ultimately hired as a full-time employee. I gave her a project to implement our Employee Engagement Survey (which we deploy twice a year). This project was the first project where she was really on her own and was supposed to take the lead on managing the project deadlines.

Ultimately, Meldina failed pretty badly at managing the project. Her failure caused us to have to stay late on a Friday trying to fix the issues and, ultimately, having to delay the deployment of the survey. How did she respond to this failure? Well, you see, Meldina is extremely smart – she had never actually failed at anything in her life before (I know, crazy right?).

Meldina is highly Analytical®[21], Strategic®, and an Achiever®, so she spent significant amounts of time thinking about and stressing over her failure to achieve a positive result (the wildflowers were growing). Until all she could see was her failure. She came to me stating she needed and wanted to be assigned simpler tasks or put in an administrative role because she lacked the capability to coordinate a project. She would never be successful because she had failed once! She also told me that she thought she didn't do a very good job because she didn't really enjoy the tasks, so she didn't care as much about the result. My reaction to this revelation was quite dramatic. I told her, point blank, the following:

"You are one of the most capable, intelligent, and talented people I have ever met. If you think for one minute this failure is indicative of your capability, you lack complete self-awareness and understanding of what you can do. Failing a project is to be expected.

---

21 CliftonStrengths® and the CliftonStrengths 34 Themes of Talent are trademarks of Gallup, Inc. Gallup's content is Copyrighted by Gallup. Used with permission. All rights reserved.

I am disappointed but pointing out the issues so you can learn, not so you can quit. We've all failed at managing a project. Anyone who has ever managed a project has failed to meet a deadline – it's impossible to get good at project management and coordination without failure. But frankly, if you don't care about what you are doing while working on this team (including the details) then you are welcome to leave right now and never come back. Seriously – you can walk out the front door right now."

I was beyond frustrated. I can tolerate mistakes, errors, issues, and learning curves. I **cannot** tolerate a lack of willingness to put in the effort, take ownership of the results, and be accountable whether you like the task or not. I shocked myself and Meldina that day. Clearly, she did not walk out that door. In fact, she worked on her level of personal accountability, she learned from the experience, focused on the future, and has achieved tremendous results working with me at Experitec.

Fast forward three years, Meldina is capable of managing and coordinating many different projects and activities all at once. If she had allowed her mindset and lack of accountability to dictate her future, she might never be where she is now. She would have given up before she had really even gotten started. In life, we must remember not to let the thoughts about the experience change our beliefs about our capability to evolve our performance. We must step back, look at the experience as one moment in time, learn what is relevant, apply it to our lives, and then move on to the next experience.

We must take time to acknowledge when our mindset needs to change. When our thoughts are not serving us or bringing us value, we can start by just acknowledging the need for change. The thought of creating the change may be too much at first – so just start by acknowledging where you are today.

WHAT IS A LACK OF ACCOUNTABILITY AND WHY DOES IT HAPPEN?

The best way I know to recognize a lack of accountability is that anytime I feel stuck and unable to move to the next step, I am probably demonstrating a lack of accountability. Everyone has different ways to describe a lack of accountability. Cy Wakeman refers to it as "BMW Driving – Belly-aching, moaning and whining"[60] or, in *The Oz Principle*, it is considered "Below the Line Thinking."[61] But no matter what you call it, the same elements indicate a lack of accountability.

The visual I find most helpful as I think about accountability issues comes from a video based on a speech by Brené Brown about Empathy.[62] The video shows a person falling into a hole, and once they are down in the hole, they get stuck. Falling in the hole, like falling below the line, happens when we demonstrate a lack of accountability. This lack of accountability can manifest as judging, criticizing, deflecting, finger-pointing, blaming, gossiping, venting, complaining, reasons, stories, excuses, resistance, conditional commitment, disengagement, evading, avoiding, and learned helplessness. Whew – we have a lot of choices for demonstrating a lack of accountability! Anytime you are stuck – whether driving your BMW or stopped at a stop sign – you aren't moving, and this is the indicator you are in the hole.

We fall in the hole because we believe we are the victim of our circumstances. We fall in the hole because we trip over our past practices. We fall in the hole because our egos cause us to miss seeing the hole altogether. We get stuck because we can't get beyond the emotions we are experiencing as a result of the situation. We get stuck because it's easier to be upset about being stuck than to figure out how to get out of the hole. We get stuck because those around us join us providing sympathy which makes staying in the hole more enjoyable (although not productive).

The first step to getting out of the hole is recognizing we've fallen into one in the first place. I've provided a few examples below of what each of these behaviors sound or look like in our lives, what causes us to fall into these holes, and what we should do when it happens. As a reminder, you can't completely avoid these holes. We all (including myself) fall in them. So, what are they?

Judging & Criticizing

* **What does it sound or look like?** This sounds like "It's not fair, why does he always get extra time off?" "They are always late to meetings; they should be more punctual," or "They never answer their phones – they should be available when I call them." We've all done this; we've all started down the "Someone should…" sentence which never leads to any valuable actions or next steps. We can all work on the frequency in which we do this – because it happens more than most of us would like to admit.

* **What is the cause?** It's easy to judge! Judging occurs when we have insufficient facts. We try to fill in the blanks without having all the information. You only have one small piece of a much bigger picture. We do this because of the fundamental attribution error – the human tendency to judge our own behavior based on context but to attribute others' behavior to their character. My favorite example of this is when we get cut off while driving. We (or at least my husband) immediately get angry and frustrated at the other person's actions. However, when we do it because we are running late, on our way to the hospital, or because we are exhausted from a personal event – we have justifications and excuses for our actions.

* **What should we do?** We need to give others the same benefit of the doubt we give ourselves. Not doing so is counterproductive. The world does not only exist from our perspective, and we are not the center of the universe!

Deflecting Finger Pointing & Blaming

* **What does it sound or look like?** This sounds like *"They* didn't tell *me* what *I* needed to know," "It's all your fault, if you didn't make a mistake, we wouldn't have this issue," or "This isn't our fault, it's their fault." We see this behavior when we are trying to shift blame to others, and we want to deflect from our own level of involvement and responsibility. Instead, we try to put the focus and attention on someone else. Oftentimes, we see this when one employee emails a manager to criticize a co-worker's efforts. Or when mistakes are made, and people begin searching for a scapegoat to take responsibility for the consequences.

* **What is the cause?** Why do we blame or point fingers at others? Blaming is much safer and easier than actually taking action or acknowledging our part in the particular issue. It is much easier to blame someone else than to admit our own contributing actions. When we think about a person "falling into the hole," imagine two people falling in and blaming each other. "I wouldn't be down here if he hadn't run into me." "Well, he pushed me in!"

* **What should we do?** Instead, we ought to be saying, "I could have looked where I was going and avoided the hole. Then neither of us would be down here." We need to look for our own part in the issue rather than focusing only on the external factors that caused it.

Storytelling, Reasons, & Excuses

* **What does it sound or look like?** Storytelling sounds like "I don't know why they said that" "They didn't respond, they must not care about me!" and "Did you see how they responded to my email?" Anytime you feel yourself making up a story about what might have happened, excuses as to why you did something, or

reasons for something that happened – you are likely in this category! I am going to admit – this is one of the hardest areas to improve.

* **What is the cause?** When we get information, our minds try to fill in the missing gaps or pieces of information. We can't actively process all the information coming at us each day; therefore, our brains make decisions to fill in the spaces based on what we typically know. The problem is that sometimes our minds fill in gaps inaccurately. We are even more likely to be inaccurate when our minds fill in gaps on topics we aren't sure about or are insecure about. Our minds will tend to put a negative spin on things and start telling stories. For example, our brains often make up stories when we get a piece of feedback, or someone seems overly critical. We jump right to "It must be because I did a bad job," "I must not have been very good," and "They must not like me."

* **What should we do?** We need to recognize first when this is happening. I will provide some techniques in the next section, but the most important thing is to notice that you are making up a story. Recognize when you are asking victim-based questions – questions that place blame and promote victim thinking, complaining, and procrastinating. A great book for this is *The Question Behind the Question* by John Miller.[63] Next, we must either let it go or choose to seek out additional information. Whatever we do, we must find the next best step we can take to keep moving forward.

Resistance and Conditional Commitment

* **What does it sound or look like?** This area is a little tricker and not as obvious but can still be extremely detrimental to our level of accountability. Resistance looks like insistent assertiveness or even aggressiveness. When we resist, we intentionally choose not

to engage or help. In other words, we are rowing the boat in the opposite direction everyone else is moving. Conditional commitment sounds like, "You're not doing it right; this is the only way to do it" or "Fine I'll do it, but only my way."

* **What is the cause?** The primary cause of resistance is a lack of clarity or understanding on the part of those who are involved. The lack of clarity or understanding leads people to fear the effects of a change, especially when there is no precedent. We are typically creatures of habit; we love routine and procedure. If something hasn't been done before, we can't see the final state, and we can't see the end when we are at the beginning! Change also interferes with our autonomy – people feel they are losing control over their situation and the ways they have always done something. These responses cause us to hold back and resist or only provide a conditional commitment rather than fully engage and help.

* **What should we do?** When we encounter ourselves in this state, we must seek out the additional information or clarity necessary to move ourselves to commitment. We must acknowledge resistance and conditional commitment are not productive choices and we need to determine an appropriate next step rather than waste time and energy.

Complaining & Venting

* **What does it sound or look like?** We all know what complaining sounds like – and we are also all guilty of doing it! Our society has actually moved to a practice where complaining is the norm – where we literally try to out-complain someone else. "Yeah, I'm exhausted, and work sucks so bad." "Oh no! You got it great. My work sucks even worse!" I am not sure when or why we decided this was helpful – but it is a serious waste of time and energy. Venting is really just another form of

complaining. Venting sounds like "Can I vent for a second? Let me tell you how awful blah blah blah interaction was." Or "I just need to blow off some steam." The problem is that when we vent to another person, we relive the experience ourselves and then expect another person to get angry or commiserate with us without moving to action. When we vent, we are sitting in our own negativity rather than trying to move beyond it. We are too upset we are in the hole to look for a way out.

* **What is the cause?** I know this is going to be surprising but the only logical reason for complaining is that for some reason we believe our workplace or life should be free of challenges and conflict. Our lives should be smooth sailing with no challenges, no frustrations, no overflowing emails, no drama, and just smooth waters. Ha! We all know better. Complaining and venting are really just a poor response to reality. We aren't ready to move forward so we get stuck in complaining, sitting in our own pool of negativity. The problem is, once again, we waste a ton of time and energy.

* **What should we do?** I used to say we should stop complaining and venting altogether. I've learned differently over the years. Although venting, especially repeatedly, does not solve the problem, it can help with processing the emotion. Instead of using venting sessions to complain about everything that is wrong, needs to change, or who is bad, we need to shift to understanding why we feel the way we do about a situation and then determining what we can productively do next. (More on this soon!)

Gossiping

* **What does it sound or look like?** I originally didn't include gossiping as an area of focus. I had an employee say to me once, "That sounds like what my teenagers go through, not what

happens in the workplace." We all know gossiping does happen in the workplace, at home, and in our communities. We want to share things with each other, want to know what is going on, and want to know what's the story, who did what, to whom, and why. The problem with gossiping is the negative impact it can have on the subject of the gossip.

* **What is the cause?** Gossiping happens because we have a desire to connect and build relationships with others, and the fastest and easiest way to connect quickly is to gossip or create a common enemy by complaining about someone. We gossip so we can connect. This concept blew my mind, but it is incredibly accurate!

* **What should we do?** Learn alternative strategies to connect with others – look for commonalities, identify ways you can learn about each other, and grow your skills in this area so gossiping is unnecessary.

Learned Helplessness

* **What does it sound or look like?** This sounds like "We've tried this before and it doesn't work," "It's fine, I don't really care," "I can't convince them anyway, so it doesn't really matter," or "We can't do that here – XYZ won't let that happen." The best explanation I have seen for learned helplessness is the flea in a jar video (Google it and you will find it). Essentially, you can train fleas to become so accustomed to there being a lid on a jar that even when you remove the lid, they won't jump out of the jar. Even their offspring will never jump out of the jar when the lid is removed! Likewise, in our lives, we learn things, see patterns, and have experiences which contribute to our effectiveness, but they can also get in our way of seeing how things could be improved or changed. We learn that we can't do something so even when the limiting factor is removed, we never try to actually do it!

* **What is the cause?** When someone faces a negative situation so many times, they actually stop trying to change their circumstances, even when they have the ability to do so. For example, have you ever seen a smoker try quitting and repeatedly fail? They grow frustrated, decide there is nothing more they can do to and stop trying. When people feel like no matter what they do, their situation won't change, they can, and oftentimes do, begin to act in a helpless manner. Our past practices are so engrained in our brains neurologically (through neural pathways) we slide right back into our learned behavior without even trying something different.

* **What should we do?** We need to challenge our thinking – what are our self-limiting beliefs which are getting in the way of solving problems? Ask ourselves what we really know for sure and ask questions to determine if our beliefs are accurate or the situation may have changed.

Disengages, Evades, & Avoids

* **What does it sound or look like?** This looks like a person trying to avoid situations, changing the subject, making vague promises, or completely ignoring a situation altogether. Avoidance sounds like "Yeah sure, I guess I can do that," "I need to work on other things right now – I'll think about it later," "Let's not go there," and "I'm not willing to talk about that right now."

* **What is the cause?** We are humans and, as such, we have very delicate human egos – if we can avoid something which might impact our ego, we can avoid the pain. We use avoidance because we believe it will reduce the stress created by the challenging situation. We avoid situations which make us uncomfortable, especially situations that might negatively impact the relationship we have with another person. Also, those with a fixed mindset

tend to use this approach. "If I don't change, then maybe I can't fail, I'll just avoid the challenge altogether." The problem with this approach is it is only temporary – a "band-aid" that will ultimately lead to even bigger challenges. Avoiding the hard things only leads to more stress and hardship.

* **What should we do?** We need to acknowledge when we see ourselves or others engaging in this technique and challenge ourselves to lean into the challenge rather than away from it. I am not going to sugarcoat this – I think this example of a lack of accountability can sometimes be the hardest one to overcome! Certainly, it feels easier and better to avoid, disengage, and evade the challenging circumstances in our lives – but easy doesn't equate to good outcomes, growth, or positive results! And certainly, it doesn't evolve our performance.

Reflection: *Which of these examples triggered a response? Which have you experienced and know you are guilty of doing? Which of these do you tend to fall into frequently and why?*

Each of these examples of a lack of accountability should resonate with everyone. We are all victims of our circumstances and occasionally miss seeing the hole, falling into a poor accountability mindset. After reviewing all the opportunities for falling into a hole, I am sure most of you recognized how frequently these occur in your lives. A few different reactions are possible at this point:

* One reaction might be to resist – begin coming up with reasons why these types of responses aren't problematic or are even justifiable in particular situations. If this was your reaction, I ask you to stay open to the possibility that this response is not valuable and there may be a better way to respond!

* Another reaction might be to feel negatively about ourselves, focusing on how bad we are and how problematic our behaviors

have been. If this was your reaction, I want to remind you falling in a hole is the human condition – we all do it and we all struggle with it – so hold tight and I will help you learn how to avoid more holes and how to get out faster when you do inevitably fall in them.

* Or you might react with self-awareness and acknowledgement. Like, "Yep! This is definitely something I do! What can I do to be better?" If this was your reaction – great! We can start looking at new ways to approach our mindsets!

Whatever your reaction was to the ways we fall into the hole, the first step to getting out of the hole is always the same – understanding and recognizing the root cause of the fall in the first place! Have you noticed a common theme amongst all the causes of the various examples? Why did we trip, why did we not see the hole, why did we fall into this type of behavior or response?

WHAT IS THE ROOT CAUSE OF A LACK OF ACCOUNTABILITY?

The root cause of a lack of accountability is always *emotion*. We are always feeling something, and these feelings are what cause us to fall in and get stuck. Emotion is what causes us not to move forward and stay in the accountability hole.

When tough things happen in our lives, we have to learn to understand, process, and then let go of the emotion. My girls were playing with balloons recently. My husband and I would blow them up and they would take the balloon holding the air hole shut and then... let them go. The balloon would shoot all over the place with the air was shooting out of them. I think this is what it feels like when we first try to let go of our emotions. Things feel out of control as our emotions come rushing through us. We realize we'd be much more comfortable if we could just "close up the hole." We are left holding the balloon of our emotions closed rather than moving on to what comes next. Letting go may seem easy, but the truth is, letting go of our balloon of emotions is really hard.

When I train employees on this topic, I put up a big chart with the many different emotions we experience as humans. Growing up, many of us were not exposed or educated on how these different emotions impact what we choose to do in our lives. For some, you may not have ever considered or even seen all the emotions we are capable of experiencing as human beings. I know when I first ask people to write a list of emotions, the list is pretty short. When I show the chart of emotions, people are surprised but appreciative. Many people struggle to identify or describe emotions. To be honest, I still frequently pull up the emotions chart so I can pinpoint my own emotions or those of the people I am coaching (or parenting)!

We have to be able to identify, understand, and process the emotion all before we can let go of it and move on to action. When we fail to do this, when we hold onto our balloon, we stay stuck in our way of operating. And we certainly can't get out of the hole by climbing a ladder or a rock wall while holding our balloons closed!

Confusion	Angry	Sad	Anxious	Hurt	Embarrassed
Uncertain	Grumpy	Disappointed	Afraid	Jealous	Isolated
Upset	Frustrated	Mournful	Stressed	Betrayed	Self-Conscious
Doubtful	Annoyed	Regretful	Vulnerable	Isolated	Lonely
Indecisive	Defensive	Depressed	Confused	Shocked	Inferior
Perplexed	Spiteful	Paralyzed	Bewildered	Deprived	Guilty
Hesitant	Impatient	Pessimistic	Skeptical	Victimized	Abandoned
Shy	Disgusted	Tearful	Worried	Aggrieved	Repugnant
Lost	Offended	Dismayed	Cautious	Tormented	Pathetic
Unsure	Irritated	Disillusioned	Nervous	Abandoned	Confused

Negative emotions typically fall into a few major categories – confusion, anger, sad, anxious, hurt, or embarrassed. Although we are familiar with these, the secret is in the details. It's the detail of why we are experiencing a particular feeling, understanding it, and processing it.

For example, take angry. We all know when we feel angry, but what leads to this feeling of angry? When you look down the list you might see 'irritated' or 'offended' or 'frustrated,' which provide much greater context as to what might actually be going on. We have to understand what is leading to or causing the anger we see on the surface. When we understand what is happening, we are better positioned to process through the challenge and move to action.

During a recent challenge, after two long weeks of very long days solving extremely tough challenges and under a high degree of stress – I snapped. Our employees use more than 70 systems to do their work (due to supplier and customer requirements). All their passwords were reset. I had spent over twenty hours the previous few days trying to remedy this particular problem.

After three hours on a Friday, I was only able to reset 30 of my 180 employees to get them functional again. I reacted with a complete lack of accountability. I was frustrated, irritated, and impatient, just to name a few of the emotions I was experiencing. I snapped at my employees to "hurry up and get it (the work they were doing) done." My patience was just gone! I started saying, "I quit, I quit, I quit. Figure it out on your own. I'm out, I'm done."

My reaction, although somewhat embarrassing (and maybe comical), was a great example of falling in a hole with a lack of accountability. Thankfully, I have trained my employees well in accountability coaching and they provided me excellent coaching and support during my accountability tantrum! I needed to acknowledge my frustration was wanting to solve a necessary problem. My irritation was due to my exhaustion and need for a break (it was Friday). I needed to let go of it all, apologize to those I had impacted, and move forward. By the next morning, I was back to myself and knew I'd come back the next week and struggle through the challenges again – no matter what it took!

The human condition is to feel emotion in response to situations. For example, if someone feels:

* Confused – they might vent or complain
* Hurt – they might tell stories or come up with excuses
* Anger – they might judge or blame others
* Anxious – they might point fingers at someone else or resist a change
* Embarrassed – they might disengage or avoid

Our job is to recognize the emotion, understand what is causing it, and seek out support to process and move forward from our hole of emotion. When we have people around us trained to do this, they step into the hole, empathize with our emotion, and then help us get ourselves out of the hole! Although there are techniques for avoiding the holes, we aren't going to completely avoid all the holes in our lives. We are going to experience challenges which lead to emotion, and when this happens, we must recognize the value of the challenge and the process for getting out of the hole.

On the last night of a recent vacation, we had a very long day filled with meltdowns (you know the kind where you go for a walk and *all three* kids refuse to walk so you end up carrying two while pushing a stroller and pulling one on a big wheel with a rope tied to the front...very relaxing!). We had just successfully gotten all three children to sleep in bed and were about to go to bed ourselves. In the instant we flipped the switch to turn the lights off, the power blew and everything in the house turned off! I didn't even have the chance to accuse my husband of doing it before all six alarms were blaring and we were scrambling to get them turned off before they woke our three exceptionally cranky children. (Thankfully, they did not wake up!) My phone was nearly out of power and the house was completely dark.

While debating our next steps in the dark, I thought to myself there surely must be a lesson in this somewhere. I came up empty.

But if this were the end of the story, it wouldn't be nearly as entertaining. Fast forward two hours later, we had relocated our son down to a bedroom with us (for safety) and were just about to fall asleep when – bam! The power came back on… along with the lights in the bedroom which, unbeknownst to us, were left on when the power went out! Once again, all six alarms were blaring. My husband tried to stop them but, ultimately, they went off on their own. My children somehow managed to sleep through all of it. Oh no, there is more! Two hours later, my son woke up crying and wanted to go back to his room because he didn't like this bed!

So… what is the lesson? The next morning, exhausted, I said to my husband, "I wonder if the music will work." You see, for the whole trip, the music in the house would not play. My husband (trained as an electrician and mechanical engineer) tried resetting every device he could find to try to reset the power, but none of it had worked. He shrugged his shoulders and responded, "Maybe it will?" and turned on the music… and it worked! We turned on my favorite Pandora station, "Happy," and my kids and I danced around the house. That's when the lesson hit me: "Sometimes we need the power to turn off completely for a time to get the music to turn back on!"

> *Sometimes in life we have to go through a dark time – a frustrating, angry, hurt, sad, lonely, exhausted, overwhelmed, period of time – before we can re-set the power and have the music of our life turn back on.*

Sometimes in life we have to go through a dark time – a frustrating, angry, hurt, sad, lonely, exhausted, overwhelmed, period of time – before we can reset the power and have the music of our life turn back on. When the music came on that morning, it played the song "Don't Worry, Be Happy." When you are struggling and it's hard and it hurts, and it just feels dark – try to remember that sometimes you just have to go through the dark to come out better in the end. Look for the lesson, look for the learning, look for the growth, and focus on what you will be, feel, and experience when it is over. Focus on the music that will come. Don't worry, you'll be happy!

Reflection: *What dark holes have you fallen into? What emotions did you experience? Why did you get stuck? Has there been a time where someone helped you get out of the hole? What did that feel like? How can we be more conscious of our emotions when we find ourselves in the hole?*

HOW DO WE IMPROVE A LACK OF ACCOUNTABILITY MINDSET?

As I mentioned in the last section, sometimes in life we just fall into a hole and the lights go out! It's dark, it's lonely, and it's hard. But we don't have to stay in that hole! Once we know we are in the dark hole, how do we get the lights to come on and the music to play again? I have learned there are a number of strategies we can use, all of which will work in different situations.

As a reminder, the first step is seeing we are in a hole in the first place and realizing why we are there – what emotion are we experiencing. What are we feeling? Then we must identify why we feel a certain way, and what's causing this (in us or others). When this happens, the lights come on and we can see the situation more clearly, then we must figure out how to get out of the hole.

Imagine you're in a deep, dark hole – how do you get out? Well, the first thing that comes to my mind is the need for a ladder. Consider each rung of the ladder as a different strategy for getting us out of the hole. Each rung is one way you can work to change your mindset and move to high accountability.

Mindset – Changing Your Thoughts

The first ladder rung is to change our thoughts about an event. Any time a particular event or circumstance occurs in our lives, our minds begin to think about them and characterize what happened. For example, given a set of facts, we can choose to think about them differently.

* *Fact: A thunderstorm:* "Wow, that was beautiful" or "Wow that ruined a beautiful day"

* *Fact: He didn't answer my text:* "He must be upset with me" or "He must be busy"

* *Fact: My boss told me I need to improve my work:* "I suck" or "I know what I can do to improve"

When an event occurs, our minds start to think about how to interpret them – depending on this choice, our result will be entirely different. What we choose to think about an event causes us to feel a particular way, our feelings cause us to take an action, and that action determines our results.

Using the last example, if I think "I suck," I am going to feel sad, uncertain, stressed, or anxious. Therefore, I am likely to "vent" or be unable to make progress on my work. The outcome is that I feel bad, and the work doesn't improve. Instead, if I think "I know what I can do to improve," then I am likely to feel empowered, energized, and focused on making the improvements. By improving, I will see better results. What we choose to think has as much to do with the result as the event itself!

Edit Your Story

Due to our brains ability to process, any time we lack details, our brains start to fill in the blanks for us based upon our past experience (our lens). Stories occur when we don't have the necessary facts and we try to fill in the blanks. As we experience negative thoughts about our circumstances or interactions, we must ask ourselves if we are "telling ourselves a story." Are we filling in the gaps with facts and information we do not actually know for certain? Cy Wakeman uses a fantastic exercise in her book *Reality Based Leadership* to "edit your story."[64]

First, we must consider whether we have the facts necessary to truly know if our understanding of the story is accurate. What do we know for certain? What does our story look like with only those facts and nothing extra? Once we understand we are in a story and identify the facts, we can move to action. The question I always ask is: "What is the next best thing I can do now?"[65]

Over many years of sharing this technique with employees, I have found that editing our stories can dramatically change our level of happiness. We can reduce wasted energy and time, and instead redirect it towards action that brings value!

Consider Your Beliefs

My father taught me from a young age that our beliefs are what impact our lives and results. If you want to change a person's behavior, you have to start by changing their beliefs. Likewise, if you want to change your mindset, you must start by considering what beliefs are holding you back. Our beliefs impact our thoughts which impact our actions and, ultimately, our results.

Belief: something believed; an opinion or conviction; confidence in the truth or existence of something not immediately susceptible to rigorous proof; confidence; faith; trust; a religious tenant[66]

What self-limiting beliefs are impacting our lives? Beliefs are assumptions or perceptions about yourself and about the way the world works.[67] They are self-limiting because, in some ways, these beliefs are holding you back from achieving all that you are capable of achieving. In the end, you will always find what you believe and then when you find even a shred of information to back it up it will reinforce your belief.

Here's an example of how it might work for a salesperson. If they believe "I've seen this a million times, I know what they need. They won't buy from us our price is too high! They always buy from competitors. Their budget was cut, there is nothing I can do." Then when the customer doesn't buy from them, they say, "See I knew I was right, we'd never win the sale!"

Do you see the problem with this approach? How are our beliefs creating our results? If we want a different result, we have to challenge any beliefs that might be hindering our success. We can do this by challenging ourselves with specific questions. For example:

* Do I fully understand the problem?

* What is my value based upon? Results or perfection?

* If I believe that, what do I think the result is going to be? What do I want the result to be?

* What assumptions am I making?

* What strengths, capabilities, experience, and skills do I have that will help me be successful?

* What do I need to believe about myself to be successful?

* Who can I work with to provide a new perspective?

* What if there is a solution I haven't found yet?

What self-limiting beliefs are holding you back or hindering your success? The most common self-limiting belief I hear constantly is "I have no more time." When we believe this, we will never achieve the goals we are setting out for ourselves. We must change our beliefs first to see the results we want.

Focus on Success

Our focus becomes our reality, so we must learn to focus on the positive – on success, happiness, and having exceptional work and life experiences! My favorite quote by Cy Wakemen is, "Whether you believe it to be possible or impossible, you will be right."[68] I love this quote so much I turned it into a key chain that I always keep on my keys so I can be frequently reminded of this mindset. Whether or not we believe success and happiness is possible is going to determine whether we experience it!

We know our brains are hardwired to focus on the negative, like all the reasons we can't be happy, successful, or live exceptional lives. Instead, we need to focus our energy on what we *can* do and how we *will* be successful. If we don't focus on success, we most certainly will not achieve it!

"Whether you believe it to be possible or impossible, you will be right."

Cy Wakeman

How do we focus on success? Shawn Achor shares a few different strategies in his books on happiness – I've summarized a few of his key elements.[69]

* Identify a Positive Target – Find meaning, purpose, success, or happiness for you.

* Zoom in on the Target – Recognize your progress towards your goals and towards achieving an exceptional life so your goal appears closer.

* Magnify the Target Size – Believe in your ability to achieve. Be growth minded. Be confident in your abilities. Recognize the strengths, capabilities, experiences, knowledge, skills, and resources you have available that can help you be successful.

* Recalculate Energy – Don't assume it's out of reach or harder than it really is. Success is possible, but we must believe it first!

We often focus so much on what we are missing that we forget all the tools we have available to help us achieve success, happiness, and an exceptional life!

Adopt a Growth Mindset

In the last section on development, we talked about having a fixed versus a growth mindset. When we fall into the hole, remembering to shift our mindsets to focus on growth can help us get out of the hole. Embrace the challenge, work through the obstacles, and find the lessons in the most challenging of circumstances! Believing that we can *improve* our abilities is even more important than believing *in* those abilities.

See Alternative Perspectives

The last rung on the ladder challenges us to look at things from different perspectives. We often get stuck looking at the world through our own lens, and when we do, we fail to see everything beyond our view. I've encountered this challenge many times over the past ten years.

The first time I faced this challenge was when our business was going through significant challenges when the oil industry collapsed. We were forced to close a significant services business, terminating about 40 employees. I had friendships and relationships with those individuals and all I could see was the negative of the challenges. My dad (and boss at the time) said to me, "Jess – you're missing it, you are missing all the good by only focusing on the bad. We are stable, the rest of the business is healthy. We made the decision early to protect all the other employee families, and we will come out of this and be successful again." He was right. I was not seeing the situation from any other perspective.

Since this experience, any time I have a bad day, get frustrated, or start to think about quitting, I begin to think about different perspectives.

* Frist, I ask: what am I not seeing, how else can I look at it, and what facts am I leaving out?
* Then I ask again: what else have I missed? Are there positives I am missing?
* Then a third time: what details of my experience have I failed to mention the first two times?

After this, I ask which reality or set of facts or information will bring me the greatest value. How can I choose the most positive reality? The most valuable reality is the one that is most valid (or true), helpful (to the best outcomes), and positive (growth-producing).[70] Typically, after even the first round I begin to feel much better as I shift my mindset and see greater possibilities. By the time I am done, I am always in a much better headspace and able to see my situation from different perspectives.

Reflection: *Which of these techniques do you think will help you get out of the hole? Which can you use with others you interact with? How can they help you in the future?*

HOW DO WE HELP OTHERS AND WORK TOGETHER TO STAY ACCOUNTABLE?

I've provided a variety of strategies that can be used to stay accountable. How do we help others when they've fallen in the hole? The worst way to address a lack of accountability is to point it out directly. "You aren't being very accountable" or "You are just blaming the other person that's not accountable!" What do you think happens when we address a lack of accountability this way?

You got it. People begin resisting, disengaging from the conversation, and they do not get out of their hole! Just as we do with ourselves, whenever we encounter a lack of accountability, we must start by looking for the emotion that is causing the issue. Taking this step with another person is not for the faint of heart. I've seen many struggle to develop the skillsets to do this effectively.

The problem is no matter how much we want to ignore what is going on with people and avoid dealing with the tough topics and emotions – we can't. Failing to address the emotion, failing to engage and connect with the person, and failing to demonstrate empathy is a significant mistake. Everyone experiences crappy situations in their lives and when they do, you can't force them to ignore it or pretend it isn't happening. You can't argue away accountability issues and, frankly, you can't just ignore or refuse to acknowledge them.

Rather, we must connect, understand, and engage with people. When we have trust, we can connect. When we connect, we can understand what is happening. When we understand what is happening, we can engage in a discussion on how to move forward.

As we discussed in the feedback section, connecting and building trust is foundational to helping someone get out of the hole. They must feel like we are with them – connecting with them and empathetic to how they feel. Then we can begin to move them to the next steps on the ladder to get out of the hole! How do we build trust in order to coach another person or group out of their accountability hole?

I'll admit it took me years to figure this out, but it truly works well and is the best method I have ever used. The answer is vulnerability. If this word makes you uncomfortable – you are not alone. According to Brené Brown, most people experience challenges associated with vulnerability and struggle to truly be vulnerable.[71] However, the only way to truly build the necessary trust to help another person out of their hole is to be vulnerable and acknowledge we've been in the accountability hole too! And remember – every person has been in that hole. It's the human condition!

By being vulnerable and willing to share our own experience and challenges with accountability, we gain credibility and those we are coaching feel more confident in our suggestions. People connect more when they feel the other person also has weaknesses. Honestly, don't we all have weaknesses? Haven't we all been in that dark, lonely accountability hole?

> **Sympathy**: feelings of pity and sorrow for someone else's misfortune; the fact or power of sharing the feelings of another, especially in sorrow or trouble; fellow feeling, compassion, or commiseration.[72]
>
> **Empathy**: the ability to understand and share the feelings of another[73]; the psychological identification with or vicarious experiencing of the feelings, thoughts, or attitudes of another[74]

I struggled for years with the concept of empathy versus sympathy and wondered which one we should use and when. I already mentioned Brené Brown's video that explains the difference, and I have to say that was the first time I really understood the difference. Sympathy is when we look down in the hole and say something like, "Man that really sucks. Yeah, you've got it tough... that's awful. It must be dark, cold, and lonely. I'm so sorry you are stuck down there. I'll pull you out and solve your problem for you." Empathy is when we get down in the hole and say, "Yeah, this is hard, and it is dark and lonely. But I've been here before, so let's work together to figure out how you can move forward and get out of the hole."

The difference is subtle, I know, but it is very important. We need empathy and support when we are in an accountability hole. The last thing we need is sympathy – that just encourages us to stay in the hole or look to someone else to solve the problem. Once you've connected and demonstrated empathy, then you can start to share the strategies or provide perspectives using the ladder to help the person climb out.

When we apply this approach, the results we see are tremendous. The level of trust increases, our connection grows, our understanding of each other improves, our commitment to achieving increases, and our resilience to challenges develops. People are capable of more than you imagine, but they need coaching and support to reach peak performance.

Reflection: *How do we focus on demonstrating empathy when we see others in a hole? What can we do to connect with them and help them see the strategies for getting out of the hole?*

HOW DO WE BUILD ACCOUNTABILITY INTO OUR PEAK PERFORMANCE?

A variety of skills can be used to help improve your level of accountability and reduce the frequency with which you fall in the hole. I like to think of these skills and capabilities as the "tools" you have available to avoid tripping or falling in the hole in the first place. We can do so by strengthening our commitment to expectations and our resilience to feedback while continuously learning for development and taking ownership for our peak performance.

Expectations

* Commit to understanding, aligning, and delivering on expectations
* Determine how your role aligns with your business, family, or communities' direction
* Continuously learn and understand how your role is impacting others

Feedback

* Actively learn about yourself (self-awareness) and others (preferences)
* Take responsibility for seeking out and giving others feedback on both success and failure
* Build relationships and cultivate resilience in the face of challenges

Development

* Continuously look for ways to grow and develop both yourself and those around you
* Learn to maximize your strengths and manage your weaknesses
* Be prepared for change and for the future by always learning new capabilities

The highest level of personal accountability is taking ownership of our results – whether they are good or bad. Be willing to acknowledge your part in any situation or challenge.

WHAT WILL BE THE RESULT OR IMPACT IF WE IMPROVE MINDSETS AND ACCOUNTABILITY?

At this point in the book, I hope it is clear why changing our mindsets and improving our accountability is critical to reaching peak performance. Many studies point to the benefits of a positive and accountable mindset in all aspects of our life.

The best example from my own life is my Grandma Tietjen. She had a little Mickey Mouse picture that said, "Happiness is a choice," and she lived by that each and every day. She passed away a number of years ago, and the day before she passed away, I was in the hospital with her. After saying goodbye, I started to walk down the hall, but my dad came out and told me that my grandma wanted to see me again. I went back in, and my grandma hugged me and said she loved me and was proud of me. I knew then that it would be the last time we would talk. She did not wake up the next day. When she died, we talked a lot about her philosophy on happiness and I guess it really just stuck with me. We *can* choose happiness.

Years earlier, when I first created Experitec's Accountability and Mindset training, I got into a debate with one of my former employees. She felt strongly that you could never achieve happiness. She said she'd only be happy if she lived in a forest far away from everyone, and even then, she couldn't be happy because she would be lonely. We debated until we landed on Mindset and Personal Accountability impacting our level of success. We chose to leave out happiness as an outcome of the training. But she was wrong, and I was wrong to let her convince me. The problem was that she didn't believe happiness was possible, and we know if you don't believe it, then you are right... you will never be happy.

I, on the other hand, after years of conducting this training for employees and applying the principles in my own life, know without a doubt that my happiness is 100% dependent on my mindset and level of personal accountability. When you choose a life of happiness then the peace, joy, and positivity spreads to all your interactions. Life is not perfect, and it never can be, but it can be exceptional.

CHECKLIST:
WHAT DO I DO FIRST?

✓ Identify your current mindset

✓ Acknowledge when you've fallen in the hole with a lack of personal accountability

✓ Identify, Understand, Process, and Let Go of the emotion to move on to action

✓ Climb the steps of your ladder: Change your Thoughts, Edit your Story, Consider Your Beliefs, Focus on Success, and See Alternative Perspectives

✓ Support and coach others by demonstrating vulnerability and empathy

✓ Cultivate your capabilities for accountability and mindset

✓ Experience the joy and success of choosing happiness

Section Four

APPLYING THE KEYS OF PEAK PERFORMANCE TO OUR ROLES

How do I implement these insights and where should I start?

> *Where we experience our roles helps shape how we interact, what we believe, and how we see and portray ourselves.*

While writing this book, I felt strongly that more context, stories, and examples were needed to help translate the concepts into actionable insights specific to the roles we serve. I struggled because, although I have personal experience in some roles, I am not an expert in all roles. For example, I am a working mom, therefore, I can only speculate about the experience of a mom or dad performing unpaid work in the home every day. Although it is impossible for me to apply this to all potential roles you may perform, I think by applying it to even a few roles, it helps to put these concepts into context and in practice.

After significant reflection, I have decided the stories and examples must carry on beyond the pages of this book. Sharing and hearing stories of people on the path to peak performance can provide far greater examples than I can include in this book. At the risk of no one participating, I will create a forum for anyone to join where you can share your role, how you apply the four keys, what challenges you are facing, and how others can support you. We will create a community of like-minded people who can continue to share how they apply this guide to the roles they perform in their lives.

At the beginning of this book, I indicated that these principles would help you determine where to spend your time and how to ultimately get time back. I believe with 100% confidence this will be the case and you will experience this benefit. However, most of us serve a lot of different roles and most of us don't have the time to make changes to our performance in all these roles at once. Therefore, if you have not applied the principles of peak performance in any role, I encourage you to choose one role (or two at most) to begin applying the four keys. This will allow you to see more significant results in one role and then you can begin to apply the same practices to another.

In this section, I will provide context and examples of how the four keys to peak performance can be applied to the roles we serve. This last section is meant to be a reference, building upon what has previously been covered. Therefore, you can read just one chapter right now and come back to the others when you are ready to focus on your performance in a different role.

The environment in which we perform a role provides significant context and understanding of the role itself. Where we experience our roles helps shape how we interact, what we believe, and how we see and portray ourselves. Therefore, I've chosen to approach the roles we serve by environment – our workplaces, our homes, and our communities. I hope these next few chapters provide helpful insights for you to think about your performance.

Before diving into the roles contained in each of the three environments, we will address one role which spans across all three

– leadership. In the world today, we need more people to see themselves as leaders in their lives. Collective leadership is critical to creating the cultures required in our workplaces, homes, and communities. Therefore, we must start by addressing leadership.

CHAPTER ELEVEN
Leading Together

How do we apply the keys to the role of Leadership?

> ### Key Insight:
>
> We will ensure great leadership exists in each area of our lives and fill the gap when we inevitability discover a lack of leadership.

In many "future of the workplace" discussions, a trend has emerged suggesting a move away from the traditional hierarchical structures of the past. Many are speculating how our organizations, businesses, communities, and even families will be structured in our new world. I've heard suggestions about leadership in families needing to change from patriarchal to matriarchal. I've heard community leaders become increasingly polarized, unable to work collectively for the greater good. I've heard some suggest we will need fewer leaders and managers in the future as we continue to automate and thereby flatten our organizations. In all areas, respectfully, I disagree. I believe we need not only more leadership, but also to modernize our interpretation of leadership.

Leadership is a word often used but frequently misinterpreted, repeatedly misconstrued, and regularly misunderstood. To me, leadership is about bringing people together, being the glue that holds people together, and helping generate greater results collectively than are possible individually.

Throughout history, the type of leadership required has varied significantly based on the culture, beliefs, and understanding at the time. The current definitions on lead, leading, and leadership all highlight the concept of "being in front" or "at the top." We've frequently observed this type of leadership – lead by, directed, and even dictated. A more progressive form of leadership has (ironically) been to lead from behind, called "Servant Leadership." This type of leadership pushes others to the front with the leader providing support from behind.

Leadership: The action of leading a group of people or an organization; the state or position of being a leader; capacity to lead; the act or instance of leading; the accomplishment of a goal through the direction of human assistants.[75]

Leading: coming or ranking first, providing direction or guidance, given most prominent display[76]

Lead: to guide on a way especially by going in advance; to direct a course or in a direction, to serve as a channel for; to direct the operations, activity, or performance of; to have charge of; to guide someone or something along a way[77]

> CCL defined leadership as "the ability to create a vision for positive change, help focus resources on right solutions, inspire and motivate others, and provide opportunities for growth and learning."[78]

Neither type of leadership seems appropriate in today's climate. When we are in front, we miss seeing what is happening behind or beneath us. Even if we know we are leading in the right direction, we lack the connection needed for people to enthusiastically follow us. When we are leading from behind, we can see what is happening but not necessarily where we need to be going. Our people must make the choices and, while we are supporting them, we are not guiding the direction of their efforts.

What if, instead of leading in front or leading behind, we are meant to be leading with and among? Instead of being in front or behind, we are right there with everyone – building together, guiding together, and generating strength and results through collective power. If we can lead together, we can create more opportunities for leadership from anywhere and in any role. In the current climate and context, we not only need more leaders, but we also need more of this specific kind of leadership – leading together.

WHY IS MORE LEADERSHIP NEEDED?

Leading together simply requires more leaders. How do I know we need more leaders? As our communities, workplaces, and families have become more fragmented, we require additional leadership to lead these disconnected groups. Community gathering has long been deteriorating as people move frequently between communities and further apart, struggling to find their tribe. Families which historically lived together, or at least close by, are now frequently spread across many cities, states, and even countries. Workplaces have people working on teams spanning the globe and, with the rise of remote work, the workplace community is likely to be challenged even further.

All this expansion has fragmented the structures we historically relied upon to ensure continuity in our lives. Our churches, communities, workplaces, and even families had designated leaders responsible for helping to shape the culture of those environments. Although those leaders are still needed, we need even more leaders to ensure our cultures don't further deteriorate. As groups are separated, experiencing fewer interactions – more leadership (not less) is necessary.

The effects of the leadership gap are noticeable. We've seen the breakdown of leadership in many businesses with far too many instances of harassment, discrimination, and toxic cultures. Our education systems are challenged to acquire adequate resources to meet the needs of our children. Our families struggle with increasing conflict and discord – balancing the challenges of work and home amongst the family. Churches and communities continue to shrink, struggling to bring people together in a meaningful way or have been faced with conflict and scandal.

In many cases, those who have been leading us lately have done so unsuccessfully – toxic business environments, systemic racism in our criminal justice system, inadequate education systems, families broken by abuse or drugs, and an inability to provide the support needed (financially or emotionally). We need a new age of leadership where everyone is taught the skills required to be effective leaders and everyone can fill that role when called upon to act for the greater good.

Call to the Wolfpack:

If you have a voice, you have influence to spread.
If you have relationships, you have hearts to guide.
If you know young people, you have futures to mold.
If you have privilege, you have power to share.
If you have money, you have support to give.
If you have a ballot, you have policy to shape.
If you have pain, you have empathy to offer.
If you have freedom, you have others to fight for.
If you are alive, you are a leader.[79]

— Abby Wambach, in Wolfpack

In my experience, leading together is truly valuable and will help us reach peak performance. I want as many people as possible to live their best life, and the only way we get close to achieving this is if more people take on the role of leader and apply these principles for those they serve.

WHAT ARE THE EXPECTATIONS FOR LEADERS?

The expectations of leaders have been written about in hundreds, if not thousands, of books. These leadership books exist on every topic, covering competencies, skills, and what "should" be expected of leaders. Everyone has a different theory on the best type of leadership; inclusive leadership, servant leadership, democratic leadership, autocratic leadership, strategic leadership, transformational leadership, delegative leadership, transactional leadership, and on and on and on! I will not discount any of them, as they all have valuable insights to bring on the topic of leadership and have likely all served a necessary purpose at one point in time.

However, the expectations of leading must be based upon the needs of those who are being led. As a leader, we must extend beyond simply performing the role we serve to actively leading others while performing the role. How we lead is directly impacted by who we are leading and why we are leading them (for what purpose). When we are leading together, we can work as a group to identify our purpose for leading alongside those with whom we are collectively generating results.

I am sure you know this by now, but my purpose is to help others to live their best life possible – whether that is my employees, my children, my spouse, my company, you the reader, or anyone in the world. As a leader, I strive to support and guide those with whom I lead in a way that enhances their ability to live their best life. For example, my workplace teams work together to define the expectations of leadership (both for me and for the team) that help us all to be successful at achieving that purpose and outcome.

Each of us has the potential within us to lead when called upon, and each of us can decide how we choose to lead. This book's purpose is for you to apply these principles and establish your own leadership style. We must, however, first view ourselves as a leader. We must recognize the opportunity which exists for us to lead. Leadership always involves influencing other people and we have the ability to lead together in a way that positively influences others, strengthens everyone, and generates meaningful results.

I recognize some may struggle to see themselves as a leader using the leadership images of the past. So, let's start with a blank slate – a clean beginning where leadership expectations can be anything we need them to be. At the Gallup®[22] at Work Summit, I heard a speaker named Lynn Perry Wooten use a leadership term I had not heard before – "Everyday Leadership." Without ever hearing the definition or description of Everyday Leadership, I can quickly

---

[22] CliftonStrengths® and the CliftonStrengths 34 Themes of Talent are trademarks of Gallup, Inc. Gallup's content is Copyrighted by Gallup. Used with permission. All rights reserved.

and easily relate to the potential for leadership to be what is required every day, by everyone and anyone, in the roles they are performing.

"Leadership can come in different forms," Wooten says. *"Especially now, just think about our everyday leadership— we've seen in the last months how essential workers have been driving our world. I like to call it 'unleashing leadership'— intentional leadership development that gives everyone the opportunity to lead. If everyone is trained and invested as a leader, it makes both that person and the organization stronger."[80]*

Lynn Perry Wooten

The beauty of everyday leadership is you can apply it in any context which makes sense for you. You can be the type of everyday leader you need and want to be in whatever context or environment you are leading. Whether you are a formal leader or not, you can demonstrate leadership as an Everyday Leader in your workplace, home, or community. What do you see as the expectations of your everyday leadership in the roles you are performing?

For example, in our business, we empower all employee owners to be leaders in our organization. When we identify employees as high potential (for taking on leadership roles in the future) and they join our iLEAD team, they are specifically tasked with being leaders of our culture – driven, positive, and collaborative. They begin leading from any role and, as a result, they have become some of the most influential leaders in our organization – regardless of title or position.

If nothing comes to mind, everyone can start with leading their own lives and families. And keep in mind, families can have more than one leader. In fact, when both parents lead together, families are even more effective. Each leader brings unique qualities and insights which allow them to be effective and provide strong leadership in different ways. One parent may lead in the areas of relationships, connection, and empathy. Another may lead in the areas of finances, direction, and goal setting. Both provide the context and insights necessary to shape a family culture.

The most important expectation of leadership is the check-in – taking the time to check-in, coach, communicate, and work with each person you are leading. To be able to check-in frequently enough and with the context of what is required, we need to be there leading **with** our teams.

"Checking in with each person on a team – listening, course-correcting, adjusting, coaching, pinpointing, advising, paying attention to the intersection of the person and the real-world work – is not what you do in addition to the work of leading. This is the work of leading."[81]

Marcus Buckingham, in Nine Lies About Work

HOW DO WE GET AND GIVE FEEDBACK AS LEADERS?

Receiving *effective and relevant* feedback as a leader is quite difficult. People are often hesitant to give their leaders the direct feedback necessary to improve. As I discussed earlier, the best way to get meaningful feedback is by building a foundation of trust. Whoever you are leading must know they are safe to provide you honest feedback. If they fear your reaction and willingness to consider their perspective – they will never tell you the truth! And, if you are so far out front or behind that they cannot easily reach you, they won't have the opportunity to give you feedback and you likely wouldn't have the necessary perspective to appreciate their feedback anyway.

A number of years ago I got feedback in our engagement survey on how my employees trusted me – it wasn't terrible, but it wasn't great either! If I am honest, this was a gut punch to me at the time. I was working hard at performance management, and this low score hurt. After falling in a hole for a bit, I recognized the survey result was telling me something important. No matter how good of a job I thought I was doing, I needed to take steps to build better trust with my team. I couldn't argue with them about it. I couldn't reject it. I needed to acknowledge it and look for what I could do differently.

I needed to look at the feedback from their perspective not my own. I was leading from out front – I saw where we needed to go and what we needed to do, but I didn't see it how those I was leading were experiencing it. Even if I thought I was doing all the right things, if they weren't creating a positive experience, it really didn't make a difference! I needed to change my practices to reflect and consider their experience and their perspective. I needed to lead *with* them, leading together.

As a result, I took steps to improve – I listened more to different opinions, left space for discussion (even holding my opinion until others had a chance to share), and I made time to engage with employees on a personal level. The changes I made took time to impact and build trust. I learned trust is a slow process and requires us to truly be *with* those we are leading. New leaders and managers don't get it right off the bat – it takes time. Time to lead with our teams, get to know them, and build up trust and understanding.

Today, our team, the people I work *with* each day, are some of the people I trust most in the whole world. They are my closest friends. Likewise, I am there for them in any situation – we have extremely high trust and work together seamlessly. Having grown the trust, I can now see the dramatic difference in culture and interactions as a result of building trust. I am glad I was able to receive the feedback and make the changes necessary.

As a leader, we must build trust and seek out feedback. When we get it, I encourage you as a leader to be open to the feedback you get – even if it feels painful at first. Sit with the feedback, be willing to see your part in it, be willing to change your perspective, and move from ahead, above, or behind to be next to those you are leading. Realize that taking steps to improve is going to help everyone! Brené Brown's words really resonated with me when she said the following: 82_{OBJ}

"I know I'm ready to give feedback when: I'm ready to sit next to you rather than across from you; I'm willing to put the problem in front of us rather than between us (or sliding it toward you); I'm ready to listen, ask questions, and accept that I may not fully understand the issue..."

Brene Brown

We must also recognize when feedback is not helpful, useful, or accurate. Remember, not all feedback is good feedback. I once received feedback that some of my choices in how I was working and leading my teams were harming my credibility with other leaders. By engaging in doing the work itself, I was harming my reputation (and that of my teams) by indicating with my involvement they were not effective or capable of doing the work on their own.

I took time to consider this input, and I recognized and acknowledged I do get involved in the work. My involvement has nothing to do with their not being capable or effective, but rather because I am energized by the work, and I want them to feel me working with them and know I am there to guide, support and coach. In doing so, I can provide them with real-time, meaningful, actionable feedback. I can give them insights into our direction while receiving insight into their perspective as the work is actually happening, rather than days, weeks, or months later. We can adjust as we learn together and thereby create greater performance outcomes and results.

The style of leadership I wish to emulate reminds me of Abby Wamback's book *Wolfpack* and her leadership as Team Captain of the US Women's Soccer Team. Abby says to "Lead now-from wherever you are."[83] I want to be the team captain. I want to know how to play the game itself. Sometimes I'm on the field with them observing, engaged, and playing the game. Other times, I'm on the bench watching, encouraging, supporting, and coaching them to be their best. No matter what, I am always right there with them, fully *in* the game. I don't want to be up in the owner's box, watching from on high and lacking perspective, experience, access, and credibility with the teams I am leading. I want to be right there with them – where we can change, adjust, guide, and support as we are not just playing, but winning the game!

After significant reflection and seeking out the perspective of those I work with to ensure my actions were not harming them directly, I concluded I care more about my credibility with those I am leading than I do about my credibility with other leaders. Especially if these other leaders are judging my behavior based upon their external, above, or behind but certainly not in, and limited view. These leaders may choose to lead differently than I do, like from in front or behind – but they lack my perspective and that of our team and, therefore, their opinions are not particularly helpful.

The advice given to you by a leader who
is not you will not necessarily work for you.

Marcus Buckingham, in Nine Lies about Work

As leaders, when we lead together, we will likely find ourselves in many situations with both positive and negative feedback. Some will be helpful, and some will not, and we must evaluate and discern which are useful in producing valuable results. For me, the most valuable feedback comes from others who are in the arena, in the game, and who know what's really happening.

"It is not the critic who counts; not the man who points out how the strong man stumbles, or where the doer of deeds could have done them better. The credit belongs to the man who is actually in the arena, whose face is marred by dust and sweat and blood; who strives valiantly; who errs, who comes short again and again, because there is no effort without error and shortcoming; but who does actually strive to do the deeds; who knows great enthusiasms, the great devotions; who spends himself in a worthy cause; who at the best knows in the end the triumph of high achievement, and who at the worst, if he fails, at least fails while daring greatly, so that his place shall never be with those cold and timid souls who neither know victory nor defeat."

Theodore Roosevelt

Likewise, as leaders it is our responsibility to be **good** leaders who provide effective feedback. Which means we must provide significantly more positive feedback! What is the worst kind of feedback? I venture a guess you thought 'negative' but actually it is 'the absence of feedback or no feedback.' When people hear nothing about their performance the level of engagement drops tremendously.[84] For many of us, this conclusion is quite obvious – when I know nothing about how I am doing I am left to make up my own stories. At least with negative feedback I know what I need to be working on. Whatever you do as a leader – give feedback, frequently, and try to point out the work you want to see repeated as frequently as you can!

HOW DO WE DEVELOP OUR LEADERSHIP CAPABILITIES?

For some, leadership comes naturally while for others leadership requires intentional development, but everyone is capable of evolving their leadership skills. However, as leaders, we often forget the need for development. I've seen many leaders get to the "position" of leadership and stop growing. They stop looking at how they can improve, stop considering what has changed and stop seeing what is needed of leadership now. They've moved so far out front that they can no longer see from the perspective of those they are trying to lead.

> *No one wins a prize for being perfect at the start*
> *– everyone has to put in effort to grow*
> *and develop first!*

If you think back 10, 20, or 50 years ago, the types of leaders of the past are quite different from those we see are needed now. The type of leadership required for managing an industrial manufacturing group of employees on the line is quite different than the knowledge workers of today. We used to believe work only happened in an office, in a cube, on a manufacturing line, and with co-workers. We now know a lot of work can truly happen anywhere. And people can be productive (actually even more productive) in other settings than the offices of the past.

This change, however, requires a change in how we lead and manage performance. We must learn new strategies that replace the MBWA (management by walking around) strategy. Our culture has changed everywhere and, therefore, our leadership must change with it. We must develop the capabilities to lead with those we are leading – by leading together!

Developing to Lead Together in Our Workplaces

As leaders, we must shift the focus of our skills development from traditional practices of providing clearly defined direction, detailed instruction, strong and sometimes aggressive approaches, hands-off and removed leadership from above, and a culture of authority and control. Rather, we must learn to lead alongside our teams, understanding the workplace challenges, collectively identifying solutions, and supporting our teams with ongoing coaching and performance development. In order to do so, we must develop our capabilities relating to empathy, understanding, people management, communication, connection, authenticity, and growth mindedness.

Developing to Lead Our Families Together

Take, for example, the history of families. In the past, the men in the family made all the decisions for the family regardless of their knowledge, capability, and impact on the family. Now, leadership in our families can become (and in some cases is becoming) more shared between spouses (of any gender). We can develop the capabilities for this shared leadership – leading together – and it can be based more upon the strengths of the family rather than on a traditional model of the ideal family. We can expand how we see our roles and improve the effectiveness of our families in our homes. We can develop the leadership capabilities necessary to lead with our families, making decisions collectively and for the greater good of the family.

Developing for Leading Diversity & Inclusion

The societal shift in culture to create more diverse and inclusive workplaces lends itself to a model of leading together. We must have leadership skilled in respect, diversity, and inclusion. We must have leaders who understand why inclusion is important and how to foster the behaviors and culture necessary to create environments of inclusion. We need leaders who demonstrate diversity and inclusion skills and help those they lead to cultivate these same skills. These skills require leaders who understand, see, hear, and value those they are leading. We must be leading alongside people in order to truly understand, see, hear, and value them as individuals.

Many businesses are beginning to train on respect in the workplace and creating a culture of inclusion, as ours has. To create an exceptional workplace, the workplace must be exceptional for everyone. Therefore, inclusion is critical to our workplaces. If people don't feel respected at work, they are never going to be engaged or feel their workplace is exceptional. I like to think about respect like good hygiene – when it's there you don't always notice, but when it's gone, everyone knows!

Although the workplace is obviously experiencing significant change, this same change is needed in our homes and communities as well. I think educators are beginning to incorporate these inclusion skillsets into classes (albeit sometimes controversially). Many religious institutions and community groups are also grappling with how to create inclusive cultures and build the skills necessary to create meaningful change.

The one place we can all have an impact is in our own homes. To be true leaders in our homes, we must learn about these culture shifts, the skills needed to lead them, and then lead our families through these changes. We can and should help our families develop the skills of inclusion and respect. We must ensure our children gain this knowledge earlier in life and demonstrate these capabilities throughout their lives.

HOW DO WE HOLD OURSELVES ACCOUNTABLE AS LEADERS?

When I think of accountability for leadership, I am reminded of when my father used to say, "You are perfectly aligned for the results you are getting." What he meant was our beliefs, culture, values, behaviors, and strategies all contribute to our results – we are getting results based on what we put into the process. Therefore, if you don't like the results you are getting, you must look at what needs to change.

As leaders, we must be the owners of the results – both good and bad – of those we lead. If what we want to see is not happening, we are responsible for making the change to improve the outcome or result. We naturally want to point the finger away from ourselves and focus on how others are failing to meet *our* expectations. But, as leaders, we bear the full responsibility and accountability for everything, even if something or someone is not working as it should. Instead, no matter the issue, we must identify it, actively work on it, and find a solution to fix it. We must lead with our people to identify what's really happening, work on the issue, and know what is truly the right solution.

In my experience, the fastest way to lose the trust of those you lead is to fail to hold yourself accountable, to point fingers, or place blame elsewhere. If you begin to blame those you lead for shortcomings, you will ultimately fail at leading them. Our people watch us to see how we behave, react, and respond during challenging circumstances. We must demonstrate the behaviors we wish to see from those we lead. I have witnessed managers fall into an accountability hole, and one by one, their team members end up down there with them, all stuck and unable to get out. As leaders, we have to ensure we maintain high accountability (or, at a minimum, return quickly after stumbling).

The importance of this in our homes is even greater. Our children need to see us admit when we make a mistake and hold ourselves accountable. "Yes, sometimes mommies and daddies yell when they shouldn't – we get frustrated and have to remind ourselves it's not okay to yell" or "No, daddy forgot flowers for mommy's birthday, it's not your fault he forgot because you were yelling on the way home." I'm sure you could come up with many examples in your own families where we begin to point fingers or place blame. We teach our children and reinforce to ourselves that blaming others is a legitimate approach. It's not. It only creates more discord, frustration, and hurt feelings. Taking responsibility and ownership of mistakes, issues, and challenges is always better than storytelling, judging, or blaming others.

The future needs less arrogance and more self-awareness; less management and more entrepreneurship; less sorting and more coaching. We need to focus less on cost and more on value, meaning, and impact.

Jeff Schwartz, in Work Disrupted[85]

In our world today, we see leaders pointing fingers, blaming others, and failing to take ownership for just about everything. We see leaders use members of their teams as scapegoats when something goes wrong. We punish leaders who admit mistakes, failures, and shortcomings. We have it completely backwards! We need leaders who take ownership of the problems, who take ownership of the solutions, and who work together, regardless of any issues, to implement the solutions. Our children need to see more accountability everywhere they look. Truly, if accountability were seen as a requirement for leadership – we would be much better off in this world.

Conclusion & Reflection

Start by looking for areas in your life that require or need greater leadership. What are the areas where you keep saying "someone should" do something about this? Where is culture struggling or needs greater leadership? What role are you already performing where you can think of yourself as a leader? Start with these areas. Frequently where we feel we are least equipped to lead is where we are called upon to demonstrate leadership. You can be the leader you know is needed – you just have to step it and do it!

Expectations: *Once you've identified who you are going to lead and why (your purpose for leading), you must think about what you will do differently. Why type of Everyday Leader will you be? How will you be leading together rather than leading in the ways of the past? Based upon your strengths, what expectations will you set for yourself in this leadership role? What type of leader is needed? What type of skills do you need? How will you know if you are being successful? What are you going to do each day as the leader?*

Feedback: *How will you solicit feedback on your performance as a leader and from who? How will you build trust so that those you lead will feel safe and free to give you feedback? How will you prepare to respond to critical feedback so you can internalize and draw meaningful insights? How will you decide whose feedback not to listen to and when to trust yourself the most?*

Development: *What will you do to cultivate the capabilities for leadership in your role? How will you purposefully grow the skills necessary to lead together? How will you grow your inclusivity skills, so people feel seen, heard, and valued?*

Accountability: *How will you hold yourself accountable for the results of the teams you are leading? What will you do to stay engaged in the game so you can adjust and respond as changes are needed? How will you set an example for accountability in leadership?*

As we develop more leaders in this world, we must actively use the keys to peak performance. I encourage each of you to think about your leadership role in the context of the workplace, home, and community. Where can you lead? How can you lead using the four keys to peak performance? How can your leadership help to change the world for those you lead and those they impact?

CHAPTER TWELVE
The Modern
Workplace

How do the keys to reaching peak performance
apply in the modern workplace

Roles: Employee, Leader, Manager, Mentor

> ### Key Insight:
>
> Evolving our workplace performance creates
> exceptional workplace experiences.

W hat do I mean by the modern workplace? We are right in the messy middle of a world that is changing how we work, live, and interact. I'm not sure yet, and no one really can be, how it will all turn out. In my workplace and on our leadership team, we are still very much debating and discussing what makes sense for our organization and how people will work in the future. We can all feel the world of work has changed, and I, personally, choose to believe it has changed for the better! If anything, I believe even more strongly that the concepts from this book, if applied effectively, can truly change our workplaces. We can all have exceptional work and life experiences.

As a three-time Gallup®[23] Exceptional Workplace Award Winner and four-time St. Louis Post Dispatch Top Workplace, Experitec has successfully created and (thus far) maintained an exceptional workplace. The path to this achievement and the practices necessary to maintain it are not expensive or highly complex. In fact, Experitec has less than 200 employees and, despite our size, implemented our approach to performance using internally developed tools and training, without external consultants, and with good old fashioned hard work! Creating an exceptional workplace *is* achievable for any business that *chooses* to put in the necessary effort to do so. Cost, resources, tools are all only partially related to success.

Success depends mostly on commitment and consistency. The path to an exceptional workplace is not easy. There is not one sure-fire way to achieve this result. Rather, the path to an exceptional workplace requires continuously evolving our performance in order to reach and maintain peak performance, being committed to consistently applying the four keys, and putting in the effort, energy, and hard work to cultivate peak performance in all people.

As a Leadership Team, implementing the principles of Lencioni's "The Advantage" we committed to creating a "healthy" organization first and "strategy" second.[86] We believed focusing on our culture, by implementing the right people and performance practices, could and would create business results. We use our Gallup® Q12® engagement scores to measure our effectiveness in using and implementing the four keys. When our business results fall short, we first look at our engagement scores and then focus on what we are doing or need to do to improve them.

---

[23] CliftonStrengths® and the CliftonStrengths 34 Themes of Talent are trademarks of Gallup, Inc. Gallup's content is Copyrighted by Gallup. Used with permission. All rights reserved.

Over our history using the Q12®[24], our engagement scores have almost always trended directly with our corporate performance. As our engagement went up so did our financial results. Even in 2020, when we experienced major disruption, financial challenges, and required a workforce reduction, our engagement scores went up. We reached our highest engagement score to date *during* these challenges.

You might be wondering... how was that possible? How can engagement go up when the business is making unpopular decisions? I believe our employee owners recognized the decisions were necessary and stayed committed to achieving results, and therefore, engagement remained high. Also, I truly believe we were already mostly operating at peak performance. We were ready, we adapted well, we acknowledged challenges, and we worked together!

Please know, I am not suggesting we will always be able to maintain such a high status of accomplishment and level of engagement. Even now, I am very much aware of the engagement challenges, performance issues, conflicts, and never-ending work to be done in the area of people and performance! Evolving our performance is never truly done! I can simplify our tools and processes but no matter what I do people are never going to be simple. Creating and remaining an exceptional workplace requires the ongoing effort of everyone working on their peak performance.

> *Tools and processes can be simplified but we can't make engaging and coaching people simple, people just aren't simple!*

---

[24] CliftonStrengths® and the CliftonStrengths 34 Themes of Talent are trademarks of Gallup, Inc. Gallup's content is Copyrighted by Gallup. Used with permission. All rights reserved.

By using the Gallup®[25] Q12® as an ongoing metric of how we are doing as an organization every six months, we can recalibrate and adjust as needed. These scores may go up, down, or stay the same, but they tell us where we need to focus and evolve our performance. They provide a guidepost for measuring how we are doing with our people and our culture. This guidepost allows us to adjust our focus and approach when inevitably issues arise. Without swift action when challenges occur the workplace is in jeopardy of no longer being exceptional.

WHY IS BETTER PERFORMANCE NEEDED IN THE MODERN WORKPLACE?

Many companies have made immense progress with respect to performance practices. However, many more have a long way to go. For the past five years or so, numerous companies have thrown out performance reviews and trialed a variety of methods for approaching performance differently. We now know and can begin to point to the success of these methods – the organizations that use them clearly see better results and create better workplaces for employees.[87]

As mentioned earlier, I think many of these approaches are quite similar. The Keys of Peak Performance are not entirely unique from other models or tools available. However, despite the availability of models and approaches, many organizations have still not shifted their practices. Yes, maybe they have removed the scores and numbers off performance reviews, but they kept the rating with words. As one HR leader told me, "Employees know exactly how the rating translates into words." They haven't truly transformed their approach to one where employees, managers, and leaders actively engage with and use the approach to execute their daily work.

---

[25] CliftonStrengths® and the CliftonStrengths 34 Themes of Talent are trademarks of Gallup, Inc. Gallup's content is Copyrighted by Gallup. Used with permission. All rights reserved.

Although some may think large companies have an advantage because they have more resources and finances to be successful, they frequently struggle the most to move away from their long-time, rigid practices. I am not sure why, but they find it hard to believe those performance reviews are doing more harm than good. They struggle to generate real value and results from most learning and development initiatives. In fact, their focus on training far surpasses that of creating true development experiences. Their effort focuses more on forms, tools, and activities than on cultivating the performance of their people. They fail to make impactful and necessary changes to truly help employees reach peak performance.

If companies can implement a better approach to performance, one which actually *evolves* performance, the result will be more exceptional workplaces! Selfishly, I might want Experitec to remain one of the very few recognized as being an exceptional workplace. However, I want more people to be able to experience helping create and work for an exceptional workplace. To live exceptional lives, we need to have exceptional workplace experiences. Therefore, I want to help all workplaces become exceptional and create these experiences for their employees so they can have exceptional lives.

Furthermore, we know exceptional workplaces produce greater results. Imagine a world where all people work for exceptional workplaces. Can you imagine the results? What could be possible? Breakthroughs in technology, healthcare, government, finance, and the environment – we might be able to achieve more than we ever realized was possible! If this concept doesn't excite you, I am not sure what will. Think of how we can change the world if we just focus on changing our performance in it!

> *We can change the world
> if we just focus on changing our performance in it!*

I know any workplace, anywhere, in any industry, with any number of employees, of any size can implement these practices and create an exceptional workplace! Even if your company is not yet ready to take these steps, as leaders and managers, we can start improving the workplace for our own teams. And as individuals, we can implement these practices to improve our performance and results! Everyone can impact and improve our workplaces, and everyone is needed to do so!

For many years now, workplaces have been concerned about improving the employee experience and likewise addressing engagement, performance, culture, and a slew of other HR-related initiatives. Instead of focusing solely on the employee experience, we must consider the full work and life experiences of employees. We must tap into what truly motivates people, helping them find both life and work satisfaction by creating exceptional experiences at work *and* in their lives.

We cannot have an exceptional work experience if our life experience is suffering and vice versa. We split our time between these areas so we must focus on strategies that allow us to improve in all parts of our lives. Although the principles in this book can be applied by anyone, workplaces must take responsibility to truly change and improve work and life experiences alongside their people.

WHAT DO WE NEED TO DO TO SET EXPECTATIONS IN THE WORKPLACE?

Every workplace is plagued with the disease of ineffective expectation setting – it is a virus we must fight frequently and consistently. Workplaces use job descriptions, how-to books, OKRs, and best practices to try to fight this disease. Unfortunately, despite their helpful insights, these tools rarely remedy the problem. Job descriptions tend to either be detailed enough to provide clarity (in which case a few months later, everything changes, and the description is no longer valid) or the job descriptions are too broad and include everything a person might be responsible for performing (in which case, they fail to provide clarity). The tool, the practice, and the technique are all helpful with setting expectations, but what really matters is consistency in communication.

I had an employee complain the job they were doing was not the job described in the job description. The feedback was fair, given I hate job descriptions and only use them for recruitment purposes. I struggle with job descriptions because they capture only one moment in time – when they were written. The world of work changes so rapidly that a job description grows stale quickly and tends to be more academic than actually useful to the employee performing the work.

I prefer an Outcomes, Responsibilities, and Goals (ORG) document (although any living document with a similar structure is likely superior to job descriptions). ORGs must be reviewed and updated frequently (weekly, monthly, or at least quarterly). If you are a leader in your workplace, consider how you could put in place expectation setting that is able to adapt to changing circumstances. As a manager, try collaboratively setting and frequently reviewing expectations with your people. If you are an employee – same advice. Create one for yourself, then ask your manager how aligned you are with what they see as your expectations. Give the process time. Active expectation setting can be uncomfortable at first as you get familiar with regular discussions on progress and changes. I promise you will see a major difference in results!

Employees need more expectations than just those necessary to perform their role. They need to understand the workplace expectations with real examples, not just platitudes placed on a PowerPoint. Workplaces must bring to life their vision, values, mission, and strategy by incorporating them into the work, providing frequent examples, and talking about them frequently in the context of performance.

At Experitec, we introduce employees at the start, and by "we," I mean our CEO. He discusses our culture with new employees, and we reinforce these elements by including them in our performance conversations. We provide examples in our monthly meetings related to our vision, mission, and values. Most importantly, we talk about our annual plan and provide regular updates on progress towards those goals we've set, helping employees recognize where their contributions are impacting our business results!

Clear and active expectation setting is not just between manager and employee, but is also necessary for different groups, roles, or positions in the organization and external stakeholders (suppliers, customers, etc.). One customer issue we dealt with provides a valuable example. Our customer wanted quotes back in two to three days from their request. Our salesperson committed to two to three days, believing it was two to three days from when we got the information, and that we'd get all the information we needed in a day or so. However, our resources responsible for quotes believed the expectation was two to three days from when they had all the information to fully quote the request. Getting all the information to fully quote the request, well... that could take weeks. As you can see, the team was set up for failure. This alignment on expectations is critical in all contexts – without it we frequently fail to deliver.

I can guarantee if you are not frequently setting and realigning on expectations in your workplace, then expectations are misaligned. Even if this is not having a major impact on your business yet, it can cause significant challenges in the future.

HOW DO WE CREATE VALUABLE FEEDBACK LOOPS IN OUR WORKPLACES?

Feedback can be valuable, but also tricky. How do we create a culture where feedback positively impacts our workplace and we avoid the drama of complaining, criticizing, and blaming? I struggle the most with this key and believe feedback can be hard in the workplace. It has taken me the longest to both give and receive feedback effectively (and I'll admit I'm still a work in progress). Since people expect to get feedback in the workplace, both positive and constructive, no feedback is undoubtedly the worst possible approach.

> **Attention:** Notice taken of someone or something; the regarding of someone or something as interesting or important; the action of dealing with or taking special care of someone or something.[88]
>
> **Connection:** a relationship in which a person, thing, or idea is linked or associated with something else[89]

I recently read what employees actually need most is attention.[90] Attention gets us partway there because they do need someone to take notice. But what they really need is connection. Employees need to have a relationship and feel like they can trust their leaders and, most importantly, their managers to tell them the truth and be direct, honest, and kind. Employees need to feel like they matter and are cared about by their managers and leaders. They need to hear how they are doing and progressing – be it positive or negative.

As always, trust is a requirement for giving and receiving feedback. Gallup®[26] Q12® includes a controversial question about having a best friend at work. When I first introduced the Q12® to our Leadership Team, two leaders had opposite reactions. One leader loved the question – it was his favorite question. The other leader wanted to remove or change the wording of the question. We are not the first or only group who has struggled with the question of having a best friend at work!

---

[26] CliftonStrengths® and the CliftonStrengths 34 Themes of Talent are trademarks of Gallup, Inc. Gallup's content is Copyrighted by Gallup. Used with permission. All rights reserved.

The employee experience behind this question relates to trust. Employees who know, like, and are truly friends with each other will inevitably trust each other. The closer our teams are, the more they are friends, and the more they trust each other, the easier it is to get work done, make decisions, and accomplish goals. By far my favorite part about our company is our friendships, relationships, and working with people I trust and like each day! Relationships and friendships matter! We spend a lot of time at work, and we need to encourage these relationships, not condemn them.

Workplaces must create opportunities for building relationships and trust. Managers cannot be effective without the trust of their teams. The days of "bad bosses" and managers who operate as dictators are coming to an end. Employees will vote with their feet by leaving organizations with bad bosses, those who fail to provide valuable feedback. For teams to work effectively, they require great managers who create a culture of trust by being willing to be vulnerable and authentic. Before we ever get to giving feedback, we must build trust within our teams and businesses.

For feedback to work, employees need to be getting more positive than negative feedback, which means workplaces need a culture of recognition. Many will grumble, "Why does everyone need a trophy?" But the truth is, our objective is to have our teams working at peak performance, and without recognition – we simply can't get there. We need to encourage team members to provide recognition regularly. People don't always need trophies, but they do need to know what they are doing is producing the right results. They need to know they are performing their job well.

Workplaces also need to create time and space for people to learn about each other so they can connect, build trust, and care about each other. We can't develop trusting relationships with people we don't know. Even in a remote environment, we must take time to ask questions, learn about how our teams spent the weekend, and ask what is happening with their children. Frankly, I struggle with this a lot. I typically want to get to my next task and chit-chatting is not my thing. But I know these moments build relationships and allow us to work more effectively together. The closer my relationships with my co-workers, the better our teams execute and operate.

Just recently, I was on a work call with a team of employees trying to solve a tough expectations alignment challenge. A few minutes into the call, while we were working together to solve the issue, one of the team members said, "Have I told you all how much I appreciate working with you lately?" I responded with, "I'm not sure that's directed at me, but I 100% agree and thank you so much for pointing it out." That felt so freaking good! A few hours later, I decided to do the same thing with another group who has been working hard to execute a ton of projects and doing phenomenal work. After discussing a number of challenges, I said, "I am so grateful this is the team of people I get to work with – you guys are just awesome!" And I truly meant it! That team is awesome, and they do phenomenal work, and it feels amazing to be on teams like this.

I wish all organizations, teams, and employees could have similar experiences. But I know from tons of interviews and conversations with employees we hire that this is not the case everywhere. We genuinely like each other, miss each other, and are friends with each other. When you know people well, have a high degree of trust, and, better yet, are actually friends – we typically always assume positive intent. And when there is an issue we go to the person quickly, ask the question, and work together to solve it. Conflict is significantly reduced.

I will not, however, pretend conflict is eliminated or that somehow a workplace becomes some idealistic utopia. Rather, we must become comfortable with the conflict, comfortable with the challenges, and ultimately comfortable with the discomfort itself. Ignoring challenges, failing to address issues, or moving on without addressing conflict fails to provide the information necessary for growth. We need to acknowledge when we are falling short and engage in meaningful discussions to find the solutions.

After a recent move of our customer service team to take on new activities, they needed input and feedback when they made mistakes so they could learn from them. With everyone's urgency, they frequently would not hear if they were right or not. In a group call, everyone agreed to be better about reaching out and messaging the other person. Remember, it's not personal – it's about reaching peak performance!

WHAT IS NEEDED FOR GROWTH AND DEVELOPMENT IN OUR WORKPLACES?

We just discussed the challenges with feedback in the workplace, but this input is necessary and required for learning, growth, and development to occur. Frequently, we hear how organizations struggle with change, and what is development but just another example of change? When we grow and develop, we are changing ourselves and our capabilities and evolving our performance. Workplaces need to reconsider how they approach growing and developing people.

Transforming How we Learn & Grow

Businesses have been trying to perfect training and development programs for decades. I am sure some would disagree, but I am not sure these efforts have been very successful. Don't get me wrong – developing understanding by getting training and learning about key concepts, knowledge, skills, and competencies is necessary. However, workplaces need to get better at more intentionally incorporating exposure and experiences.

New opportunities with VR/AR could transform our ability to do this in the very near future. At a conference, I saw a demonstration of technology that trained people on responding to a live gunman in the workplace. They lived through the experience of being confronted with a gun without putting their lives actually at risk. These types of training, whether with technology or the old school way of simulations and roleplay, are critical to development. Everyone groans when they hear roleplay, but we learn much more when we are forced to practice.

When Experitec trained managers on having Compensation Conversations, each manager practiced giving the conversation and fellow managers provided feedback. When we conducted workplace respect training, our leadership team facilitated discussions around roleplay examples, giving each employee the opportunity to practice being the victim, the bad actor, the bystander, and the manager. They took turns describing what they would say and do in the situation. Most employees gave feedback that it was helpful to practice saying the words and, in many cases, they learned things they didn't know from the situations themselves.

As workplaces, we must assume people don't have the necessary experiences. In most instances, no matter how long you have worked, you could still use additional experience to perform better. By providing employees the chance to practice and experience situations, we ensure they are better prepared when they encounter them in the workplace.

As I developed tools and strategies around the four keys, I first used every single one myself. The ones that failed didn't make it in this book! I totally believe in experiencing any tool, technique, approach, or strategy before recommending it. I've tried to have my TM Generalists also experience management by managing interns – they need to know what it feels like and how hard it can be. When you read the words, it sounds much easier than it is in reality when you have to think on your feet and respond in the moment.

Likewise, exposure to others is underutilized as a development tool in the workplace. Years ago, there were apprenticeships, and people learned their jobs almost solely from others. Today we have mentorships, coaches, and partners – with varying degrees of success. We want and need employees to observe how others handle particular situations, so they know how to respond, what to say, and what to do. Those in manager roles need this type of exposure even more so to improve their performance management skills. Opportunities to practice conversations, responses, and strategies must become a regular part of our interactions. We must encourage this type of roleplay and preparation, as it will certainly create much better outcomes in the performance of our people.

The challenge with creating these opportunities is going to grow as more workplaces move to hybrid models. Therefore, opportunities to observe must be more intentionally considered and created for employees to truly learn and grow. My team members tell me all the time how they have picked up on things from watching me and seeing how I lead and work. Let's not lose this critical element of development!

Strengths Based Development (rather than weakness fixing)

We must stop focusing on what is wrong with people and trying to "fix" them. The more we focus on weaknesses, or where people struggle, the less opportunity we have to see them grow to their full potential. Leveraging strengths in the workplace is incredibly powerful and beneficial to our teams and businesses.

As I mentioned previously, my sales team does regular development calls around sales competencies. The more everyone sees these as an opportunity for growth, to share and learn from one and other, and that by doing so they will see greater results in their performance (and pockets!) the more the momentum grows! Rather than resist the sales assessments, they are embracing them and identifying strategies to enhance their performance and generate greater sales results.

On a personal note, I'd put my sales team (and really our whole company) up against almost any sales team. Their focus on performing even better than they already are today will help them be the best in the world at what they do. We aren't playing to just beat our competition; we are playing to beat our own best performance! I'd like to think every business wants to do the same. As a business, we must incorporate these practices into how we performance manage our organizations.

Many businesses hold talent reviews to discuss and consider the development of employees. (Note: A talent review is not a performance review, rather, it is when the manager presents their employee's development and current performance to our leadership team and discusses their plan for continuing to develop the employee. Then the Manager meets with the employee to provide them feedback and development actions.) When we do talent reviews, we include each employee's Top Five Talents while we discuss that employee. Frequently, the greatest challenges or issues with that employee are centered around the basements of their talents. By keeping them top of mind, we can highlight how to coach the employee around those limitations and identify strategies to leverage their strengths instead. We can achieve the same outcomes with different talents, but we have to coach employees on how to use and develop them! We hold talent reviews annually for all employees – this keeps employee growth and development in focus and every employee on our radar as leaders.

We also need to develop teams which have complementary talents. My lowest talent (34) is Analytical®[27] – I struggle with spreadsheets and numbers! I have a team member who has Analytical® in her top 5 (as does my husband and sister) and I frequently partner with them to help me when I have something that requires that skillset. Something that might take me days only takes

---

[27] CliftonStrengths® and the CliftonStrengths 34 Themes of Talent are trademarks of Gallup, Inc. Gallup's content is Copyrighted by Gallup. Used with permission. All rights reserved.

them a few hours. Likewise, I can draft an email or frame a written document with ease. When something needs to be communicated, I'm your gal! In our businesses, we need to consider creating teams with this balance. Rather than making individuals well-rounded, we need to review our teams and help make the team well-rounded!

Completely New Learning and Career Models for Work

The historically successful model for learning has been a "scalable efficiency model" where the primary focus is on performing complex tasks efficiently and reliably at scale.[91] "The alternative... scalable learning [is] the ability to learn faster at scale... learning in the form of creating new knowledge by confronting situations that have never been seen before and developing new approaches to create value. It's learning through action, not just sitting, and reading books or thinking great new thoughts. Rather than standardize all tasks, the most efficient way to respond to rapidly changing contexts will be to learn faster about the new approaches that will deliver the most value efficiently."[92]

Our future requires a new approach to learning which is scalable and ever-changing. Our traditional career ladders will not be useful much longer as our organizations are challenged to re-invent how we execute work, grow in our careers, and change roles or responsibilities more frequently. We will need to find ways to learn completely new roles as we grow throughout our careers. Instead of moving from one specific job up to the next rung on the ladder, we will be growing our capabilities for the next role while still in our current role. And the next role could be entirely different as we navigate changing organizational structures and new workplace requirements.

HOW DO WE ENSURE CULTURES OF ACCOUNTABILITY IN OUR WORKPLACES?

Usually, performance issues in the workplace are the result of one of three things: unclear expectations, misalignment with the role, and most often – a lack of accountability. When addressing performance issues, the first two can be addressed to help the employee be successful. But accountability is much harder to improve. Although, I've seen moderately accountable people improve their accountability mindset, I have rarely seen someone with a complete lack of accountability improve substantially. And I've noticed the further into a career an individual is the harder it becomes to make a change in their mindset.

What's worse is anytime you have an employee with a lack of accountability, it spreads like a weed. That person pulls someone else in and soon they are complaining and blaming together, then they pull another person in and so on. Until they hit a person with an accountability mindset, it truly spreads like a disease through your office.

One of the most significant contributors to a lack of accountability is resistance to change. Change is not quite as complex as many consultants and experts would like you believe. Ultimately our mindset, with respect to our own ability to change, is the greatest factor in reaching peak performance. Maybe a better way exists than creating complex change management processes, multi-step communication strategies, or coaxing and convincing our people to change. What if, instead, we prepare our people for change by helping them develop the capabilities necessary to be successful in any change they may experience with an accountability mindset?

Being truly accountable means that we don't run away from the discomfort and change. Rather, we embrace the discomfort and learn to operate in the space of discomfort. We allow all the chaos and complexity to happen around us and stand firm in our belief that we have the ability to be successful.

Many, many, many books have been written on accountability. I think virtually every business knows its importance to achieving results. Why then is an accountability mindset so elusive in our workplaces? I think the challenge is incorporating accountability into workplace practices and explaining how it fits together. We talk about accountability rather than identify ways to incorporate and embed it into everything we do. And, even more importantly, when we see a lack of accountability like a weed, we need to deal with it right away before it grows and overtakes our gardens.

Accountability is intentionally cultivated and developed over time. My level of accountability has grown as I have worked to develop my capabilities. Workplaces must spend as much time on accountability as they do on other training. They need to incorporate accountability into their performance practices, both managers and employees need to be trained, and the culture must promote it. Then, every person is empowered to respond and address issues as they arise. All employees in the workplace must take ownership of and accountability for the engagement, culture, and results of the organization. Unless everyone is contributing, creating true accountability is not possible.

In our organization, accountability is so well-trained that people admit when they are about to demonstrate a lack of accountability before they even do it. They say, "Well this is probably just complaining or venting, and I probably shouldn't go down this path but I'm about to go in a hole!" I think this self-recognition is great. It means we know what we are doing, and we know it's probably not productive. I'll allow the person a few moments to express their emotion – frustration, exhaustion, insecurity – and then together we can ask, what is the next best thing we can do? I now have employees beat me to the words – they say, "I know you are going to say what is the next best thing we can do?" and immediately start telling me what they are going to do!

We must remember we can't eliminate a lack of accountability – it will happen, it's the human condition. But we can help people see it, acknowledge it, give them the skills to get out of it, and move on to more productive behavior. Simply, how do we keep them from falling in the hole, get them out quickly, and give them the tools to avoid the hole in the first place! I've seen the benefits of our efforts here probably more than in any area – I see our teams work well together most of the time and handle issues very effectively. We still have our challenges, but this effort has gone a long way to creating an exceptional work experience.

Conclusion and Reflection

We are nearing "The Great Resignation," a period of time when more people will be resigning from jobs possibly than ever before. As employees re-evaluated their lives during the pandemic, they discovered a desire to live and work differently. People recognized the benefits of working remotely on their families, health, and overall well-being. Many people used the time to self-reflect and determine their purpose and what they want from their lives. As a result, employees are reconsidering how they want to work and live their lives and choosing new careers as a result. As workplaces, we have an opportunity to embrace or reject this shift in culture and either evolve our workplaces or risk the effects of failing to do so. As individuals considering how we want to work and live, we have the ability to influence our futures by choosing what is best for ourselves and our families. We can apply the four keys to evolve our performance and reach peak performance in the workplace.

Expectations: *Consider how you can ensure all expectations are visible. How can you incorporate them into your performance practices and conversations? How can you relate what people are doing to your strategy and corporate goals? How will you ensure ongoing alignment and clarity?*

Feedback: *How can we make sure we learn about and build trust with those we are working with in the workplace? What will we do to learn about the strengths of our teams and spend time developing meaningful relationships? How* *will we provide regular feedback on what employees are doing well and what we want them to keep doing? How will we continue to improve our performance?*

Development: *As workplaces change and our careers evolve, we must develop new and different capabilities. How will we identify these capabilities, incorporate learning opportunities, and frequently experience growth? What can we do to incorporate strengths into our development and increase our ability to be successful at developing?*

Accountability: *How will we incorporate accountability into our workplace cultures? What will we do to train our employees to get out of the hole?*

CHAPTER THIRTEEN
Navigating our Homes

How the keys to Peak
Performance apply at home?

Roles: Spouse, Parent, Child, Sister, Brother, Grandparent

> ### Key Insight:
>
> By evolving my performance in
> my role at home, I can create better
> outcomes for my family.

Ever seen right at the beginning of a major thunderstorm how the clouds are moving towards each other from different directions? When the fronts come together, they create friction, which is what causes the thunderstorm. When systems collide, the clouds turn dark, lightning strikes, and thunder roars, shaking our homes. During the storm, it can be loud, dark, and scary or it can be beautiful, brilliant, and exciting, depending on your perspective. When the storm is over, the calm, quiet, and peace returns, the sun comes out, and sometimes we even get to see a rainbow.

My grandfather, Robert Zimmermann, served as a
sailor in the US Navy and used to reference the old
adage, "Red sky at night, sailors delight. Red sky in the
morning, sailors take warning." He knew a red sky in
the morning meant a thunderstorm may be approaching and the
sailors needed to be warned to prepare the ship for the storm. He
was also an avid fisherman, who preferred not to get caught in a
storm while fishing!

Our family relationships can be like these storms – with fronts
coming together from different directions (different lives,
experiences, perspectives, personalities, and ideas about life). When
they come together, conflict is inevitable, and it can be quite the
storm! During the family storm, it can feel overwhelming, chaotic,
and too much to handle. When we are surrounded by the mess of the
storm – screaming children, unhappy spouses, family dysfunction,
and our own anger and exhaustion – our boat is knocked around by
the storm. If unprepared, we may lose our footing, the boat can be
thrown off course, and it can be scary.

The challenge we face is preparing our boat (our family) for the
storms we will face. So, when the storms come, we remain calm
amidst the chaos. We can keep the boat on track even as the wind
and waves try to knock us off course. We must be prepared for the
storm, knowing what to do when it happens. We must develop the
skills to navigate the storms and the tools to light our way through
them. We must know what is expected to traverse through the storm
and safely come out the other side together! Even when prepared, we
may still be knocked around, but we will maintain our course, and it
can be beautiful and exciting.

We've all experienced these family storms and we know what to
expect. When we consider the role we serve in our homes, our
greatest challenge is to prepare, navigate, and enjoy the calm after the
storm. The experience and lessons of the storms are what create the
opportunity to celebrate the rainbows of life. Our families will have

moments of joy and moments of struggle – we can learn to celebrate both by evolving and reaching peak performance!

As we move from our workplaces into our homes, I may lose some readers who feel this is too invasive to their private lives. However, I felt it was important to address the roles we serve outside the workplace. These roles are often even more important to us than the ones we perform in the workplace, and rarely do we get the framework and tools to impact our performance at home.

I want to recognize and acknowledge everyone's family is different. I actually love the variety we see within families today and the relationships that develop as a result. I can't possibly address every family dynamic or relationship in your home; therefore, I ask you to reflect on your own relationships and relate where you can to the examples I provide. Please know I respect your family, your choices, and your performance in your home.

One final note – for those in abusive, neglectful, or otherwise harmful relationships in their homes – I encourage you to seek out expertise. Although I believe these principles can be applied in our homes – they are not meant to solve the problems created by dysfunction, abuse, and harmful relationships. By all means, take what is valuable, but know that this alone will not be a remedy for the unique challenges you face.

WHY IS IMPROVING PERFORMANCE IN MY HOME IMPORTANT?

For me, my family relationships have a significant impact on my overall life satisfaction. When I am in conflict with my spouse, parent, or child, it inevitably impacts everything in my life. Although most everyone will recognize how important these roles are, we rarely put additional thought into evolving our performance in them. We take these roles for granted. We fail to prioritize anything which isn't required including evolving our performance. However, evolving our performance is necessary for creating a better life and future for everyone in our home.

Take, for example, our earlier analogy of the walls in our home. If our house is built on a poor foundation, the walls actually will move, the floors will crumble, and everything, no matter how beautiful, built on top of this wobbly foundation can (and probably will) be destroyed. When I think of this, I think of divorce. If we fail to build a good foundation in our marriage – no matter how beautiful our careers or our parenting – it may all crumble due to the cracks in the foundation. But if we see and fix these issues early enough, we may be able to avoid future damage.

Regardless of where you are in your role today, whether things are wonderful or challenging, the storms will come – conflict will happen, challenges will arise, and storms will rock your home. Preparing our families with a good foundation of performance practices will make a significant difference during the storm. And, if you are already struggling amidst a storm, consider using the performance keys to fix your foundation, navigate the storm, and come out able to appreciate the growth you've experienced.

We must recognize evolving our performance in these roles is critical for having an exceptional life. In fact, without putting effort into our performance at home, we are going to struggle to have an exceptional life. And even if your efforts are solitary at first, I am willing to bet if you start working these keys for yourself and your own performance – your family members will notice, and they will want to make similar improvements. I mean – why wouldn't we all want to have exceptional life experiences together with our families?

HOW DO WE ESTABLISH EXPECTATIONS IN OUR HOMES?

While workplaces have job descriptions for discussing expectations, our homes do not. Although books exist on nearly every topic, most of us don't approach these roles the same way we do in the workplace. Unlike the workplace, we don't set aside time for clarifying expectations (barring a religious or cultural expectation). We don't go to school to get a degree, take courses, or get coaching. We don't take time to learn how to be effective. We might take a class for a few hours before the birth of our child that covers the very basics of childbirth and parenthood. But I spent eight years in school (college, grad school, and law school) to learn my profession. I barely spent eight days learning how to be a mom.

When conflict and storms arise, we may seek out assistance, look for answers, and try to address the issues we see during the storm. But rarely do we take the time to build the skills and acquire the tools or experience to be prepared for the storms and how we handle the storms. Although the information and research are readily available to evolve our performance in our roles at home, we typically don't see these roles as requiring intentional effort. However, by creating clear expectations we can better weather the storms, improve our interactions, and create exceptional life experiences in our homes!

Creating Expectations in Marital Relationships

For most of us, our marital or spousal relationship is probably the most critical and foundational to our life satisfaction and happiness. When we get caught up in life's chaos, our marriages are often the first place we fail to set and align expectations. When spouses have different expectations of the marriage, conflict is inevitable. I'm early in my marriage and won't claim to have life-long wisdom, however, I do have two sets of grandparents that were married over fifty years and my parents, who have been together since high school, and married for over forty years. Their example, combined with my early years of marriage, provide the basis for my insights.

Both prior to and early on in our marriage, my husband and I spent time discussing our wants and needs for our relationship and the future, in other words our expectations. However, these discussions couldn't have and certainly didn't take into consideration the many things that would be different from what we expected, planned, and anticipated. For example, we both wanted children, but we never anticipated having twins. We both wanted to work, but we never anticipated the challenges of us each having careers involving travel with young children. We anticipated challenges, but we never anticipated the significant health issues I experienced and their impact on our lives.

As change occurs in our lives, we must evaluate how it impacts our marriage expectations. I read an article that older individuals are getting divorced more than ever before. The article shared people are beginning to recognize their lives have changed and their relationships are no longer desired in this new life. I believe, based upon my own observations, that unless we find a way to change and grow together – we will grow apart. Simply operating in life side by side, in the same bed, sharing the same experiences is not enough. We must consciously choose to connect, share, communicate, learn, and grow *with* each other. The only way we can accomplish this objective is to be consciously and continuously realigning on marriage and family expectations.

We must take time to learn about, discuss, and align on expectations. As long as our expectations are mis-aligned we will experience conflict, frustration, and discord in our marriages and thereby our families. We must be clear on our family values, our vision for our families and how our personal visions fit with them, the direction we are going as a family, who has which responsibilities in the family, what we hope to accomplish as a family, and how we want to live as a family. These conversations may be some of the most important ones we ever have in our lives. They can shape the future of our families and our children.

Once again, I am not suggesting that healthy equals perfect. There is no perfect marriage. Marriages involve bringing people together, and any time you have people, you can't have perfect. We are all different, complex, and interesting human beings with differences that are beautiful but inevitably cause conflict. Rather, healthy means always striving for a balance in our relationship that keeps things as productive and purposeful as possible. I recognize this will be a life-long objective – but at least I'll be working at it with my best friend in the best way I know how!

Our Role as Parents

As parents, children do not come with an instruction guide (believe me I've looked!). I've always found it baffling to drive a vehicle, practice a profession, or become a citizen, we have to pass a test, but to have a child, which is certainly the most difficult thing we ever do in our lives, there is no such test. I am a mother to three children – a son and twin girls – and fully appreciate that parenthood does not come with a manual!

Parenting is the single hardest, most challenging, and also the most rewarding role we play in our lives. Many books have been written on pregnancy, childbirth, and parenting – and they have changed dramatically over the years. If you look back at older books, they recommend lots of blankets to keep the baby warm, in current books the exact opposite is recommended. Over the decades, parenting advice has changed over and over again – corporal punishment is needed, any physical punishment is detrimental, time-outs are good, time-outs are bad, and time-ins are better, and so on.

The rapidly changing advice, and therefore expectations of parenthood, make finding clarity even more challenging. Every parent (barring some psychological or developmental condition) wants what is best for their children and tries to make good choices. However, the secret every parent knows (but no one tells you until you join the club) is that all parents are just guessing! We don't really know what we are doing, rather we just do our best and hope we don't screw it up!

I distinctly remember realizing one night after nursing both my girls and putting my son to bed, "Holy crap, I am really an adult and in charge of these three children! When did that happen? How did I get here?" Don't get me wrong, I love and adore my children with all of my heart, but I never anticipated what it would feel like to realize suddenly you are fully a parent. I never experienced the transition of having to learn parenting. Parenting is special in that you continuously learn in the process and get very little preparation.

What is the purpose, goal, or outcome of our role as parents? What are we supposed to be accomplishing? Are we simply supposed to keep our children alive or are we meant to do more in our role as parents?

> *As parents, we are meant to nurture our children through life so they can learn, grow, and evolve as human beings.*

We must set expectations for ourselves which help us to achieve this purpose. We must identify how, what, when, and where we want our children to learn, grow, and evolve. We must determine the beliefs we want them to hold and purposely perform our role as parents.

Unfortunately, understanding how we purposely perform as a new parent is difficult. As new mothers, we are often left guessing regarding our experiences. I learned (after having three children) that all mothers experience dark intrusive thoughts and these are actually natural and normal occurrences after the birth of a child. What are intrusive thoughts? They are the thoughts born of exhaustion, pain, and lack of sleep that cause tremendous irrational fear of harm coming to your child, or that you will cause harm to your child, or that you want to walk away because you can't keep doing what feels impossible. When I went through these feelings, I thought something was wrong with me (as I am sure many women do). I had no idea they were normal because no one had ever set the expectation – and the lack of communication on this topic causes many to struggle.

By better understanding the knowledge and information related to parenting, we can better prepare and evolve our performance as parents. We must determine for our families what expectations we will operate based upon, and these must not be built using social media as the guide. We must build our foundation of expectations based upon our family values, vision, goals, and needs.

I know many mothers who struggle significantly with the beautiful pictures posted on Facebook by other parents as the bar set for what you "should" be doing as a parent. You know the pictures and posts I am talking about – the first day of school, family photos at pumpkin patch/zoo/vacation, perfect 1st birthday cake, beautiful hospital newborn baby, completely organized home, and many more! I give the mothers and parents who are able to accomplish these objectives many props and congratulations – I have often wished I could measure up to those expectations. I, however, have learned motherhood and parenting expectations are different for me, and I have created expectations to fit my family's personal values, vision, life goals, and needs.

We must carefully craft these expectations to fit what is reasonably necessary to create exceptional home life experiences – and not expectations created to impress others! We must not expect more than any human being is capable of achieving. I know well what it feels like to be torn between failure as a mom or failure at work – always failing never succeeding. I have had to let go of the fear, control, guilt, and shame and make the choice that feels right for my family, accepting that time apart helps us feel joy when we are together again.

We must trust ourselves to choose the right expectations and goals for our families and learn to adjust as needed. No one, not your parents, not your friends, not even your religious leader or counselor can tell you what the right decision is for *your* family, in *your* situation, in *your* life. We must trust ourselves to know what expectations are needed in our family. And then we must do the work to create and align on them. Then, we must take action on them to move our vision for our family forward with goals to achieve those exceptional experiences.

We thrive when we have a positive goal to move toward, not just a negative state we are trying to move away from.

Emily & Amelia Nagoski [93]

As a result of my life experiences – health issues, knowledge, self-awareness, upbringing, learning – I determined what type of parent I would be and what was most important to my parenting. As a result, I have vowed as a parent:

*   To be present in the moments I spend with my children, called Lifetime Movie Moments!
*   To say **yes** whenever I can and enjoy their requests whenever possible.
*   To encourage all feelings and emotions – good, bad, and sad.
*   To recognize everyone experiences challenges when processing these feelings and emotions.
*   To strive to avoid shaming my children.
*   To do my best to always do what I believe to be best for my children trusting my own instincts.
*   To nurture my children, helping them to learn, grow, and evolve.

* To support them and who they are and want to be – no matter what that is. (Even if my son wants to be an astronaut and that terrifies me as a mother!)
* And, when I inevitably make a mistake, to simply acknowledge the mistake and change for the better.

I use these guideposts for myself as expectations to help me stay on track and make good decisions as a parent. Try crafting some expectations for yourself that will serve as a guide and make sure you align these expectations with your children's other caregivers. I've been through a painful experience where the caregiver for my child did not share my beliefs and my child suffered as a result. We must respect the fact that expectations are different in every family. We cannot judge another family by the standards and expectations of our own. Each family must set expectations with their children based upon what is needed and unique to the members of that particular family.

HOW DO I GIVE AND RECEIVE FEEDBACK AT HOME?

Many of you may see the word feedback and cringe in response to this concept in our homes. Honestly, we don't really want or need unsolicited feedback from outsiders in the roles we perform especially at home. Or at least, we don't want feedback from most people. I 100% understand this feeling! How dare that other mother or sister-in-law or man judge you and disguise their criticism as "feedback!" They don't know you, they don't know your family, and they don't have a right to tell you what to do.

In the chapter on feedback, I mentioned the need to build your pyramid one brick at time and to learn what is below the surface of the iceberg. These concepts are probably even more important in our homes than in our workplaces. If we want to have deep, meaningful, loving, caring connections with our families, we must truly get to know who they are as people. We can't assume because we've spent years with them that we fully understand them. In fact, as I mentioned earlier, many people go their whole lives without ever developing self-awareness. If they are not yet personally self-aware, learning about others will be similarly challenging.

Learning about our Spouses and Family Members

Each relationship is based upon the unique talents, values, and beliefs of those in the family. Early in my marriage, my husband took the Gallup®[28] StrengthsFinder® assessment, and the results forever changed our marriage. I know that sounds dramatic, but the insights were significant. Two of my husband's top strengths are Deliberative® (which means he takes his time making decisions in order to evaluate and mitigate risk) and Responsibility® (which means he takes psychological ownership of anything he commits to, whether it is large or small, and feels emotionally bound to follow it through to completion). In a general sense, I knew these things about him, but did not appreciate how much they were impacting our marriage.

> **Deliberative®:** People exceptionally talented in the Deliberative theme are best described by the serious care they take in making decisions or choices. They anticipate obstacles.
>
> **Responsibility®:** People exceptionally talented in the Responsibility theme take psychological ownership of what they say they will do. They are committed to stable values such as honesty and loyalty.

---

[28] CliftonStrengths® and the CliftonStrengths 34 Themes of Talent are trademarks of Gallup, Inc. Gallup's content is Copyrighted by Gallup. Used with permission. All rights reserved.

> **Strategic®:** People exceptionally talented in the Strategic theme create alternative ways to proceed. Faced with any given scenario, they can quickly spot the relevant patterns and issues.
>
> **Adaptability®:** People exceptionally talented in the Adaptability theme prefer to go with the flow. They tend to be "now" people who take things as they come and discover the future one day at a time.

His strengths of Responsibility® and Deliberative® meant he needed time to think and, once he decides, you can always trust him to carry through. Unlike my husband, I do not have high Responsibility® so when I said I would do something and didn't (ran out of time or didn't prioritize it), he would get really frustrated! I never understood why he was so upset, but he was expecting me to follow through on my commitments like he would. My mind was blown! He also requires time to think about big decisions or discussions. Anytime we have a big topic, I will plant the seed a few days before – say we need to talk about buying a car, a trip, my career – and then give him time to think before we do!

Our different strengths allowed us to better understand why we would behave in particular ways. This has allowed us to leverage each other's strengths in our marriage and balance each other out. I like to plan (Strategic®[29]), and he is always able to deal with surprises (Adaptability®). Our strengths are different, and we're married – so of course there is conflict. Once we had the language of strengths to talk about why we are the way we are – we could actually come up with solutions. Now when we have conflict (which, of course, every married couple does) we are able to give each other the feedback in a way that helps it be well received.

---

[29] CliftonStrengths® and the CliftonStrengths 34 Themes of Talent are trademarks of Gallup, Inc. Gallup's content is Copyrighted by Gallup. Used with permission. All rights reserved.

The belief that the people around us will reciprocate in proportion to what we give them is called "trust."

Emily Nagoski, in Burnout[94]

We must also build a foundation of trust. Developing trust and a connection with your family can be harder than you think. In fact, sometimes being vulnerable with our families can be more difficult because the reaction (like rejection, criticism, or judgement) can hurt more than those in the workplace ever could. Let me make this very clear – until you know each other AND trust each other to respond in a way that works for everyone, feedback is never going to help!

Feedback From our Children

Thinking about the elements of feedback with our children or even other family members gets even trickier. Children are not particularly equipped to provide feedback. Their feedback is filtered through their lens which lacks perspective. We must remember we are not parenting our children to win an award from them or for them to like us best. Rather, we need to parent our children, so they recognize and reward us as adults with lives that demonstrate they learned, grew, and evolved successfully. We are making decisions as parents not for this moment, but for the many years to come. And we will need to take their feedback and input with a grain of salt.

However, we must not ignore the information our children are sharing. I mentioned having a challenge with a childcare provider and expectations. At the time, my son was barely 3 years old and switched from happy and sweet to acting out, angry, yelling, and occasionally being violent. I knew something had changed, but thought it was a phase. I was wrong and he was trying to tell me something. He was trying to tell me his care provider was causing him harm. He would cry when he knew we were leaving him with her (previously he loved spending his days with her).

One day I checked the cameras in our house. What I saw certainly could have been much worse, but my breath caught in my throat and my stomach turned over. My son was being screamed at daily, sent to his room for hours, and put in "time-out" for long stretches of time. When he remained upset, she pinned him to the ground between her legs, twisted his arms, and he cried out in pain. She was our care provider his whole life, but we parted ways that weekend and never saw her again.

I tell this story because I think it's important to listen to what our children are telling us. Pay close attention to what they are saying, why they are saying it, and ask *lots* of questions. We don't necessarily have to internalize all the feedback, but we should at least consider what they are telling us and ensure we understand. This is how we build trust with our children, connect with our children, care for our children, and motivate our children.

We must also celebrate the uniqueness of our children. Even my twins are completely different with totally different personalities. I try to foster what they enjoy, encourage, and support them, and seek opportunities to expose them to new experiences. I also secretly (or not so secretly, since I'm writing it here) regularly try to guess what their strengths will be some day. I'm fairly certain my son will have Woo®[30] and Communication® – he loves to win others over, makes friends anywhere he goes, and talks more than me (which is not an easy accomplishment). My daughter, Arabella, will most certainly have Command® (or I hope she will) – she is strong, opinionated, and confident even with the big kids. My Scarlett is my little bird – I think she will have Focus®. She can concentrate on single tasks for such a long time for such a little baby! I may be wrong, or I may be right, but I love watching them grow and learning more about them every day.

---

[30] CliftonStrengths® and the CliftonStrengths 34 Themes of Talent are trademarks of Gallup, Inc. Gallup's content is Copyrighted by Gallup. Used with permission. All rights reserved.

Recognition, Recognition, and more Recognition

Trust your body. Be kind to yourself. You are enough, just as you are right now. Your joy matters. Please tell everyone you know.

Emily & Amelia Nagoski, in Burnout

Once you establish trust and relationships, then you can provide healthy and valuable feedback. Positive reinforcement is 1000% more important at home than in the workplace. The work we do for our families in our homes deserves recognition as much, if not more, than what we do in the workplace. We are often far too critical of ourselves and our performance in our roles at home. We must recognize our learning and growth as spouses and as parents to reinforce these behaviors. And we must look for opportunities to do the same for others!

When giving feedback, start with *only* positive examples. Spend as much time as you can providing your family members with positive reinforcement on what they do that you like, love, or even just want them to keep doing. Like I mentioned earlier, my husband and I developed a habit to say thank you for every little thing we do! This practice has carried over into my other family relationships – I try my best to show gratitude and point out when my family members do something worthy of mention. I've watched some of these moments transform the day for my sisters. When one of us gives the other support, positive feedback, and acknowledges our performance – the feeling is indescribable.

I think this is especially important for heads of household (or those who do the majority of the unpaid work at home). Those roles don't get peer feedback, and generally kids are giving the opposite of recognition. The massive amount of work that gets accomplished in the home goes completely unnoticed and unacknowledged most of the time. This work is *very* real work – we need to reinforce how meaningful it is for the other person to do it! Take, for example, a world without houses getting cleaned, dinners getting made, children fed, bathed, dressed, and sent off to school. Our worlds don't work without the household work also getting done. For those who have to accomplish it all let me just say this:

> You are amazing! You are superheroes and superwomen! You deserve a round of applause and a standing ovation! Thank you for keeping up with this work. Thank you for doing it even though you aren't paid for it. Thank you for everything you do and every sacrifice you make to get this work done! (And anytime you need it – come back to this page and re-read this little bit of recognition. Or, better yet, go post on the group page and let others who understand the need for recognition and reinforcement do it for you!)

I am blessed in life to share much of this work with my husband – in fact, we've tried to split it based on what we enjoy most and how our strengths align best. For me, vacuuming, mopping, and cleaning counters feels good using my Achiever®[31]; organizing allows my Maximizer® to feel I am making things great; and talking with my kids allows me to use my Communication®! My husband ensures the work required on deadlines like trash, recyclables, and doctor appointments are completed on time using his Responsibility® strength, and he keeps up with the daily dishes created by our children using his Adaptability® strength. I encourage you to play with your strengths in the household work and find a division that works in your family.

Leading up to this past Mother's Day, I saw a Facebook post in one of the Working Women Facebook groups I am a part of saying:

---

[31] CliftonStrengths® and the CliftonStrengths 34 Themes of Talent are trademarks of Gallup, Inc. Gallup's content is Copyrighted by Gallup. Used with permission. All rights reserved.

"Ok Ladies, tell us what you bought for yourself this Mother's Day!" I loved, I mean really loved this post. I commented, "Can I just say I love love love 💜 this! I love we all care enough about ourselves and being mothers to make sure even if no one else does we recognize ourselves! Way to go mamas! You all rock and deserve everything you buy yourself!!!!!"

Likewise, I think we all need to do this for ourselves. Take the time to recognize all the great things you are doing and treat yourself occasionally! The roles we perform at home are hard and the work we do deserves recognition – in some cases we may just need to recognize ourselves.

HOW DO I DEVELOP AND GROW IN MY HOME?

Earlier I shared we are meant to nurture our children through life so they can learn, grow, and evolve as human beings. We are meant to do this with all family relationships – to learn from them, grow together, and evolve our performance in new and better ways. Despite intuitively knowing growth and development are important to the evolution of our roles and relationships at home, we rarely allocate the time to focus on improving. We tend to perform our roles and not think much about our performance in them. We are missing a significant opportunity for development. Our families mean so much to us, why not continue growing and developing on purpose in these roles?

Our growth at home is essential to weathering the storm. Think of the tree in a storm – if the tree's roots lack strength, the tree will be ripped from the ground during a storm. Likewise, we must identify our strengths and leverage them to grow our roots – the things we are naturally talented at – to be prepared for the storms which will come. We can't run away from the discomfort and change we will face in our lives. Rather, we must embrace the discomfort and learn to operate in this space. We must allow the wind to blow and storms to rage while we stay rooted in our own beliefs, capabilities, and trust in ourselves.

Initially, those in a new marriage or who have become new parents are experiencing frequent growth and development. I know I have been transformed by motherhood both physically and emotionally. And marriage – well that's been a growing experience for sure! When we are new at something we are almost always learning and growing, but over time we get comfortable and believe we have mastered a role (or at least are pretending we have so no one realizes our perceived deficiency!).

Our culture has historically supported tradition in our family practices based upon many people continuing to perform the way things have always been performed. Ever heard the song from Fiddler on the Roof about tradition? In my family, anytime we talk about change someone bursts into singing this song!

Tradition, tradition... Tradition
Tradition, tradition... Tradition
"Because of our traditions, we've kept our balance for many, many years. Here in Anatevka we have traditions for everything... how to eat, how to sleep, even, how to wear clothes. For instance, we always keep our heads covered and always wear a little prayer shawl... This shows our constant devotion to God. You may ask, how did this tradition start? I'll tell you - I don't know. But it's a tradition... Because of our traditions, everyone knows who he is and what God expects him to do."

Who day and night
Must scramble for a living
Feed the wife and children
Say his daily prayers
And who has the right

As master of the house
To have the final word at home?
The papa, the papas... Tradition
The papa, the papas... Tradition
Who must know the way to make a proper home
A quiet home, a kosher home

Who must raise a family and run the home
So papa's free to read the holy book?
The mama, the mama... Tradition
The mama, the mama... Tradition[95]

Deviating from tradition feels uncomfortable and so we tend to follow what we know, what we've seen, and what we've experienced. This approach isn't wrong per se, but it fails to incorporate the learning and growing necessary to improve and evolve. The emphasis on tradition is certainly not due to a lack of new information. The knowledge and resources to support learning and development as parents and spouses certainly exist and are exploding with new data on how best to improve our families.

The challenge with moving away from tradition is accepting that in order to evolve, we must learn and grow, and that means we must **change**. We struggle with changing from what feels comfortable and recognizing there is a different way, a better way, or a newer way based upon all the knowledge we have collected over our existence. Doing things differently does not have to mean bad or wrong – different can be good.

Take, for example, marriages which have changed significantly and continue to evolve. Historically, one spouse was responsible for doing all the unpaid household work (typically the wife). As we have progressed and recognized other marriage models can be successful, our marriages have begun to look different. We've seen responsibility be divided differently. We've seen relationship dynamics change in how partners treat each other. We've seen new family structures successfully create positive results. We are creating a future where success and satisfaction is possible for both spouses. One does not have to suffer. However, we are going to have to develop, grow, and change, how we think about and approach our marriages.

After the birth of my son, I advocated for a parental leave policy for our male employees. I had read about and personally experienced the impact of having your husband (the father) home after a new baby is born. Research shows fathers who are home during the first two weeks develop better caretaking skills, are more bonded with the children, and there are even long-term positive effects on the child's development.[96] Any parent knows those first few weeks are hard – really hard. As new fathers at home during those early weeks, they get the experience needed to be a better parent by changing diapers, responding to crying, seeing the pain and struggle of their wives, and being present for all of it. I couldn't imagine why we wouldn't want them to get this growth and development?

We must think about our roles at home in this capacity. What skillsets are required and how do we ensure the time necessary to develop them? I know all businesses don't offer this same opportunity, although they certainly should!

The growth we experience at work helps us at home and the growth we experience at home helps us at work. In fact, I realized after the birth of my children that I experienced a major shift in my level of empathy and understanding. I became a much better manager and leader as a result. I could better understand alternative perspectives and, more importantly, I wanted to understand them. This growth has been tremendously valuable for me.

Likewise, a traditional approach to growing and developing in our roles at home will not work in today's context. Rather, we must learn from the past, look to prepare for the future, and stay present in the moment which is our greatest opportunity for growth. The growth opportunities in our homes abound if we are willing to change our paradigm and approach them just as we would our professional roles. Look for opportunities to evolve our families in ways that will improve our lives and create exceptional life experiences for all. Remember, we are growing our entire lives – it's never too late to start working on evolving your performance for your family.

HOW DO I CREATE A MINDSET OF HIGH ACCOUNTABILITY IN MY HOME?

Our ability to cultivate accountability in our homes will ultimately determine the success of our children, marriages, and families. Without a mindset of accountability our families will continuously struggle as they encounter the many challenges we experience throughout our lives. As long as we are blaming our circumstances, judging, criticizing, complaining, we will not be demonstrating the productive behaviors necessary for successful outcomes.

Children who lack any training, skills, and understanding are going to be the most likely to fall into those holes. They are going to experience frustration, exhaustion, confusion, fear, and so much more, and when they do, they will fall right into that hole. As parents, we must be equipped to help them build the skills to learn how to get themselves out of the hole, how to navigate looking for the holes, and how to respond when they encounter others in a hole. The human condition is to fall into a lack of accountability, and we see it early in our children.

Anytime my not yet 2-year-old daughter gets frustrated because she can't do something, she throws her body on the floor face down while screaming, crying, and kicking. She appears inconsolable and the easy thing for me to do would be to just do it for her – put her shoes or socks on, build the tower, or fix her food. But she must learn – at least how to move herself from the hole to the first step of the ladder. I certainly engage; I show her empathy, 'I know you are frustrated, and it is hard to learn at first,' provide support 'I am confident you have the skills to figure this out,' and then work with her 'let's see how we might figure it out together.' I've been doing this longer with my 5-year-old son – he now tries to pre-empt me with "I've already tried everything mom," to which I say, "Well let's see what happens if you try one more time" – and most of the time he gets it!

Our first job as parents must be to demonstrate accountability, *then* call our children to accountability, and help them to create the skills for themselves. Demonstrating accountability can actually be the hardest part – our natural tendency is to blame, shame, and complain. Instead, we must admit our mistakes, issues, and challenges. We must allow our children to see us say "I shouldn't have yelled at you – Mommies and Daddies get frustrated and make mistakes too." We must show them what accountability looks like – providing them significant exposure to these skills.

Although we are meant to guide our children, we must also have this accountability in our adult relationships. When we fall into the hole and start blaming other family members, we are failing to see our part in the situation. Anytime I encounter an issue at home, if I start from a place of how my actions have contributed to the situation, the discussion is far more productive. When we start with "I may have not been clear in what I was asking for," "I didn't follow through and that was my mistake," or "I am also struggling" – we make space for the other person to share their perspective without pulling out the battle guns.

Ever seen a family fight escalate from something small to something major as each side begins to lob shots at the other based on totally unrelated topics? Inevitably, the dangerous words of always and never come out, and suddenly what was a minor event has become a full-fledged multi-hour (or day) battle. Instead, we must always start from a place of what is my part in this, what might the other person be feeling, and how can I have a productive conversation rather than enter into Family War 5,273!

In our homes, our families (whatever they look like) are our responsibility, and we must foster cultures of accountability and positive mindsets. We want to embody changing our thoughts, editing our stories, considering our beliefs, focusing on success, having a growth mindset, and seeing alternative perspectives. The more we are able to demonstrate these skills with our families, the more experiences our families will have and be able to carry the lessons into their lives.

Conclusion & Reflection

Our roles at home are essential to creating an exceptional life experience – even if we love our workplace, the challenges at home are going to impact our effectiveness and overall level of happiness. Using performance practices at home feels unnatural at first, but it actually makes complete sense to do so. With a little bit of intention and effort, we can evolve our families and create far better outcomes for everyone in them. Take a few moments now to reflect on your current role. Based upon that role – what do you hope to achieve for your family, what is your vision? Using the four keys below, how can you chart a course to navigate to that destination and stay on course even when the storms come?

Expectations: How will you define expectations for your role in your home? What guideposts will you create for yourself to better understand the choices you make in your family? How will you establish clear expectations with your spouse, children, and other family members? What goals can you set to ensure you make progress on evolving your performance at home?

Feedback: What are you going to do to increase recognition in your home – for yourself, your kids, your spouse? How can you better learn about your family members and use that knowledge to improve the family operations? How can you provide feedback in a way which is well received and constructive to building the family relationships?

Development: *What can you do to grow and develop your capabilities in your role at home? What areas of opportunity exist to grow your role or that of your children or other family members? What additional skills would bring value to your marriage and children?*

Accountability: *What will you do to demonstrate accountability in your home? What will you do when you fall in the hole? What will you do when someone else falls in the hole? What steps will you take to ensure we connect, demonstrate empathy, coach, and, most importantly, create cultures of accountability in our homes?*

CHAPTER FOURTEEN
Creators of Community

How do the keys of Peak Performance apply in my community?

Roles: Advocate, Church or Faith Leader (Christian, Jewish, Muslim, etc.), Government Leader, Educator, Servant

> **Key Insight:**
>
> We must create the opportunity for our communities to evolve in and reach their peak performance.

As human beings, our mission in life must be about more than just surviving. My grandfather, Rev. Dr. John H. Tietjen, once said, "We know what it means to fight for survival. We have to make mission, rather than survival, the goal for our life together." When we are focused on survival, we are expressing a selfish emotion – one which causes us to fight to survive, no matter the consequences, no matter who is harmed. We put our own needs, wants, and desires above all others. When we are focused on our mission, we are expressing a selfless emotion – one which causes us to serve the greater good, even at the expense of ourselves. We put the needs of the greater community, of humankind, above our own and, through this focus, we create what is required to evolve as a species.

> **Survival:** the act or fact of surviving especially under adverse or unusual circumstances; the act or fact of living or continuing longer than any other person or thing; a person or thing that survives or endures.[97]
>
> **Mission:** A specific task with which a person or group is charged; a pre-established and often self-imposed objective or purpose; An important goal or purpose that is accompanied by strong conviction; a calling or vocation.[98]
>
> **Thrive:** grow or develop well or vigorously; prosper; flourish[99]

I respect all beliefs on original creation – a tremendous energy source, seven days of creation, or any other belief. Regardless of your religious beliefs regarding creation, as human beings, we were all created and brought to life from the womb of a woman. Our creator created everything we see, which means we are all the beautiful work of the divine creator. Creating runs through our veins and every ounce of our being innately desires to create. It's why parents feel the desire to create children. It's why we invent new things. It's why we discover medicine, cook meals, build houses, make cars, create art, innovate technology, and continuously uncover new ways of seeing the world.

For all our existence, humans have created, and our creations continue to improve. We continue to get better, smarter, faster, stronger, kinder, and capable of more than we dreamed possible. At the same time, we've also been distracted by darkness. The darkness wants to stand in our way because the more we create, the lighter, kinder, more joyful, and beautiful the world becomes. Creating from love is the antithesis of darkness, which seeks to fade, wither, and expire our existence. To create, we choose to bring something new into existence. When we bring new things into existence out of love, we defeat the darkness.

Our creator has been waiting patiently, caring for us as growing creations (like children) until we reach the state of existence in which we can live together peacefully. Just like a baby at birth does not recognize their existence separately from their mother, we must recognize our mother, our creator, who has been guiding us along as her children. She is guiding us to create – to create out of love – to create joy, goodness, protection, success, happiness, and victory over the darkness. Our shared mission as humans is to create in our communities. We are meant, through our creations, to thrive rather than just survive through our existence.

When you live good values.
Your mind will think things that will help you create positive change.
Your eyes will see things that will help you create positive change.
Your heart will feel things that will help you create positive change.
Your attitude will embrace things that will help
you create positive change.
Your mouth will say things that will help you create positive change.
Your life will attract things that will help you create positive change.
Your feet will lead you to do things that will create positive change.[100]

John C. Maxwell, in Change Your World

This chapter covers the roles we *must choose* to serve in our communities. These roles are a choice we make to serve our mission to create together with love. These are roles where we focus on advancing our existence as a society by creating opportunity, support, and protection for everyone. These are roles we perform because we believe we are called to do so; we perform them because we care. When we serve our communities, we are doing so out of a devotion to the mission to create with love – to support, care, help, serve, guide, nurture, teach, coach, and protect. We will look at the roles we serve in our religious, government, education, and other communities and how the keys to peak performance can help us on our mission to create better results for our communities and those we serve.

In his book, *Change Your World*, John C. Maxwell, and Rob Hoskins challenge the belief that changing the world requires extraordinary efforts and instead suggest changing the world always starts with doing something, no matter how small. I believe, like Maxwell shared, "Everyone can do something, and when they do, it makes it better for everyone."[101] As you consider your role in the community, think about what you can do, no matter how small, to make the world better for everyone!

WHY DO WE NEED TO CONSIDER OUR PERFORMANCE IN THE COMMUNITY?

As human beings with a higher capacity for thinking, we have the opportunity to choose what we do with our lives, including where we spend our time, what we do with the time, what we experience during our lives, and what impact we leave as a result of our lives. At a basic level, all humans must first survive – acquiring food, shelter, water, and safety. Humans cannot survive alone and require communities for basic needs to be met. Only through the contributions of all the members of the community can we meet even these most basic needs.

Once our basic needs are met only then can we pursue our purpose or mission. We are meant to do more than just survive this world; we are meant to thrive in the world. Just as we need communities to survive, in order to thrive we must work together to further our mission of creating in our communities. We must perform in order to create opportunity, safety, resources, support, and connection for everyone. By reaching peak performance, we can create exceptional experiences for our entire community.

I grew up watching my mother demonstrate leadership in the community. She served on the council at our church (many times), she chaired committees, served on the PTA, supported non-profits, and much more. While my dad ran his business, my mom was committed to serving the community. Her leadership, performance, and commitment went unpaid and often unrecognized. Watching her throughout my life shaped my belief in the need for strong performance in our communities. We require our best and brightest performers to help improve our communities and provide the much-needed services necessary to do so.

However, "the reality is that most of us are waiting for somebody else to do something about the problems we see. We want change, but we hope that some*one* some*where* will do some*thing* to bring it about."[102]

We wait for the government to do something. We want the health care system to do something. We believe education will do something. We look to business to do something. We imagine media will do something. We wish arts and entertainment would do something. We think sport will do something. We hope religious institutions will do something.[103]

John C. Maxwell, in Change Your World

Despite our waiting, wanting, believing, looking, imagining, wishing, thinking, and hoping much of what needs to be done is simply not accomplished by anyone. Rather, we must recognize the first step toward creating a better world, is the one I choose to take!

Deciding to take the first step to change the world, in even the smallest of ways, is the energy required to create change. If we all take even one small step forward to change the world for the better, imagine the energy created and endless possibilities for positive change! If we could multiply the one small step, we would see a tremendous increase in the service of our communities.

> *The first step toward creating a better world is the one I choose to take!*

Why are more services needed? As lives are more filled, time constrained, and isolated than ever before, our community groups have struggled. The community groups lacking adequate resources may cease to make progress or even exist. Many community organizations are challenged with bringing people together to serve a greater purpose. Our religious groups are plagued with membership challenges, increasing fragmentation, and a struggle to connect those of different beliefs. Our governments are extraordinarily polarized with an intense focus and emphasis on campaigning, more so than on actually governing and creating results in our communities. Our schools are challenged with limited resources and funding to meet the necessary requirements for advancing the capabilities of our children while navigating a world with polarized views on education.

Generally, we lack the necessary practices to move from surviving to thriving. Our world and the communities which serve it are struggling to create the changes needed. If these changes can truly be made to last, they can transform lives for the better. I'll admit this is a gross overgeneralization and many groups and organizations are likely making amazing progress in their efforts to change the world. However, as a whole, we are clearly struggling to make the changes needed in the world today to truly transform lives, improve outcomes, and create experiences where everyone can thrive!

Without a doubt, there is significantly more work to be done to change, improve, and evolve the world today to be better than the world of yesterday.

Once we've overcome the hurdle of deciding to take the first step, we must then consider our performance when doing so. Although we are driven to perform these roles out of mission, personal belief, conviction, or calling, this alone does not create peak performance. Rather, we need these community organizations to intentionally bring about the change needed to evolve our performance and the world as a whole.

We need faith-based or religious communities to bring people together, support growth in faith and spirituality, and serve the needs of the community. Historically, these groups have struggled with the accumulation of power thereby corrupting the beliefs and spirituality itself. The beliefs become a reflection of those in power rather than of the divine creator. Instead, we need these groups to perform a different role, one which promotes the needs of the community over the beliefs of the leaders in the community. One which creates from love and sacrifice rather than for selfish reasons.

> **Spirituality:** recognition of a feeling or sense of belief there is something greater than myself; a solitary experience of the divine[104], the quality of being concerned with the human spirit or soul as opposed to material or physical things.[105]
>
> **Religion:** involves a group of people brought together by their common faith or beliefs about the divine, a particular system of faith and worship, a commitment or devotion to a religious faith or observance.[106]

We need our government communities to provide what is unachievable by the private sector. Governments can transform their results by focusing on the performance of their greatest asset – our people! Imagine the impact we would have if we got even 1% more out of our government resources. I feel a strong sense of urgency to redirect our government's mission and operation to focus on creating for the benefit of those the government serves. With good leadership, focus, and commitment, many underperforming elements of the government could be dramatically transformed.

We need our schools to teach students lessons that support their future growth and the evolution of their performance. Education must be transformed to include key skillsets such as mindset, accountability, resilience, positivity, grit, authenticity, vulnerability, respect, gratitude, communication, self-awareness, and reflection. The education of our children, and what they can do with this wisdom, is one of the greatest avenues for growth and changing our world!

I also believe we must build more communities to support our growth and the evolution of our performance. I have struggled finding a community for myself and my family. Although my personal experience may be impacting my view, given my health issues, work challenges, children, and the difference in spiritual beliefs between myself and my husband, but maybe – just maybe – I'm not alone. Maybe others also struggle to create meaningful connection and develop communities where they belong. Maybe other moms juggling work, home, and so much more each day struggle to carve out time for anything else. Maybe others who are single struggle to find relationships and friendships with those in the same phase of life. Maybe I'm not the only one who struggles to find a community where I belong.

Recently, I stumbled on a Facebook post of a mother asking other women how much time they spend with their friends. Although a few individuals had answers of a few times a week, month, or year, the vast majority of answers were variations of "What is a friend?" "Friends?" "You have friends?" "How do you get friends?" If I am honest, this response was also my first response to the question. We all desperately feel this desire for community and yet we struggle to find connection and build friendships.

If this is the case and I'm not alone, then how do we come together again? How do we support each other and build connections with one another? How do we create rather than embrace the ever-dividing rhetoric which exists in the world today? I am tired of hearing about how our differences divide us rather than unite us as we support and learn from each other. How do we find a way to evolve our performance in our communities, allowing all of us to thrive and grow together?

We must shift from control, direction, and power to a new world with support, guidance, and devotion to the greater good. When we focus on what we bring rather than what we need, we are able to see beyond ourselves and achieve greater results. I will identify some strategies and suggestions for approaching this challenge, but it will take far more than I can do alone. I hope this provides a catalyst of sharing, connecting, conversing, and creating ideas which might turn the tide. I welcome and encourage the conversation to continue beyond the pages of this book.

Reflection: *Think about what you are doing today to serve in the community. Where could your strengths, skills, and capabilities bring value to the broader community? How might you take one small step in service or to better the broader community? How might you impact schools, governments, churches, or other communities? Where might you best contribute or begin on a path to improve and evolve your performance in the community? One suggestion is to consider looking into John C. Maxwell's Transformation tables at Changeyourworld.com. They are free and available to anyone!*

HOW DO YOU ESTABLISH CLEAR EXPECTATIONS IN COMMUNITY-BASED ROLES?

For the most part, the same expectation principles apply to community roles: they require clarity, direction, and alignment. Herein lies the challenge – expectations are often overly complex, ill-defined, or nonexistent. Our community groups tend to be extraordinarily complex, steeped in tradition, and slow to evolve and change. This complexity makes understanding expectations extraordinarily difficult. However, we must create clarity, so everyone knows how to create and contribute to a better and brighter future. **What is the purpose and expectations for community groups?**

Historically, we've focused on processes and specifying exactly what must be done rather than focusing on the values we hold and the outcomes we seek for our communities. As a result, we developed complex systems which require professional degrees to navigate and where even the people performing them are confused.

Churches and non-profits are burdened with complex governance systems and struggle to navigate a complex world of varying viewpoints. Governments are actual governance systems with complicated administrative practices and little consideration for culture and values. Education systems require a focus on meeting test scores rather than the true development and growth of our children. Even social media groups have complex rule systems for what you can share, where, when, and with whom. New forms, new processes, and new confusion at every turn. But we aren't really focused on what needs to happen... instead it's all about following the written laws, rules, or processes.

Take immigration – a very controversial and hot topic. I know from personal experience the complexity and insanity of our immigration system. My uncle is from Sierra Leone, Africa – he married my aunt and moved here. I watched them struggle for years to figure out the process to get him here legally. Even now, he wants to become a US citizen and fears making a mistake in the process.

My uncle is a Lutheran pastor and an amazing human being. He is definitely an example of who we want in this country.

In the workplace, I've worked with student visas, H-1B visas, and green cards. Despite being a lawyer myself, I required outside counsel expertise to navigate the complexity of our system. The process was expensive, complicated, and anything but straightforward. I also have a close friend whose husband runs a lawn care company and brings employees from Mexico to work in his business each summer. He struggles each year to get them here. When he can't, he struggles to find anyone sober, willing to reliably show up, and correctly do the work!

Why is this so hard? Why do we need to spend so much money administering a process as complex as this one? Could we do it differently? Could we improve our systems by focusing more on values and outcomes rather than process, more on people than policy and laws, and more on creating results rather than punching a clock?

What if we applied this to education? What if the outcome we were working towards was: "To become the most educated, employed, capable, talented, and happy society in all of history?" How would this change the goals we set and the decisions we make about our schools? If this were our outcome, we could begin with new objectives such as: ensuring all children receive an education based on current best practices, identifying strategies to support child well-being, and considering programs to build skills for better employment opportunities in the future. Most importantly, we could only achieve this goal or outcome by working together to find ways to be successful.

Early in my career I spent months working on Visio process flow diagrams, which were a best practice for defining processes and clarifying expectations. What I learned was that diagrams don't make expectations any clearer. Rather, the communication around the expectations and actively discussing the process, the steps, the outcomes is what created clear expectations. The world is constantly changing, and our community groups need to be practicing the same best practices that are readily found in workplaces. We must create clarity with good communication and frequently re-visit and realign on expectations.

These expectations may be formal or informal, shared, or personal. For example, what is expected of our faith-based roles? I'd prefer to hear my direction from the "boss" directly – others seek input from various religious organizations and teachings. Whatever your belief or approach – take time to truly consider what you expect of yourself in the role of your faith. Not sure if you have faith? I can tell you I recently incorrectly assumed that faith did not have a major impact on my life – I now know with 100% certainty a faith-based or spiritual life is a necessary factor to an exceptional life.

HOW DO WE GIVE AND RECEIVE FEEDBACK IN THE COMMUNITY?

Many communities are deteriorating with increasing polarization, unhealthy dialogue, disparagement, and generally negative communication. If we aren't part of the same "group," we assume we are different and, therefore, unable to connect and relate to one another. We stop listening and understanding different perspectives from our own. We believe we are superior in our experience, personal practices, and beliefs.

We couldn't be more wrong. In fact, no single group is superior to any other. We need each other. We exist in a world where to survive; we must work together – we are not self-sufficient in our ability to support our basic needs. Rather, we need our collective abilities to perform different functions and jobs that produce different results and meet the needs of our communities. We must leverage the strengths of all the people in our communities to find solutions to the challenges we face. We were not all gifted with the same strengths for a reason, we are meant to work together. We will learn so much more from each other, working together rather than working separately.

Knowing who you are – and who you are not – is essential. But it is only a starting point. All the talent, motivation, and hard work in the world will not be valued or remembered if it does not help another human being. Most people agree that life is not about focusing on self-oriented or monetary ambitions. It is about what you create that improves lives. It is about investing in the development of other people. And it is about participating in efforts that will continue to grow when you are gone. In the end, you won't' get to stay around forever, but your contributions will.[107]

Tom Rath, in Life's Great Question

My grandfather (the pastor) believed in unity – he wrote about Lutheran unity, Christian unity, and believed in unifying faiths to work together. When we come together, we can solve more problems, identify more solutions, and learn more about how to improve the world. We are a society-based species, never meant to exist alone. We are capable of so much if we can learn about, trust, and listen to each other and then provide feedback to share experiences, ideas, and information.

Our religious institutions must begin to look for ways to work collectively rather than separately to solve the challenges of today. Our communities need more faith leaders who are willing to meet people where they are and welcome them into their churches. Faith leaders who actively work with members of all faiths to bring about greater collaboration around the problems and our growth as a society.

Our governments, and especially our politicians, must stop focusing on what will win personal favor. As voters and as a society, we need to give feedback to our politicians that trust, collaboration, and positive outcomes are what matter. They must be willing to work together rather than create division by perpetually promoting differences. I don't expect every person to agree with every bit of feedback – but we must get better at how we receive and reflect on this input to create better results. We must not simply deny every bit of information which contradicts our own limited point of view.

All of this starts with learning more about each other and building a foundation of trust. When we don't understand another person's background, life experiences, or religious beliefs, we can't possibly claim to know their intent, purpose, or objectives.

> *When we are skeptical and lack trust of those who think differently, we tune out or casually dismiss relevant information for solving problems in our communities.*

How do we begin to build trust? How do we look at everyone as individuals, each with their own thoughts, feelings, experiences, personalities, beliefs, strengths, values, and abilities to contribute? If we can take the time, reserve the space, and purposefully learn about one and other's preferences, maybe we can begin to build trust and ultimately relationships. When we trust others, we are far more open to hearing what they have to say. We can sit on the same side even when we have different perspectives or beliefs.

We are all on this planet and in our communities together. We cannot remove or eliminate those with whom we disagree. Instead, we must learn to co-exist peacefully and proactively work together to evolve our performance and the results we achieve together.

Then we can engage in healthy conversations about important topics. We will work collectively to solve problems we all agree exist – rather than focus on differences. We will find ways to reduce violence in our communities, improve education, support new mothers, increase health and wellness, and live better lives. As we learn more, we will find new solutions. As we stop repeating the same age-old debates and focus on new challenges and new perspectives, we may find ways to resolve issues we never thought possible. I'm not naïve; I know we may still argue, still fail to solve, or disagree on particular issues, but at least we will be making progress.

Certainly, everyone would like to be thriving rather than suffering or struggling. By understanding the needs in our communities, engaging in meaningful discussions, learning about each other, and building trust, we will be able to reach peak performance in our communities. And everyone will have the opportunity to have more exceptional work and life experiences.

HOW DO WE CREATE GROWTH AND DEVELOPMENT IN OUR COMMUNITIES?

I recently read a theory on why the human race has evolved over time. The theory is based upon evidence that women's brains actually change as a result of pregnancy and motherhood.[108] The composition of the brain and how it operates is altered. Yes, I really am a neuroscience nerd! This information did not surprise me in the slightest. I bet most mothers would agree motherhood has transformed how they think and operate. The transformation is largely based upon the intense need to protect our children. As a mom, I feel this tremendous intensity to protect and make the world better for my children. It goes beyond desire and feels like a biological imperative – and, in fact, it might be!

This transformation and desire to protect is what the theory purports may have been the primary reason for evolution.[109] As a result of the change women experience, they take steps to protect and improve the life of their children – physically and emotionally. If you think about it, this makes sense, to help our children, we created tribes to protect them, agriculture to feed them, medicine to save them, schools to educate them, and so much more.

*Some scientists argue that the development of maternal behavior –
heightened sensitivities, empathy, attention, skill – actually spurred the
mammalian brain to evolve... because the puzzle of keeping a
terrifyingly dependent creature alive had to be worked out, human
beings could move on to developing agriculture and smartphones.*[110]

Sara Menkedick, in Ordinary Insanity

I love this theory, not just because it highlights the tremendous value women have brought throughout time, but because it demonstrates that we are meant to keep growing and developing. Each generation is meant to push a little further, protect our children a little better, grow our minds, increase our capabilities, and keep evolving. We know this is true. Look at any IQ chart and it's clear that we are getting smarter and more capable as a species, and as communities, over time.

Unfortunately, some of our "improvements" have also created challenges – guns to protect which also kill, schools to educate with bullies who harm, medicine to save but also viruses that kill, agriculture to feed us and also make us sick. We have to keep learning from each of these experiences, identifying the lesson, and looking for opportunities to develop and grow individually and as a community. Tremendous opportunity exists for our communities to continue to grow and change the world.

I mentioned earlier how we create walls in our lives that prevent us from seeing the future and having experiences necessary for growth and development. When we create walls, we also lock out someone – the most important being in our life – our higher power, our God, our Divine, our Creator. We get overly confident in our ability to handle issues, thinking we must manage our lives and protect our egos. But we are wrong. We need trust and connection more than management and protection. We need to trust God's plan for us, for our experiences, and our future. We need to be able to connect with God, which is impossible when we are surrounded by walls. We were never meant to live this life on our own – and yet we try to do so. We stop seeking divine guidance for our lives, which prevents or hinders our growth and development.

The images of those suffering alone are present in my mind. The bullied child who feels things will never get better and the pain is all consuming because they are ill-equipped to handle the challenges they face. The new mom, overwhelmed and exhausted, feeling isolated, alone, and unsure whether her experience is normal (it is!) or whether she truly needs help (which I believe almost everyone does!). The husband who feels broken, and alone – unable to share the emotions he is experiencing as he was taught and tries to "take it like a man." There are countless situations where people are suffering alone, apart from God and away from others, unaware of the freedom that comes from connecting with others and trusting God more than ourselves.

I won't profess to be an expert. My grandfather was a Lutheran Pastor but I'm a long way from my childhood of weekly Sundays in the front row (thank you mom and dad!) and active participation at church. In fact, I am incredibly good at convincing myself that I can handle things on my own. I am so good at it that God can fade to the background, and I begin to think she should help others who need her more. As I've worked on this book I've realized once again (this ain't my first rodeo) how mistaken I am. You see, God wants to use us for good and when we cut him off, he can't! God can't help us unless we invite God to do so – unless we invite him or her into our lives to support, guide, and direct our experiences.

Growing our relationship and connection with God is essential to having exceptional lives. Only once God is directing our lives can we truly lean into the growth and development that comes from those experiences. We can look at each experience we are having as an opportunity to find the lesson, to learn a new skill, to identify how we can improve and grow ourselves to contribute to the world in new and meaningful ways. Our communities need us to develop and grow, and God is prepared to give us the experiences we need to evolve.

> *We can look at each experience we are having as an opportunity to find the lesson, to learn a new skill, to identify how we can improve and grow ourselves to contribute to the world in new and meaningful ways.*

Looking for ways to evolve our performance in our communities is critical to our future as a society. These communities create connection and provide resources and opportunity for many in the world today. They are needed now more than ever because they provide opportunity for growth outside our homes and workplaces. More people truly need this growth, and more people are avoiding it today than ever before. How do we create more growth and development within our communities? How do we drive our communities to strengthen and grow?

One possibility is to look to our government (I know you thought I was smart until this point, but bear with me here). Our government has been focused primarily on execution and delivery of services. What if our governments shifted their focus to be more about values, outcomes, and performance? If our governments placed a greater focus on creating opportunities and experiences for growth and development – for our children and our workforce – maybe it would generate the growth in our economy and results we want to see from our performance. What better entity is equipped to potentially impact the most people by simply changing their approach and focus? Alright, I might be oversimplifying but it also isn't impossible or unachievable.

Even more than our workplaces and homes, our communities need to experience the growth and development of new skills and capabilities. Everyone must be growing and evolving in order for us to truly change the world.

HOW DO WE CREATE A MINDSET OF ACCOUNTABILITY FOR OUR COMMUNITY CULTURES?

When we encounter a challenge where the answer is not readily available and the problem is not easily solved, we tend to get stuck. We aren't sure of the solution, so we choose instead to do one of the following: ignore the problem, decide the problem is not solvable, decide the problem is someone else's to solve, identify someone else who is causing the problem, or try to convince everyone the problem is not a problem at all. The last one is my favorite – my five-year-old son loves to come up with reasons why whatever he just did wrong is not actually wrong!

When we do this, we fall in the hole and get stuck in our own helplessness and lack of accountability. And what we don't do is actually solve the problem. Instead, when we are stuck, we need resources beyond ourselves more than ever. We need a different perspective to help us move beyond our own point of view and discover the solution to our challenge.

How we see things determines how we say things, and how we say things always influences – and often determines – how they turn out. When we live on the other side of yes, you believe there is always an answer. In fact, you feel certain there is not just one answer; you believe there are many good answers. That makes you willing to do the work to find them, and it also fires you up to be part of them! [111]

John C. Maxwell

The culture in our community is going to determine the mindset of accountability. If this mindset is absent, our community will struggle to overcome challenges, discover solutions, create opportunity, make progress, and evolve in their performance and results. Our ability to cultivate mindsets of accountability will be the single greatest factor in the outcome and results produced in our community. Whether you learn the principles of mindset and accountability at church, school, work, or from the government – it will determine the results we experience. Unless we all take personal accountability for our community and the challenges we encounter, we will continue to struggle.

As I mentioned in prior sections, we've missed opportunities to incorporate research we know to be true into our lives in more meaningful ways. Our schools, our governments, and our churches have not universally incorporated critical knowledge regarding mindset and accountability into their practices.

As I write this section, I believe even more strongly in the importance of developing these skillsets earlier in our lives. In the St. Louis area, a recent news story shared our mental health behavioral units were filling up with children suffering from mental health issues calling it a "pediatric behavioral health crisis."[112] We need to act now to help equip our children with the skills and tools necessary for this new world.

In *Chatter*[113] by Ethan Kross, he mentioned a number of research projects to study the impact of incorporating similar principles in the education process. I am excited this is being piloted, but I also think it is critical we take these insights and make change happen now! Our education systems and children could benefit greatly from these skillsets. Their impact on this crisis could be transformational for many children and even save lives.

In the news, we've seen the increase in school shootings, depression, mental health crises, drug addiction crises, domestic violence, and abuse – all of this can be positively impacted by developing these critical life skills earlier in life. We have the knowledge as a society to improve our communities, but we must share this knowledge and actually use it in order to make it possible.

As members of our communities, we must begin to think about and advocate for these changes. We must look for opportunities to incorporate this knowledge into our community organizations, churches, schools, and even government!

Whatever changes you have fought for and won in the past should inspire you to believe you can change again in the future. And those changes – even incremental internal changes – will help you to make changes in your world.[114]

John C. Maxwell

Similar to COVID, our communities are likely to continue to experience new and unexpected challenges as the rate of change increases. Battles that were once fought on the battlefield will now be fought virtually and digitally as the battle for power and money shifts and changes. We are no longer fighting over land but fighting over intellectual property, virtual money, and resources. As criminals change how they conduct crime and theft shifts to online data scams and threats – we have to re-think how we prepare, react, and respond to these new challenges. Our communities and the people in them need to be educated in ways that were never required before. And they need to be prepared to bounce back when challenges occur.

Conclusion & Reflection

In today's world, we have resources, knowledge, technology, and capabilities to afford everyone on the planet the ability to survive and thrive in this world, though it would certainly require significant culture change. The culture today seems uncomfortable with the shift from surviving to thriving. The 24/7 news cycle consistently finds a life-or-death situation on which to focus our attention, resources, and energy. But, by staying in a survival mode, we fail to evolve in our ability to create more than we imagined possible. We have both the ability and resources to change the world should we choose to perform our mission. Take a moment now to consider your role in the community and, if you do not yet have one, what role you want to pursue.

Expectations: *What expectations do you have for your role in serving the community? How do we identify expectations focused on what we hope the outcome to be, rather than the process of execution? What expectations or goals will you set to positively impact your communities? Where do you need clarity of expectations for your role in the community? What could you do to help create clarity in values, outcomes, or results rather than the process?*

Feedback: *How will we learn more about our communities and the diverse perspectives everyone brings? How will we expand our awareness of the value of our differences? How can we apply these differences to help improve our communities? What will we do to engage in meaningful conversations, providing input and feedback, positive and constructive, to bring about necessary change? How will we build trusting relationships in our communities?*

Development: *What do we need to learn in order to grow and develop capabilities to improve our communities? How will you learn to trust God and seek divine guidance for your life's purpose? Where can you grow in your service and participation in the community?*

Accountability: *How do we leverage the many capabilities of our communities to solve challenging problems? What can we do to provide greater awareness to the power of a mindset of accountability? How do we teach these principles so everyone can benefit from a better mindset?*

Conclusion
WHERE DO WE GO FROM HERE?

O ne of my favorite books and movies growing up (and possibly of all time) was *Gone with the Wind*. In fact, I loved the main character Scarlett O'Hara so much I named my daughter after her! One of my favorite quotes by Scarlett helped to shape my lifelong philosophy. Anytime Scarlett would become overwhelmed in the book she would say

---

"I can't think about that right now. If I do, I'll go crazy. I'll think about that tomorrow. Tomorrow is another day."[115]

Margaret Mitchell

I recognize that I've included a lot of strategies, concepts, and ideas in this book. You may be feeling overwhelmed by the information, unsure of its value, stressed about how you will implement it, intimidated by the amount of change necessary, or exhausted at the idea of having to apply so much energy to reach peak performance. Throughout my life, anytime I become overwhelmed, unsure, stressed, intimidated, exhausted, or just didn't have the answer to a problem, I always came back to the quote "I'm not going to think about that right now, I'll think about that tomorrow."

In life, sometimes we torture ourselves by continuing to think about things which are not bringing us value or are causing us distress. We need to know when to put it down, take a breath, deal with it later, or sometimes just move on. If we truly want to reach our peak performance we must learn to differentiate between when we act, when we wait, and when we move on. All three strategies are appropriate at the intersection of different challenges in life.

I'll tell you a secret I learned early on in my career and have used successfully to this day. Sometimes when we allow a problem to sit for just a bit, we find the problem solves itself. Early in my career I worked closely with salespeople redlining and negotiating contracts. The salespeople (and I hope they will forgive me for doing this) would always email me with this tremendous sense of urgency "Need this redline done ASAP." In the beginning, I would stay up late at night completing the redlines, wearing myself out and getting frustrated with the quick turnaround timelines. Then inevitably the next day they would say, "Never mind, new plan, no need for redline or don't need it for another few weeks."

In our lives, sometimes people will come to us, or problems will arise that appear to have a tremendous sense of urgency. We must determine when we need to simply take a breath and give it time to see what happens next. With my salespeople, nine out of ten times, if I waited just a bit, I would learn something that changed my next step, saving me time and frustration.

I want to emphasize that I am not suggesting we ignore our problems. When we continue to think about a problem or issue without acting, or we bury it within us, it causes tremendous internal conflict and even physical effects. Rather, I am suggesting occasionally we need space and time to consider the problem to either work out the solution or have the solution become more obvious. Often, when we allow time to pass and ourselves to reflect, perspective is gained and occasionally what appeared at first to be a problem or challenge looks more like just another experience. As you reflect on the concepts contained in this book, I encourage you to consider which personal challenges require you to take action, which require more time for reflection, and which you need to simply acknowledge and move on.

As I draw this book to a close, I ask you to imagine the following: You now stand at the base of your performance mountain, armed by your self-awareness, talents, and capabilities, equipped with the guide of the four keys, developed by our recent experiences, and prepared with examples of peak performance in workplaces, homes, and communities. Now imagine you are standing at the edge of a trail which leads to the top of a completely new mountain. A mountain no one has ever climbed before. Maybe this new mountain is even on Mars. A mountain only discovered as we reach further into space and explore entirely new frontiers.

Like the space frontier, the opportunity for everyone to have exceptional lives represents the newest frontier in the world today, a whole new world of opportunity. We have the opportunity to leverage what we already know in order to create exceptional lives for everyone. We each have everything we need to reach peak performance and change our lives forever. I encourage and invite you to take the first step up this new mountain, evolve to peak performance, and begin creating your own exceptional life.

Climb every mountain, Search high and low
Follow every highway, Every path you know

Climb every mountain, Ford every stream
Follow every rainbow, Till you find your dream

A dream that will need, All the love you can give
Every day of your life, For as long as you live

Climb every mountain, Ford every stream
Follow every rainbow, Till you find your place

Climb every mountain, Ford every stream
Follow every mountain (every mountain)
Don't you ever give up, no oh
Climb every mountain (every mountain)
There's a brighter day on the other side
Follow every rainbow, Till you find your dream[116]

Acknowledgements

Writing this book has been one the greatest professional joys thus far in my life, and without the support of my amazing husband Greg – it never would have been possible. Greg, thank you for embracing being the opposite of a traditional marriage, being a phenomenal care provider to our children, and shouldering a greater load so I could work nights, weekends, and vacations to complete this book. Your partnership, willingness to engage, and loving support are beyond what I could have ever anticipated when we married. Thank you for being you.

To my children, who are too young to realize what "mommy writing a book" really means. Wyatt, you always make people laugh, bringing joy to everyone you meet. You fear no one and say hi to everyone. Never stop being this person! You were the first one to teach me how to be a mom and I had no idea what I was doing – thank you for your patience. Arabella & Scarlett – thank you for teaching me what it means to do *really* hard things in life. I never imagined I would have twins – and yet here you are – challenging me but also loving me every day. Arabella, may you always be my fierce lion with courage, strength, and daring. Scarlett, may you always be my gentle bird with focus, kindness, and intensity. Wyatt, may you always be my silly, funny, happy, goofy, fun, interesting, and talented son!

The greatest teachers in my life, who have helped me discern, learn, research, experiment, and grow in this space, are the employees who have worked **with** me on our teams, past and present. I would like to especially recognize Jamie Meinert, Cara Wells, and Meldina Sabotic for being talent management crusaders and helping me develop capabilities I never dreamed possible. I also want to thank Justin, Julie, and Lindsey for allowing me to work with you and your teams and see the success they have been able to achieve (of course amidst the challenges as well!). I also want to thank Allison Seiler for assisting with the book and being one of the first to read the book and affirm its value! You are incredibly talented, and I am so grateful to be working with you.

To my crazy family who ends up all together on one call just because we call each other so frequently! Starting with my parents, who helped shape me through my life. My mother, Christie Tietjen, thank you for teaching me about service and setting such a phenomenal example of motherhood for me to follow. Larry Tietjen, thank you for your guidance and all that you taught me during our years working together. You are a tremendous leader and I hope to make you proud. Thank you to you both for loving, supporting, and guiding me through life. And, most importantly, loving, supporting, and guiding my children!

To my sisters and my best friends, Jennifer Tietjen and Carrie Tietjen, thank you for your friendship, insight, love, and support – you are always there when things get tough, and I am blessed to go through life with both of you. To my sisters-in-law, Amy Huschka – thank you for your love and companionship in motherhood; and Sister Sophia Grace – thank you for your sisterhood and becoming a fourth sister to me as we talk about and share the most amazing experiences, especially those related to our shared faith. Thank you to Dave Maupin, my brother-in-law, for his beautiful photos in this book! A huge thank you to my mother-in-law, Kathy Huschka, who has loved, supported, laughed, and cared about me as a daughter. Your support means more than you will ever know! And to all my aunts, uncles, and cousins for their love and support and a special Thank You to my Aunt Catherine - your mentorship, coaching, and guidance helped me evolve my performance many times throughout my life.

I want to thank my grandparents, although most are now deceased. Thanks to Rev. Dr. John H. Tietjen (deceased) for teaching me to think for myself, talk about, and debate hard topics; Robert

'Bob' Zimmermann (deceased) for loving me so much and treating me as precious as a diamond; Ernestine Tietjen (deceased) for always being proud of me and kind to me; and Gloria Zimmermann, my 90-year-old rockstar grandma who is still fishing, boating, laughing, and living her best life! Thank you for loving me, counseling me, supporting me, and being there for me my whole life.

To my coach and friend, Keira Poulsen, for helping me to awaken and birth this book into existence. Thank you for your guidance, healing, and incredible support through the writing of this book – you responded to my messages at all hours and supported me through everything! To Sara Calton, my editor, who not only edited this book but also supported, encouraged, and went above and beyond to help make it the best it could be, thank you! For the many women also writing and working with Freedom House Publishing – thank you for your words of support and guidance along the way. I hope I am able to help you bring your books into the world the way you have helped me!

To my professional HR mentors, thank you for your friendship, advice, coaching, and guidance when I was young and didn't know what I was doing. Kelly Mutuc, Susan Poynter, Sue Deegan – your influence over my career cannot be understated! Thank you for everything, and especially the late-night hotel bar conversations over Baileys!

To my leadership mentors who each taught me something about myself and helped shape me into who I am today. Thank you, Mark Franklin, for always being willing to debate and discuss tough topics with me. Thank you, Brad Fisher, for supporting me and advocating for talent management. Thank you, Don Scobey, for being my first real manager and mentor, and for helping me get Talent Management started at Experitec. Thank you to Larry again for your unparalleled example of leadership and teaching me that if you treat people right, they do right by you!

To my life-long friends, I don't have many but the few I have are true and no matter how long we are apart we still come back together as if no time has passed at all! To all my teachers who taught me to write and helped cultivate my love for books! Thank you for finding my talent and nurturing it!

A huge thank you to the Experitec Employee Owners, past and present, who have helped to create a Gallup®[32] Exceptional Workplace! You are amazing people who are working every day to serve our customers and improve performance!

To the many thought leaders who I have spent the last ten years following and reading all the amazing books you have written: Shawn Achor, Brene Brown, Marcus Buckingham, Tom Casey, Don & Jim Clifton, Glennon Doyle, Angela Duckworth, Dr. Beverly Kaye, John C Maxwell, Matthew McConaughey, Tim Pollard, Tom Rath, Cy Wakeman, and Abby Wambach. I look forward to reading your future works, as well as those from many more authors who have amazing contributions to make in the world through their writing. Thank you to Gallup and all my friends at Gallup – your partnership, thought leadership, research, and insights bring tremendous value to the world and its leaders.

And last, but certainly not least, I want to thank God for directing me and guiding me to write this book. Thank you, Divine Mother, for all your guidance, input, visions, and insights which helped to bring the words of this book to life. My faith in you is not only renewed but transformed into a beautiful and amazing relationship which will only continue to grow as the days pass. I am incredibly grateful for my faith, God's guidance, and the light that is transforming my life and its purpose.

---

[32] CliftonStrengths® and the CliftonStrengths 34 Themes of Talent are trademarks of Gallup, Inc. Gallup's content is Copyrighted by Gallup. Used with permission. All rights reserved.

Awards and Licenses

GALLUP-CERTIFIED

Strengths Coach

GALLUP EXCEPTIONAL WORKPLACE AWARD

2021 WINNER

GALLUP EXCEPTIONAL WORKPLACE AWARDS

2020 WINNER

GALLUP **GREAT WORKPLACE AWARD**

2 0 1 9 WINNER

Welcome to the R-Evolution to create Exceptional Lives!

Did you love this book?
Want to help spread the Exceptional Life R-Evolution?
Don't forget to leave a review!
Each review matters... a lot!

It would be amazing if you could head over to Amazon, or wherever you purchased this book and leave a review! Thank you, thank you, thank you.

Jessica Tietjen

References

1 Boring-Bray, Wendy, ed. "Wisdom: Definition, Synonyms, and Meaning." Betterhelp. BetterHelp, November 4, 2018. https://www.betterhelp.com/advice/wisdom/wisdom-definition-synonyms-and-meaning/.

2 Brain Forest Centers. "What Is Peak Performance and How Do I Reach It?" Brain Forest, August 18, 2018. https://www.brainforestcenters.com/news/what-is-peak-performance-and-how-do-i-reach-it.

3 Kotler, Steven. "'Flow' or Peak Performance Is Supported by Science." Time. Time, April 30, 2014. https://time.com/56809/the-science-of-peak-human-performance/.

4 "Evolve." Dictionary.com. Dictionary.com. Accessed July 20, 2021. https://www.dictionary.com/browse/evolve.

5 "Evolve." Dictionary.com. Dictionary.com. Accessed July 20, 2021. https://www.dictionary.com/browse/evolve.

6 Rath, Tom. *Life's Great Question: Discover How You Contribute to The World*, 7. Silicon Guild, 2020.

7 Morris, Donna. "Death to the Performance Review: How Adobe Reinvented Performance Management and Transformed Its Business." Adobe. WorldWork Journal, 2016. https://www.adobe.com/content/dam/acom/en/aboutadobe/pdfs/death-to-the-performance-review.pdf.

8 Buckingham, Marcus, and Curt Coffman. *First, Break All the Rules*. Simon & Schuster, 1999.

9 Buckingham, Marcus, and Curt Coffman. *First, Break All the Rules*. Simon & Schuster, 1999.

10 Buckingham, Marcus, and Curt Coffman. *First, Break All the Rules*. Simon & Schuster, 1999.

[11] "INSIGHT English Definition and Meaning." Lexico Dictionaries | English. Lexico Dictionaries. Accessed July 20, 2021. https://www.lexico.com/en/definition/insight.

[12] "Reflection." Dictionary.com. Dictionary.com. Accessed July 20, 2021. https://www.dictionary.com/browse/reflection.

[13] LePera, Nicole. *How to Do the Work: Recognize Your Patterns, Heal from Your Past, and Create Your Self*, xxii. Harper Wave, 2021.

[14] Maxwell, John C. *Everyone Communicates, Few Connect.* HarperCollins Leadership, 2010.

[15] Sutton, Robert, and Ben Wigert. "More Harm Than Good: The Truth About Performance Reviews." Gallup.com. Gallup, June 25, 2021. https://www.gallup.com/workplace/249332/harm-good-truth-performance-reviews.aspx.

[16] Morris, Donna. "Death to the Performance Review: How Adobe Reinvented Performance Management and Transformed Its Business." Adobe. WorldWork Journal, 2016. https://www.adobe.com/content/dam/acom/en/aboutadobe/pdfs/death-to-the-performance-review.pdf.

[17] Patterson, Kerry, Joseph Grenny, Ron McMillan, and Al Switzler. *Crucial Conversations: Tools for Talking When Stakes Are High.* New York: McGraw-Hill, 2012.

[18] Nagoski, Emily, and Amelia Nagoski. *Burnout: The Secret to Unlocking the Stress Cycle.* Ballantine Books, 2019.

[19] Gales, Peter Anthony. "What Does 'Respect' Mean?: Peter Anthony Gales." Peter Anthony Gales, June 12, 2014. https://peteranthonygales.com/2010/08/13/does-respect-mean/.

[20] "GRIT English Definition and Meaning." Lexico Dictionaries | English. Lexico Dictionaries. Accessed July 20, 2021. https://www.lexico.com/en/definition/grit.

21 "RESILIENCE English Definition and Meaning." Lexico Dictionaries | English. Lexico Dictionaries. Accessed July 20, 2021. https://www.lexico.com/en/definition/resilience.

22 Duckworth, Angela. *Grit: The Power of Passion and Perseverance.* New York: Scribner, 2018.

23 "GRATITUDE English Definition and Meaning." Lexico Dictionaries | English. Lexico Dictionaries. Accessed July 20, 2021. https://www.lexico.com/en/definition/gratitude.

24 Duckworth, Angela, and Giacomo Bono. "Gratitude." Character Lab. Accessed July 20, 2021. https://characterlab.org/playbooks/gratitude/.

25 Barker, Eric. "This Is the Most Fun Way to Make Your Life Awesome (Pandemic Edition)." Barking Up the Wrong Tree, March 30, 2020. https://www.bakadesuyo.com/2020/03/pandemic/.

26 *Defining Work-Life Harmony. Practicing Work-Life Harmony.* Workhuman Certified Professional Program Work-life Harmony Module.

27 Leichty, Trish. *Brave Naked Truth, 32.* Freedom House Publishing, Co., 2021.

28 Willyerd, Karie. "What High Performers Want at Work." Harvard Business Review, March 8, 2021. https://hbr.org/2014/11/what-high-performers-want-at-work.

29 Brown, Brene. "Finding Shelter in a Shame Storm (and Avoiding the Flying Debris)." Oprah.com. Oprah.com, March 21, 2013. https://www.oprah.com/spirit/brene-brown-how-to-conquer-shame-friends-who-matter.

30 Brown, Brene. "Finding Shelter in a Shame Storm (and Avoiding the Flying Debris)." Oprah.com. Oprah.com, March 21, 2013. https://www.oprah.com/spirit/brene-brown-how-to-conquer-shame-friends-who-matter.

31 Cherry, Kendra. "Why Cultivating a Growth Mindset Can Boost Your Success." Verywell Mind, April 29, 2021. https://www.verywellmind.com/what-is-a-mindset-2795025.

[32] Achor, Shawn. *Before Happiness: The 5 Hidden Keys to Achieving Success, Spreading Happiness, and Sustaining Positive Change*, 149. New York: Crown Business, 2013.

[33] Achor, Shawn. *Before Happiness: The 5 Hidden Keys to Achieving Success, Spreading Happiness, and Sustaining Positive Change*, 148-180. New York: Crown Business, 2013.

[34] "Remarks by President Biden in Address to a Joint Session of Congress." The White House. The United States Government, April 29, 2021. https://www.whitehouse.gov/briefing-room/speeches-remarks/2021/04/29/remarks-by-president-biden-in-address-to-a-joint-session-of-congress/.

[35] "Social Distancing." Merriam-Webster. Merriam-Webster. https://www.merriam-webster.com/dictionary/social%20distancing.

[36] Wolpert, Stuart. "UCLA Neuroscientist's Book Explains Why Social Connection Is as Important as Food and Shelter." UCLA. UCLA, May 10, 2019. https://newsroom.ucla.edu/releases/we-are-hard-wired-to-be-social-248746.

[37] "Facebook Groups." Facebook. Facebook Groups. Accessed July 20, 2021. https://www.facebook.com/groups/232023321811251/.

[38] McConaughey, Matthew. *Greenlights*, 198. Crown, 2020.

[39] Maxwell, John C., and Rob Hoskins. *Change Your World: How Anyone, Anywhere Can Make a Difference*, 72. HarperCollins Leadership, 2021.

[40] "DIRECTION English Definition and Meaning." Lexico Dictionaries | English. Lexico Dictionaries. Accessed July 20, 2021. https://www.lexico.com/en/definition/direction.

[41] "VALUE English Definition and Meaning." Lexico Dictionaries | English. Lexico Dictionaries. Accessed July 20, 2021. https://www.lexico.com/en/definition/value.

[42] "Outcome." Dictionary.com. Dictionary.com. Accessed July 20, 2021. https://www.dictionary.com/browse/outcome.

43 ROLE English Definition and Meaning." Lexico Dictionaries | English. Lexico Dictionaries. https://www.lexico.com/en/definition/role.

44 "Responsibility." Dictionary.com. Dictionary.com. https://www.dictionary.com/browse/responsibility.

45 Harder, Natalie. "Leadership Strengths." Natalie Harder, n.d. https://edspace.american.edu/nh5200a/leadership-strengths/ .

46 Lencioni, Patrick, and Charles Stransky. *The Five Dysfunctions of a Team*. New York: Random House, Inc, 2002.

47 Fredrickson, B. L., & M.F. Losada. (2005). Positive Affect and the Complex Dynamics of Human Flourishing, *60*(7), 678–686. American Psychologist, 2005.

48 Zenger, Jack, and Joseph Folkman. "The Ideal Praise-to-Criticism Ratio." Harvard Business Review, June 27, 2017. https://hbr.org/2013/03/the-ideal-praise-to-criticism.

49 Brown, Brene. *The Gifts of Imperfection: Let Go of Who You Think You're Supposed to Be and Embrace Who You Are*. Hazelden Publishing, 2010.

50 Magee, Julie, et al. "The Next Era of Human Machine Partnerships." Institute for the Future. Dell Technologies, 2017. https://www.delltechnologies.com/content/dam/delltechnologies/assets/pe rspectives/2030/pdf/SR1940_IFTFforDellTechnologies_Human-Machine_070517_readerhigh-res.pdf.

51 Schwab, Klaus, and Richard Samans. "The Future of Jobs and Skills." The Future of Jobs. Accessed July 20, 2021. https://reports.weforum.org/future-of-jobs-2016/chapter-1-the-future-of-jobs-and-skills/.

52 Schwartz, Jeff, and Suzanne Riss. *Work Disrupted: Opportunity, Resilience, and Growth in the Accelerated Future of Work*, 66. Wiley, 2021.

53 Dweck, Carol S. *Mindset: The New Psychology of Success*. Ballantine Books, 2007.

54 Kaye, Beverly L., and Julie Winkle Giulioni. *Help Them Grow or Watch Them Go*. Berrett-Koehler Publishers, 2012.

[55] Eagleman, David. *Livewired: The Inside Story of the Ever-Changing Brain.* P 16 Patheon Books. New York. 2020.

[56] Rigoni, Brandon, and Jim Asplund. "Developing Employees' Strengths Boosts Sales, Profit, and Engagement." Harvard Business Review, September 1, 2016. https://hbr.org/2016/09/developing-employees-strengths-boosts-sales-profit-and-engagement.

[57] Wakeman, Cy. *Reality-Based Leadership: Ditch the Drama, Restore Sanity to the Workplace, and Turn Excuses into Results.* Jossey-Bass, 2010.

[58] "MIND-SETS." MINDSETS. Accessed July 20, 2021. https://mind-sets.com/info/mindset/.

[59] DiSalvo, David. "Your Brain Sees Even When You Don't." Forbes. Forbes Magazine, June 23, 2013. https://www.forbes.com/sites/daviddisalvo/2013/06/22/your-brain-sees-even-when-you-dont/?sh=38bb8ea0116a.

[60] Wakeman, Cy. *Reality-Based Leadership: Ditch the Drama, Restore Sanity to the Workplace, and Turn Excuses into Results.* Jossey-Bass, 2010.

[61] Connors, Roger, Tom Smith, and Craig Hickman. *The Oz Principle: Getting Results through Individual and Organizational Accountability.* Prentice Hall Pr, 1994.

[62] Brown, Brene. "Brené Brown on Empathy." The RSA. YouTube, December 10, 2013. https://www.youtube.com/watch?v=1Evwgu369Jw.

[63] Wakeman, Cy. *Reality-Based Leadership: Ditch the Drama, Restore Sanity to the Workplace, and Turn Excuses into Results.* Jossey-Bass, 2010.

[64] *Wakeman, Cy. Reality-Based Leadership: Ditch the Drama, Restore Sanity to the Workplace, and Turn Excuses into Results, 22-26. Jossey-Bass, 2010.*

[65] Wakeman, Cy. *Reality-Based Leadership: Ditch the Drama, Restore Sanity to the Workplace, and Turn Excuses into Results,* 22-26. Jossey-Bass, 2010.

[66] "Belief." Dictionary.com. Dictionary.com. Accessed July 20, 2021. https://www.dictionary.com/browse/belief.

[67] "Self Limiting Beliefs and Behaviors." Foundations Asheville. Accessed July 20, 2021. https://foundationsasheville.com/blog/self-limiting-beliefs-and-behaviors/.

[68] Wakeman, Cy. *Reality-Based Leadership: Ditch the Drama, Restore Sanity to the Workplace, and Turn Excuses into Results.* Jossey-Bass, 2010.

[69] Achor, Shawn. *Before Happiness: The 5 Hidden Keys to Achieving Success, Spreading Happiness, and Sustaining Positive Change.* New York: Crown Business, 2013.

[70] Achor, Shawn. *Before Happiness: The 5 Hidden Keys to Achieving Success, Spreading Happiness, and Sustaining Positive Change*, 149. New York: Crown Business, 2013.

[71] Brown, Brene. "'The Power of Vulnerability.'" TEDxTalk. https://www.ted.com/talks/brene_brown_the_power_of_vulnerability/transcript?language=en.

[72] "Sympathy." Dictionary.com. Dictionary.com. Accessed July 20, 2021. https://www.dictionary.com/browse/sympathy.

[73] "EMPATHY" English Definition and Meaning." Lexico Dictionaries | English. Lexico Dictionaries. Accessed July 20, 2021. https://www.lexico.com/en/definition/empt.

[74] "Empathy." Dictionary.com. Dictionary.com. Accessed July 20, 2021. https://www.dictionary.com/browse/empathy.

[75] "Leadership." Dictionary.com. Dictionary.com. https://www.dictionary.com/browse/leadership.

[76] "Leading." Merriam-Webster. Merriam-Webster. https://www.merriam-webster.com/dictionary/leading.

[77] "Lead." Merriam-Webster. Merriam-Webster. https://www.merriam-webster.com/dictionary/lead.

[78] "Everyday Leaders, Everyday Leadership." CCL, March 13, 2021. https://www.ccl.org/articles/leading-effectively-articles/everyday-leaders-everyday-leadership/.

[79] Wambach, Abby. *WOLFPACK: How to Come Together, Unleash Our Power, and Change the Game*, 42. Celadon Books, 2019.

[80] Krentzman, Jackie. "The CRISIS Leader." Diversity Woman | Leadership Empowerment for Women Who Mean Business, October 14, 2020. https://www.diversitywoman.com/the-crisis-leader/.

[81] Buckingham, Marcus, and Ashley Goodall. *Nine Lies About Work: A Freethinking Leader's Guide to the Real World*, 49. Boston, MA: Harvard Business Review Press, 2019.

[82] Brown, Brene. *Daring Greatly: How the Courage to Be Vulnerable Transforms the Way We Live, Love, Parent, and Lead.* Avery, 2012.

[83] Wambach, Abby. *WOLFPACK: How to Come Together, Unleash Our Power, and Change the Game*, 33. Celadon Books, 2019.

[84] Buckingham, Marcus, and Ashley Goodall. *Nine Lies About Work: A Freethinking Leader's Guide to the Real World*. Boston, MA: Harvard Business Review Press, 2019.

[85] Schwartz, Jeff, and Suzanne Riss. *Work Disrupted: Opportunity, Resilience, and Growth in the Accelerated Future of Work*, 109. Wiley, 2021.

[86] Lencioni, Patrick. *The Advantage: Why Organizational Health Trumps Everything Else In Business.* Jossey-Bass, 2012.

[87] Need to find some sources for this

[88] "ATTENTION English Definition and Meaning." Lexico Dictionaries | English. Lexico Dictionaries. https://www.lexico.com/en/definition/attention.

[89] "CONNECTION English Definition and Meaning." Lexico Dictionaries | English. Lexico Dictionaries. https://www.lexico.com/en/definition/connection.

[90] Vozza, Stephanie. "Feedback Is Overrated–This Is What Employees Need Instead." Fast Company. Fast Company, March 19, 2019. https://www.fastcompany.com/90318711/feedback-is-overrated-this-is-what-employees-need-instead.

[91] Schwartz, Jeff, and Suzanne Riss. *Work Disrupted: Opportunity, Resilience, and Growth in the Accelerated Future of Work,* 144-145. Wiley, 2021.

[92] Schwartz, Jeff, and Suzanne Riss. *Work Disrupted: Opportunity, Resilience, and Growth in the Accelerated Future of Work,* 146. Wiley, 2021.

[93] Nagoski, Emily, and Amelia Nagoski. *Burnout: The Secret to Unlocking the Stress Cycle.* Ballantine Books, 2019.

[94] Nagoski, Emily, and Amelia Nagoski. *Burnout: The Secret to Unlocking the Stress Cycle.* Ballantine Books, 2019.

[95] Williams, John, Sheldon Harnick, and Jerry Bock. Lyrics to "Tradition." *Genius,* https://genius.com/Topol-prologue-tradition-main-title-lyrics#song-info.

[96] Colantuoni, Francesca, Shaibyaa Rajbhandari, Gila Tolub, Wahi Diome-Deer, and Karl Moore. "A Fresh Look at Paternity Leave: Why the Benefits Extend Beyond the Personal." McKinsey & Company. McKinsey & Company, April 20, 2021. https://www.mckinsey.com/business-functions/organization/our-insights/a-fresh-look-at-paternity-leave-why-the-benefits-extend-beyond-the-personal#:~:text=Recent%20research%20supports%20this%20point,mother%20and%20strengthening%20parental%20relationships.

[97] "Survival." Merriam-Webster. Merriam-Webster. https://www.merriam-webster.com/dictionary/survival.

[98] "Mission." Merriam-Webster. Merriam-Webster. Accessed July 30, 2021. https://www.merriam-webster.com/dictionary/mission.

[99] "Thrive." Merriam-Webster. Merriam-Webster. Accessed July 30, 2021. https://www.merriam-webster.com/dictionary/thrive.

[100] Maxwell, John C., and Rob Hoskins. *Change Your World: How Anyone, Anywhere Can Make a Difference,* 129. HarperCollins Leadership, 2021.

[101] Maxwell, John C., and Rob Hoskins. *Change Your World: How Anyone, Anywhere Can Make a Difference,* 72. HarperCollins Leadership, 2021.

[102] Maxwell, John C., and Rob Hoskins. *Change Your World: How Anyone, Anywhere Can Make a Difference*, 7. HarperCollins Leadership, 2021.

[103] Maxwell, John C., and Rob Hoskins. *Change Your World: How Anyone, Anywhere Can Make a Difference*, 72. HarperCollins Leadership, 2021.

[104] "What Is the Difference Between Religion and Spirituality?" Happier Human, March 17, 2020. https://www.happierhuman.com/difference-religion-spirituality/#:~:text=Spirituality%20is%20a%20solitary%20experience,to%20the%20adherence%20of%20rules.

[105] "Spirituality English Definition and Meaning." Lexico Dictionaries | English. Lexico Dictionaries. Accessed July 30, 2021. https://www.lexico.com/en/definition/spirituality.

[106] "What Is the Difference Between Religion and Spirituality?" Happier Human, March 17, 2020. https://www.happierhuman.com/difference-religion-spirituality/#:~:text=Spirituality%20is%20a%20solitary%20experience,to%20the%20adherence%20of%20rules.

[107] Rath, Tom. *Life's Great Question: Discover How You Contribute to The World*, 11. Silicon Guild, 2020.

[108] Gritters, Jenni. "This Is Your Brain on Motherhood." The New York Times. The New York Times, May 5, 2020. https://www.nytimes.com/2020/05/05/parenting/mommy-brain-science.html.

[109] Menkedick, Sarah. *Ordinary Insanity: Fear and the Silent Crisis of Motherhood in America*, 15. New York, Patheon Books, 2020.

[110] Menkedick, Sarah. *Ordinary Insanity: Fear and the Silent Crisis of Motherhood in America*, 15. New York, Patheon Books, 2020.

[111] Maxwell, John C., and Rob Hoskins. *Change Your World: How Anyone, Anywhere Can Make a Difference*, 177. HarperCollins Leadership, 2021.

[112] Onge, Kim St. "Missouri Facing Pediatric Behavioral Health Crisis; Hospitals Running out of Beds for Kids." KMOV.com, July 15, 2021.

https://www.kmov.com/news/missouri-facing-pediatric-behavioral-health-crisis-hospitals-running-out-of-beds-for-kids/article_cf9d6e00-e510-11eb-9df3-b7371bcd1e44.html.

[113] Kross, Ethan. *Chatter: The Voice in Our Head, Why It Matters, and How to Harness It.* New York: Crown, 2021.

[114] Maxwell, John C., and Rob Hoskins. *Change Your World: How Anyone, Anywhere Can Make a Difference*, 47. HarperCollins Leadership, 2021.

[115] Mitchell, Margaret. *Gone with the Wind.* Warner Books, 1936.

[116] Hammerstein, Oscar, and Richard Rodgers. Lyrics to "Climb Every Mountain." Performed by Guy Sebastian, Sony Music, 2010. *Genius*, https://genius.com/Guy-sebastian-climb-every-mountain-lyrics.

Made in the USA
Monee, IL
15 October 2021